P9-CPY-727

NEWLY REVISED & EXPANDED

KNOWING GOD'S WILL

Finding Guidance for Personal Decisions

M. Blaine Smith

Foreword by Richard C. Halverson

INTERVARSITY PRESS
DOWNERS GROVE, ILLINOIS 60515

Second Edition © 1991 by M. Blaine Smith
First Edition © 1979 by InterVarsity Christian Fellowship of the United States of America

All rights reserved. No part of this book may be reproduced in any form without written permission from InterVarsity Press, P.O. Box 1400, Downers Grove, Illinois 60515.

InterVarsity Press is the book-publishing division of InterVarsity Christian Fellowship, a student movement active on campus at hundreds of universities, colleges and schools of nursing in the United States of America, and a member movement of the International Fellowship of Evangelical Students. For information about local and regional activities, write Public Relations Dept., InterVarsity Christian Fellowship, 6400 Schroeder Rd., P.O. Box 7895, Madison, WI 53707-7895.

All Scripture quotations, unless otherwise indicated, are from the Revised Standard Version of the Bible, copyright 1946, 1952, 1971 by the Division of Christian Education of the National Council of the Churches of Christ in the USA and used by permission.

ISBN 0-8308-1308-X
Printed in the United States of America

Library of Congress Cataloging-in-Publication Data

Smith, M. Blaine.
    Knowing God's will: finding guidance for personal decisions/M.
Blaine Smith.
        p.   cm.
    Includes bibliographical references.
    ISBN 0-8308-1308-X
    1. God—Will.   2. Christian life—Presbyterian authors.
I. Title.
BV4501.2.S53438   1991
248.4—dc20   *91-30124*
                                                            CIP

---

15   14   13   12   11   10
03

To my wife, Evie

Acknowledgments

I'm greatly indebted to Evie, my wife, for her ongoing encouragement of my writing efforts and for typing the manuscript of the original edition of this book.

In that first edition I also saluted Dr. George Scotchmer and the session of Memorial Presbyterian Church in St. Louis, who provided most of the time in which that volume was written. That salute bears repeating, as I remember with gratitude their important support of my writing time when I was assistant pastor of that church.

Added to these acknowledgments is a very special thank you to Dr. David J. Gyertson, president of Regent University. It was he who first put the thought in my mind of expanding this book, and it was his decision to use it as a text for Living By The Book, the home study program of the Christian Broadcasting Network, which helped provide the incentive to do it. This led to the opportunity to record the lectures for the course, which is entitled "Guidance By The Book." Mark Wilson, general editor of Living By The Book, and his staff were most helpful and supportive and should be commended for their creative and diligent work on the course.

I must also acknowledge my considerable debt to the members of the Nehemiah Ministries board, Robert Newell III, Tom Willett, Glenn Kirkland, Jon Werner and Dr. Patrick Hartsock. They have been a vital source of friendship and direction since the inception of this ministry thirteen years ago.

Finally, I'm especially grateful to Jim Sire, Don Stephenson and Andy Le Peau at InterVarsity Press for their support and encouragement in my writing. And heartfelt appreciation goes to Joan Guest and Linda Doll for their excellent editorial work on the first and second editions respectively.

Foreword

While attending seminary, I was a member of what we called "Deputation Teams." Various churches in the Northeast area of the country invited us for special services—usually youth conferences on weekends. As part of this weekend there was nearly always a question-and-answer time during which we seminary students would respond.

Invariably one question asked had to do with the will of God—"How can I know God's will for my life?" or some variation of that theme. In the course of college and seminary I had developed a simple little formula which had been gleaned from several sources. With a great degree of confidence I would prescribe this formula, after which the matter was settled as far as I was concerned.

Unhappily for those who raised the question, this was not so. The formula proved to be artificial and mechanical, and it lacked biblical insights which came much later for me.

On reading this book, I wished that I had been able in those seminary days to give the instruction so ably presented here.

Blaine Smith writes on the subject with extraordinary maturity and careful attention to the Scriptures. As I read his first manuscript it seemed that he had thought of everything. Now in this expanded version, he gives even more help in some crucial areas.

He begins by facing and eliminating the most common misunderstanding relating to the subject. Briefly and incisively he puts away false notions held by many and often propagated with devastating effect.

His treatment of the relationship between divine sovereignty and human freedom and responsibility is excellent, as is his distinction between moral and nonmoral issues.

Here is a presentation on knowing God's will that is carefully thought through, well annotated, comprehensive, exceedingly practical and compellingly readable.

Richard C. Halverson
Washington, D.C.

Part 1
First Considerations

1
A Critical Concern

Key Questions:

■ *Why do we as Christians sometimes experience confusion over God's will?*
■ *Why the need for this book, and what areas will be covered?*

*W*hen Paul was confronted by Christ on Damascus Road, he inquired, "Who are you, Lord?" When the response came, "I am Jesus of Nazareth whom you are persecuting," Paul asked only one question: "What shall I do, Lord?" (Acts 22:8-10). There is no record of Paul's requesting any further information from the Lord. His sole concern was to know and do what Christ willed for him to do.

As we follow Christ today, Paul's prayer echoes across the centuries and reflects our own. "What shall I do, Lord?" is so often the question on our mind which far outweighs all the others.

It is an understatement to say that guidance is a major concern of Christians today. For many, it is the *primary* concern.

This is unquestionably true for students. We can still heartily agree with Joseph Bayly's claim:

If there is a serious concern among Christian students today, it is for guidance. Holiness may have been the passion of another generation of Christian young men and women. Or soul winning. Or evangelizing the world in their generation. But not today. Today the theme is getting to know the will of God.[1]

Yet guidance is not only the interest of students and young Christians who see their life as a blank canvas before them but a chronic concern of many older believers as well. It is not unusual for retirees to attend my seminars on knowing God's will, aware they have important time remaining to serve the Lord yet as confused as ever about what direction to take. A remarkable widow in her seventies confessed to me that knowing God's will was her ongoing concern.

Spiritually mature Christians seem to wrestle with questions about God's will as greatly as young believers and those with little Christian experience. This is true even for pastors and those with considerable biblical knowledge. I think of a pastor friend who had two excellent job options open to him and for some time struggled with which to choose. He admitted to me that he was tiring of having well-meaning friends ask him which he wanted more or which he was more qualified to handle. "I'll be happy doing *anything* as long as I'm confident it's where the Lord wants me," he said. "The question is, *how* do I know?"

Our concern with knowing the will of God is not hard to understand. It springs from curiosity and a natural need for direction. On the deepest level it reflects our desire to be accountable to Christ and a profound concern to accomplish something significant with our life.

I'll never forget the way one young woman expressed it to me: "When I stand before Christ at the end of my life, I want to feel good about what I've done and to have some confidence that I've accomplished what he placed me on this planet to do."

She added, though, that she was plagued with the fear that her life was not as effective for Christ as it should be. It was baffling to her to understand where her potential really lay and what she could do that would truly make a difference. If she only knew what Christ wanted her to do, that would settle things.

Christians often voice this frustration. They long to see their lives count for something yet have no clear sense of what direction to take. I once heard a schoolteacher summarize it well. Although he was successful in his position and meeting many needs, he was frustrated by the lack of a clear calling to the teaching profession. "The Bible declares that St. Paul was commanded by God to be an apostle," he noted. "My problem is that I don't feel *commanded* by God to do anything!" Like so many Christians today he was uncertain how God's call to a particular profession might be known and wondered why he didn't receive a call as unmistakable as Paul's. Lacking this clear sense of calling, he found his work regrettably mundane.

Of course, our need for guidance comes not only in career choices but in many other areas as well. Not the least of these is the whole murky area of relationships and decisions about marriage. When I wrote *Should I Get Married?* several years ago, I noted that the majority of Christians seeking my counsel at that time were looking for advice about whether to marry a particular person. That remains true today. Even as I'm writing this paragraph a woman phones—a mature Christian in her thirties wanting direction for a relationship. While there are many factors involved in a decision to marry, serious Christians almost always wrestle with how to recognize the Lord's guidance in it. Everything comes back to the question, "What shall I do, Lord?"

A Maze of Options
The concern for guidance is nothing new. Christians have always sought to know God's will and have always wrestled with questions about it. What *is* new is the level of concern. Certain factors in modern life make the need for guidance greater for believers today than at any prior time in history.

Chief among these factors is the unprecedented diversity of choice which we face in most major decision areas today. If you had lived a century ago, chances are good you would have followed the profession of your parents. Even if you didn't, your options would still have been very limited, restricted by geographical and other boundaries which only the most adventuresome would transcend.

Today, as young Christians especially, we tend to think of our vocational options as practically unlimited. The ease of travel, too, greatly expands our horizons for where we might live and work, yet so often leaves our geographical identity at no fixed address.

And then there's the media. The incessant, pervasive media. The daily march of personalities and role models and graphic pictures of human need, on television especially, but through radio, newspapers and magazines as well. Constantly we're presented with images of life, images we compare to our own life, images which leave us wondering if there is something different we should be doing with our life.

It's the nature of modern life to present us with options. On one level this is a wonderful benefit to life at the end of the twentieth century, for it greatly expands our possibilities for serving Christ. But it greatly magnifies our confusion as well, and deepens our need to know God's will.

Many of the factors of modern life which dizzy our mind in career choices render decisions about marriage confusing as well. The ease of mobility, for instance, leaves many wondering if they've dated enough or met enough potential candidates to know for certain that they've found the right person to marry. And it removes many from the support base of family and local culture which in past generations played a much more central role in helping individuals find someone suitable to marry.

In addition, the media bombards us with images of romance and marriage which often have little to do with what sort of marriage relationship would be best for us personally. Yet these images are hypnotic in their effect and cloud our understanding about what makes for healthy marriage. They become an unfortunate filter through which we consider the possibility of marriage and weigh the Lord's guidance. We may be too quick to think we've found the perfect match in someone who measures up well to the popular stereotypes. Or we may miss the marriage potential in a good relationship because we're comparing it to an ideal that is based on fantasy.

No Lack of Advice

Unfortunately, the teaching we receive in Christian circles on how to know God's will often serves to confuse us even further. Perspectives on guidance, presented through sermons, lectures, books and counseling, typically are not well integrated. A talk on guidance may present valid principles yet not show adequately how they apply in different circumstances. The listener is left with an oversimplified approach to guidance which may prove misleading.

Too many times the intricate biblical teaching on guidance is reduced to a single idea or formula. Many pat formulas for guidance float around the body of Christ—simple and foolproof solutions to knowing God's will, intended to cover all of life's contingencies. These do not always apply so easily in real-life decisions.

Even worse, the simple and foolproof solutions sometimes contradict each other. One person says, "Love God and do what you wish," while another insists, "To find God's will, you should *deny* your desires." One teacher says, "God's will is normally the most logical alternative," while another points out, "Abraham 'went out not knowing whither he went,' so God's will is likely to seem illogical to you." One counselor says, "God's will is known through your intuition," while another argues, "Feelings are misleading; God directs through our rational thought process."

We hear many other formulas touted for seeking God's will. Some promote the practice of "putting out a fleece." Others stress the role of supernatural guidance through signs, visions or prophecy. Still others claim that God's will is best found through certain chain-of-command relationships. And some Christians even encourage the use of secular forms of guidance, such as astrology, Ouija boards, seances and palm reading.

All in all, it is no wonder the typical Christian is baffled by the prospect of finding God's will.

In some cases the results of this confusion can be tragic. A young woman came to me convinced God had told her to kill herself. Assuming God was speaking to her through her impulses, she took her suicidal urges as divine guidance. Although her case is clearly extreme, it dramatizes the problems that can arise.

More typically the result is not such a tragically wrong conclusion about God's will but no conclusion at all. Many Christians are left genuinely confused about what direction God wants them to take in their decisions. Yet this is tragic in itself, especially when the decision involves a major life choice, for many conclude they must stumble through it without assurance of God's will. Not only does their well-being suffer but often their fruitfulness as well, for they are not as motivated as they would be if they had stronger confidence of the Lord's leading.

The Goal of This Study

We cannot remove all of the challenge involved in knowing God's will. Yet we can remove much of the frustration. And we can reach a point of confidence that we are following God's will and making decisions which reflect his best intentions for our life.

But for this to happen, we need a broad understanding of biblical teaching on guidance. I stress *broad* understanding, for as we're noting, the tendency is to oversimplify. Far from reducing the matter to a pat formula or two, the Scriptures present a number of principles of guidance which apply to different aspects of our decisions. The mature Christian needs to understand and embrace all of these principles to be at a point of thinking clearly about the Lord's will in critical choices.

I must hasten to say that this doesn't mean that you must understand all of these principles before you can follow God's will faithfully. When our heart is right before God, he takes an uncanny initiative to guide us within his will, even where our understanding is lacking. Yet as we'll note, many wonderful benefits come from deepening our understanding of how God guides us.

Not the least of these is a greater assurance that our decisions are reflecting his will, which leads to a stronger confidence that our life is accomplishing something significant. It takes a significant commitment of time and study to come to grips with the full range of biblical teaching on guidance. Yet once understood and appreciated, it provides a valuable map for working through our decisions from the standpoint of God's will.

The challenge of making these decisions remains. Yet our confidence of walking within the Lord's will increases, and the decision process itself becomes much more of the enjoyable adventure it was meant to be.

My purpose in this book is to present a systematic study of biblical principles of guidance. Step by step we will work through the teachings of Scripture which most directly relate to understanding God's guidance for major personal decisions. Our goal will be to develop a solid foundation for making these decisions within God's will.

If you have read the first edition of this book, you may still benefit from studying this expanded version. While most of the material from the original book is included and the key points remain the same, there is further elaboration on a number of important points; many illustrations have been added and some additional chapters as well. I share my own experience, too, much more in this volume than in the first. Like you, I remain very much a seeker in the matter of knowing God's will. I find I must continually make the effort to apply these principles to the realities of my own life.

I've also added an appendix critiquing the perspective of Garry Friesen's *Decision Making and the Will of God*, which is that God does not have a specific will for our personal decisions. Questions about his thesis have been raised to me numerous times by thoughtful Christians, and these deserve a careful response.

Another important addition to this book is a set of study questions at the end of each chapter. While it isn't necessary to work through them in order to understand the major points of the book, they do help to amplify some of the principles we'll examine and provide a further basis in Scripture for many of them. You will find it helpful to write your answers—or new questions which come to your mind—in a notebook as you go along.

Many of the questions are designed to help you apply the principles to your own life. While some of these questions can be answered quickly, most of them are purposely meaty, and many will require fifteen to thirty minutes of study and reflection. For this reason they can provide a good basis for group Bible study.[2]

Where We're Headed

Before moving ahead, it will help to give a brief overview of the book. In this introductory section we'll look first at types of decisions we face and clarify more fully what our focus of concern will be. In chapters three and four we'll consider the step-by-step nature of God's guidance in the Christian life; understanding this is foundational to everything else we discuss. In chapter five we'll give some reassuring emphasis to the initiative God takes in guiding us.

Part two examines our responsibility for knowing God's will in the most basic sense. We'll note that this responsibility has four aspects to it: willingness to do God's will, commitment to prayer, understanding the guidance already given Scripture, and the need to think through a decision carefully. Particular stress will be given to the importance of using the mind God has given us and taking responsibility for reasoning through a decision. The remainder of the book will amplify this point in various ways.

In part three we'll look at exceptions to this principle, examining direct supernatural guidance, prophecy, putting out a fleece and the role of mystical impressions ("inward guidance").

Then in part four we'll look more closely at how to make a responsible decision that glorifies Christ. We'll provide some guidelines for weighing four areas that almost always factor into our major decisions: personal desires, personal ability and potential, circumstances and the counsel of others. In appendix one we'll look further at issues for knowing God's will involved in what are called "chain-of-command" relationships. Finally, in appendix two we'll give careful consideration to the argument that God does not have a specific will for our personal decisions.

As you begin this book, you may be tempted to skip to the chapter that seems most interesting. But I believe the study will be most beneficial to you if you work through the chapters in order. They build on one another to some extent, and some of the later chapters would be difficult to understand fully without the concepts established in the earlier ones.

It is my hope and belief that you will find this study helpful in your personal search to know God's will. And it is my prayer that it will lead you to a deeper experience of joy in the Lord.

For Personal Study:

1. Though most of the questions in this book will involve direct study of Scripture, some are designed purely for personal reflection. Here at the outset of this study, take a moment to reflect on how you hope to benefit from this book. The following are some reasonable goals to have in working through this book. Note any of them which represent needs for growth in your own life and make them your personal goals as you read:

☐ Developing a biblical framework for working through my personal decisions.

☐ Gaining a greater trust in God's willingness to guide my decisions.

☐ Gaining a deeper desire for God's will.

☐ Gaining the courage to tackle decisions and to take risks when necessary.

☐ Realizing the motivation to use my abilities and spiritual gifts.

☐ Feeling the freedom in Christ to be the person he has made me to be.

☐ Developing the wisdom to counsel others in their decisions.

2. Now, list one to three personal decisions which you are presently facing, or expect to face in the future, for which you hope to gain some insight through this study.

3. Finally, note specific questions about God's guidance which you hope to resolve through this study.

2
Types of Decisions We Face

Key Questions:

■ *What different types of decisions do we confront as Christians, and what do they imply for seeking God's will?*
■ *What area of decision making will we focus upon in this study?*

A physicist friend of mine tells me that in his work fifty per cent of a problem is solved if you can simply identify the question you are trying to answer. Pinpointing the question is not just a beginning step in problem solving but often a crucial step toward finding the solution.

Of course, in major problems or decisions there are usually not just one but a variety of questions that must be addressed. Broadly speaking, these fall into two areas—*overriding questions* and *secondary questions*. It's especially important to be clear about the overriding questions before delving into an issue; otherwise you can end up running down many rabbit trails.

Frankly, our confusion over guidance often begins exactly here—we haven't clarified the overriding questions. We ask, "How can I know God's will?" yet may not be clear in our minds what sort of decision it is for which we want to know God's will. Actually we face a variety of types of decisions as Christians, and each of these implies a different approach to knowing God's will. The vital first step is to be clear about the nature of the decision we're seeking guidance for.

Second, we're often unclear about how much information we should expect when God guides us. Typically, we expect too much insight, more than may actually be needed to take the next step of faith. It's vital to understand how much guidance is reasonable to expect before looking at the further question of how to *recognize* the guidance God gives.

In the next three chapters we'll address these fundamental questions. In this chapter, we'll look at different types of decisions we face and clarify what the focus of our study will be. In chapters three and four we'll consider how much insight God typically provides when he shows us his will and what this means for our approach to guidance.

Moral and Nonmoral Decisions

It has been helpful to me to make a distinction between two basic types of decisions we face as Christians. On the one hand, we have what we can call straightforward moral decisions. These are the ones to which a single, clear moral principle can be applied. They include, for instance, decisions about stealing, killing or extramarital sex. These are areas of behavior which require the same type of response every time. The moral principle tells us what that response should be. In this sense, once a particular moral principle is understood, God's will in that area becomes a matter of application. We don't have to rethink or pray about the problem every time it arises.

If I know that God doesn't permit adultery, for instance, I don't have to waste mental energy deliberating whether he might be leading me to have an affair with my neighbor's wife. The simplest moral decisions are straightforward, clear and direct, because a single biblical principle applies directly to them.

On the other hand, there are those personal decisions to which moral principles have no relevance. Straightforward *non*moral decisions deal with our choice about actions which have no moral implications at all. For example, no biblical principle applies to whether I wear a blue shirt today or a yellow one. This is a very simple decision and one which is clearly nonmoral in character.

Perhaps the easiest way to conceive of the relationship between moral and nonmoral decisions is to picture them as forming a continuum (see illustration).

straightforward moral decisions   complicated moral decisions   gray area decisions   complex decisions   straightforward nonmoral decisions

The Shades of Decision Making

At one pole are the simplest, most obvious moral choices, and at the other pole are the simplest nonmoral decisions. As we move from left to right on the continuum, our decisions become less clearly settled by a single moral principle and our liberty of choice increases. We encounter more complicated moral decisions, such as abortion, a Christian's response to war and so on. These are issues which require careful deliberation and a delicate balancing of two or more moral principles.

Next we come to what have traditionally been called "gray area decisions." These have to do with areas of moral behavior where the Bible clearly leaves the individual Christian some freedom of choice. In Paul's day this included questions of eating certain meat (Rom 14:2) and observing certain holidays (Rom 14:5). In the twentieth century, Christians have often been concerned with matters such as smoking, drinking, dancing or gambling.

Then we come to choices which I call complex decisions. These are important personal decisions which have to do with more than merely matters of moral behavior. Complex decisions include major questions such as what profession to choose, what college to attend, whether and whom to marry and where to go to church. They also include decisions about priorities: how should you spend your time and money? In general, questions such as these cannot be resolved simply by applying moral principles to them. In most cases we are left with a good deal of freedom of choice. These are unique decisions which may require very different responses from time to time and from person to person.

This does not mean that complex decisions have no moral aspects to them. Certainly most of the important decisions we confront in life involve moral issues in one way or another. But what I mean is that moral principles will not finally settle these questions. Moral principles may simplify them or narrow the area of focus.

For instance, if I'm wrestling with God's will for a job position, I can rest assured he does not want me to become a palm reader or manager of a brothel. But no moral principle will give me the final insight into God's will if I'm trying to decide between becoming a doctor or a lawyer, a bookkeeper or a welder, a pastor or a missionary. Such decisions are complex because they cannot be conveniently settled by reference to moral principles alone.

In this book we'll be interested purely in the question of knowing God's will for complex decisions. This is the area of decision making that usually causes the most difficulty and where we most often experience confusion over God's will. Usually when we talk in Christian circles about needing *guidance* from God, we're talking about his leading for this sort of decision.[1] Therefore, when we use the term *guidance* in this book, we will always use it in this sense. (Much of what we will say will also have relevance to making a gray area moral decision. There are, however, certain additional guidelines for the gray area decision.)[2]

Please note, too, that from this point on when I use terms such as *personal decision, personal guidance, God's personal will, God's individual will,* or just *God's will,* it will always be in reference to the area of complex decision making. This will allow us a fuller vocabulary for discussing the topic.

Not a Magic Answer Book

Much of the value in drawing these distinctions between different types of decisions lies in helping us understand the role which the Scriptures should play in our decision making.

Since the Bible is our prime source of moral principles, we should expect to find the answer to a moral decision in the Bible. At times a single moral principle will give the answer clearly and directly. In other cases a weighing of various principles will lead to the right answer. But since complex decisions cannot be resolved by moral principles alone, we shouldn't expect the Bible to provide us with final answers to these choices. A person seeking God's will for a profession, for instance, shouldn't expect to find a biblical passage telling him or her to become an accountant. Someone considering whether to marry a particular person shouldn't expect to find a verse which finally settles the question.

I realize this goes against the grain of much popular thinking on guidance. It's often taught that the answer to any conceivable decision is given in the Scriptures. We just need to find the right passage. This causes some people to end up in a frustrated search for a biblical principle which will resolve their decision. Others turn their search for guidance into pure superstition by seeking guidance from irrelevant words or passages. (A classic example is the man who decided to marry a woman named Grace on the basis of the verse, "My grace is sufficient for thee.")

Many people blindly open the Bible, place their finger on a verse and take guidance uncritically from it.[3] I love the illustration Paul Little gives of this approach:

> Some people treat the Bible as a book of magic. You have probably heard of the fellow who opened the Bible and put his finger down on the phrase, "Judas went out and hanged himself." This did not comfort him very much, so he tried again. And his finger fell on the verse, "Go

thou and do likewise." That shook him terribly, so he tried it one more time, and the verse he hit on was "And what thou doest, do quickly."[4] Only when we recognize the futility of such an approach to guidance can we really be free to seek God's will in a mature and responsible way.

This doesn't mean that the Bible should play no role in making personal decisions. It is through the Bible that we learn the principles of guidance which tell us how to seek God's will, and throughout this book we'll be looking at these principles. Also, through the Bible we learn moral principles which must not be sidestepped in discerning God's will. We will, in fact, devote an entire chapter to looking at the positive role of Scripture in guidance, as there is a good deal more that needs to be said about it (chapter nine).

For now, however, we're simply saying that we shouldn't expect to find the final answer to a personal choice magically revealed in the words of Scripture. We should avoid the crystal-ball approach to the Bible which looks for easy answers to difficult decisions and seeks to escape from our God-given responsibility for careful decision making.

Does God Really Care What Decisions We Make?

I realize that at this point some readers may be raising a more basic question about the fundamental assumption underlying this study. Is it correct to assume that God has a will for the personal decisions we face? Isn't it more accurate simply to say that he gives us freedom of choice in complex decision areas, just as he does in nonmoral decisions?

While Christians seldom asked this question when I published the first edition of this book, it is more often raised today, due largely to the influence of Garry Friesen's *Decision Making and The Will of God* (published about a year after my book). In his book Friesen argues that God does not have an ideal will for us in personal decision areas but leaves such choices to our own discretion. In appendix two I examine this issue in some detail and critique some of the points which Friesen raises in his book. The fact that I've chosen to look at this issue in an appendix section is not meant to minimize the importance of it. But because a meaningful response to it involves some detailed biblical analysis, as well as frequent references to a book which many readers will not be familiar with, it seemed best to address it in an appendix rather than interrupt the flow of the book at this point.

If the question of God's having a specific will for our personal decisions is troublesome for you, you may want to go ahead and read through the material in appendix two now and then come back to chapter three. Even if you're comfortable with the notion of God's having a personal will, you may benefit from working through the appendix material at some point. It should help you better establish why you believe as you do and give you a basis for responding to any challenges to the contrary. Feel free to study that material now or to delve into it once you have finished the rest of the book.

In the next chapter we'll begin to look at the process by which we can rightly discern God's leading.

For Personal Study:

1. Each of the following passages illustrates or refers to one of the five decision areas which we discussed in this chapter. Read each passage and note which decision area it best represents:

☐ Genesis 2:15-16

☐ Luke 7:31-35 (the difference in perspective between Jesus and John the Baptist)

☐ Genesis 39:2-10 (Joseph's choice in this passage)

☐ 2 Kings 5:9-19 (Naaman's choice regarding bowing in the temple)

☐ 2 Kings 6:1-4 (the decision to move made by the company of prophets)

2. It is sometimes claimed that God does not have a will for our personal decisions but is pleased with any responsible decision we make. Read Acts 20:22-24. What evidence does Paul's statement provide (particularly v. 24) that he believed God had distinctive work set out for him to accomplish?

☐ How important was this belief to his motivation?

☐ What lessons for our own life do we gain from Paul's example?

☐ Read also Colossians 4:17 for further reference.

3
Seeing God's Will Dynamically

Key Questions:

■ *How much information does God provide when he shows us his will?*
■ *Should I expect him to reveal the future to me?*

*O*nce in seminary I was assigned lengthy papers in two courses. The first took much longer than I expected, and I became increasingly anxious that there wouldn't be enough time to produce the second. But almost as soon as I finished the first paper I realized that it might also be adequate for the second course. The professor agreed. The amazing thing is that I didn't realize the relation of the two projects until I had finished the first. If I'd plowed into both at the same time, I might have ended up doing a lot of extra work.

A business executive once asked a time-management consultant to help him become more organized and productive. The consultant responded that he would give the businessman a single piece of advice. The businessman should experiment with this idea and see how it works. The consultant added that he wouldn't charge a stated fee for his counsel. Rather, the businessman should judge from experience just how helpful it was, then send the consultant a check for what he thought it was worth.

The advice? *Work on only one task at a time.* Give all your energies to finishing it. Then, when it's done, move on to the next responsibility. That was the sum total of the principle.

Though it seemed absurdly simplistic to the businessman, he agreed to give it a try. He was so pleased with the results that he sent the consultant a check for $10,000.[1]

That principle seems to be a law in human life. It is the cardinal principle we hear espoused so often in architecture and home decorating: Tackle one project, finish one room at a time. The satisfaction and insight that come from completing one task will clear the mind to think creatively about the next. If I try to remodel my kitchen, bathroom and bedroom all at once, I'll probably find my concentration spread too thin.

Of course, we don't always have the luxury of tackling big projects one at a time. But when we do, our minds seem to function better. The human brain can hold only so much information at once; we do better when we can focus.

Understanding this fact helps us to appreciate one of the most fundamental dynamics of God's guidance shown in Scripture. And it undoubtedly helps to explain some of the reason for this as well. Consistently Scripture shows that God guides his people not through elaborate revelation of the future but only step by step. His guidance comes incrementally, one insight at a time.

On the positive side, God does give us all the information we need to know his will for a decision. He provides all the insight needed to take the next step in front of us.

But no more than that.

The God who created our minds gives us only as much information about his will as he knows we can handle at a given time. And it becomes essential that we move forward in light of that information in order to be in a position to understand his guidance for the step beyond.

Just Enough Light

This thought is expressed in a marvelous analogy in Psalm 119. Speaking of God's Word, or his instruction to us, the psalmist declares, "Thy word is a lamp to my feet and a light to my path" (v. 105). The statement is especially interesting for what it does not say. God's Word is not depicted as a massive light, such as the raging fire Moses encountered in the burning bush, or the pillar of light the Israelites experienced in the desert. Rather it is said to be a *subtle* light—illumination for our feet, for the path right in front of us.

The metaphor is remarkable for its practical implications. Think of yourself walking through the woods on a very dark evening with a light in your hand (a torch or lantern when the psalm was written, a flashlight today; the effect is the same). Just how much illumination does that light give you? *Merely enough to take the next step or two in front of you.* Only as you walk into that light are you then in position to cast the beam out further to see clearly for the next few feet ahead.

This is precisely the way God's guidance is pictured in Scripture. He's shown as one who gives light for the decisions his people face—indeed critical light—yet there's a limitation to it as well. It's generally just enough for the path right ahead. The mystery of the future remains intact. And illumination for the next jump in the trail comes only as one stays in motion.

The Problem of Vocabulary

As basic as the point is, it's usually missed by young Christians, who assume God will guide in a more dramatic fashion. It's often overlooked by older believers as well, who continue to think that God should give them more guidance than what they need to take just the next step of faith.

It's widely assumed—and often taught in popular Christianity—that when God guides us, he provides a window on our personal future. He gives us a perception of what's coming up, of what's "out there." Or if he doesn't furnish a revelation of our future per se, he at least imparts a *mandate* for our future—a distinct directive which locks us into a course of action for a considerable time, perhaps the duration of our lives.

This assumption comes across constantly in the terminology used to talk about God's guidance. A prime example is the word *call.* It's used often by those speaking of going to the mission field. Only occasionally do we hear someone say, "I've decided to serve the Lord in China." Much more typically it's, "I've had a *call* to China." The term is commonly used by those speaking of choices for other ministerial professions, such as the pastorate, Christian schoolteaching or parachurch work. "I've had a *call* to this church." Or, "I've been *called* into campus ministry." Not a few denominations and mission boards expect candidates to give evidence of a call before being certified.

It's not uncommon for those in non-ministerial professions to use the term as well: One has had a *call* to be a teacher, a *call* to be a nurse, a *call* to be an attorney, a *call* to go into business for Christ.

Those who aren't convinced they've had a call to their profession may still feel they *need* a call, or express frustration over not having one (my schoolteacher friend in chapter one, for example). Those considering marriage sometimes use the term too. "I've been called by God to marry Crisandra." Or, "I need to be more certain of God's call before I agree to marry Stephen."

But what sort of perspective on guidance is implied by a "call"? Most obviously it suggests a direct, binding command from God, telling you what the focus of your responsibilities will be for some time to come. It suggests having no doubt whatever about what God has told you. It signifies that if you haven't heard the audible voice of God, you've at least experienced such a strong inner impression or outward confirmation that God's will is now non-negotiable. You've had a *call;* God has spoken definitively, resolutely, giving you guidance not merely for the present but for the years ahead.

This isn't to say that everyone who uses the term means to imply these notions. But many do. And there's no question that many assume these implications when they hear the term.

Similar notions are conveyed by another recurring term in our guidance vocabulary: *vision.* Though not heard as frequently as *call,* it's still used commonly by Christians to speak of God's direction. One may say, "I need a vision from God for my future." Or someone declares, "I've had a vision of the man God wants me to marry."

Again, many use the term benignly. "I need a vision" is simply another way of saying one needs a goal or some sense of direction. There's no intent to imply a prophetic insight into future. But others who hear the term assume clairvoyance is implied. It must mean a revelation from God of what's ahead.

Or take the word *plan*. Christians often talk about the need "to know God's plan" or the importance of "walking in God's plan." Seldom is any distinction made between God's ultimate, mysterious intentions for one's life which cannot be known ahead of time and his immediate, personal will which can be discovered. The term *God's plan*, in fact, is frequently used as a virtual synonym for God's individual will.

Certainly the popularity of the term *God's plan* springs, in part, from its prominence in *The Four Spiritual Laws*, the most widely distributed evangelistic tract in the world. Law 1 of the *Four Laws* declares, "God loves you and has a wonderful plan for your life." In the context of the *Four Laws* the term refers to Christ's salvation and his lordship in the Christian's life, and isn't meant to convey a theology of guidance. Bill Bright and Campus Crusade, who have produced an excellent evangelistic aid, are not to blame for the misuse of this concept. Christians, though, often quote the statement apart from its context in the *Four Laws*. And understandably so, for it's greatly reassuring to be reminded that God loves you and has a wonderful plan for your life.

Yet when no explanation is given as to what is meant by *God's plan*, it is easy to jump to unwarranted conclusions. The all-too-natural assumption is that it refers to a blueprint for your life which must be discovered. Since a plan is a map for the future, it's assumed you must know something of God's future intentions before you can walk in his will in the present. Knowing God's will for a current decision becomes predicated on understanding his future plan for your life.

The problem, of course, is more than just vocabulary. Christians have long cherished the notion that God reveals the future or gives a mandate for the future when he shows his will, and this conviction will continue to be held regardless of the terminology used in speaking of God's guidance. Yet the common use of expressions such as *call, vision* and *God's plan* do tend to reinforce the concept for many. And these terms help to draw many others into the belief as well.

When We Expect Too Much Guidance

To be sure, the belief that God gives insight into the future through his guidance is often held with the most sincere and reverent intentions. Yet it just as often leads to frustration and disappointment for those who bank on it.

For one thing, it leaves many unnecessarily ambivalent in the face of taking major steps. Even when there's convincing evidence a decision should be made, one hesitates for fear that God's guidance hasn't been clear enough. Bill is a typical example.

Since graduating from college four years ago, Bill has directed the singles ministry of his large suburban church on a volunteer basis. He has found considerably more satisfaction in this role than in his job in retail sales. Many have affirmed his potential as a pastor, as well, and his spiritual gifts in this area are obvious. In short, Bill would like to go to seminary and enter the pastoral ministry in his denomination.

All the practical factors seem to line up, and his church has even agreed to help with financing. The one missing factor is a clear sense of call from God to enter the ministry. So Bill waits . . . and waits. Even officials in his denomination tell him not to go ahead until he's certain of God's call.

Or take the case of Linda. She has dated Harry for over three years. Both are mature Christians in their late twenties who are ready for marriage and want to marry each other. But while Harry is eager to go ahead, Linda feels she must wait for a clear confirmation from God that the marriage is from him and will be blessed by him. "I need certainty that this marriage is in God's plan," Linda insists.

The tragedy is that both Bill and Linda have abundant evidence that the choices they would like to make should be made. Unfortunately, their belief that they must wait for God to give a special call or revelation of some sort leaves them unreasonably cautious.

While this perspective on guidance leads to hesitation in the face of major decisions, it also tends to rob confidence once decisions are made. Many lack assurance about where they are right now—even though they may be exactly where God wants them—because they haven't had a call or dramatic guidance to be there. They may be too hasty to bail out of their present situation as a result. If not, their experience of Christ's joy in the situation is still much less than it should be, and their fruitfulness usually suffers as well.

Perhaps the most serious problem with this perspective is that it can make Christians prone to read too much into the guidance from the Lord which they do receive. Those who believe they should receive a revelation of the future when God guides them may be too quick to think this is actually occurring through feelings or impressions they experience, or through unique factors in their circumstances.

When Visions Fail

I understand this problem well, having fallen into it headfirst several times as a young believer. The most mortifying episode occurred when I was twenty-five. Though I'd known the Lord for over five years at this time, I was still operating with rose-colored glasses when it came to guidance.

I took an afternoon to pray and mull over God's direction for my life in a pleasant mountain park setting. Since I was eager for marriage at this time in my life (as I'd been at most previous times), my reflecting naturally wandered into this arena as I pondered the future. For whatever reasons, my thoughts began to focus on a young woman in the college fellowship of my church whom I barely knew. I mused over what it might be like to be married to her. I was surprised to realize how attracted I was to this possibility. As the mental image of her as my wife came into sharper focus, I was certain God was giving me a vision of the years to come. I knew I'd been ordained to marital bliss with this young lady.

For some time after that I cherished the belief that I'd been privy to a private screening on God's future plan for my life. The dream of being married to her naturally blossomed and grew.

It finally came to a screeching halt one evening when I had the audacity to share my "vision" with her, and she bluntly told me that God hadn't spoken to her in any such way.

Well, not exactly a screeching halt, because for some months after that I did continue to hope that she would eventually come to her senses and see God's will as I did. Gradually, though, reality sank in (especially when she became engaged to someone else), and I began to accept that I might have taken more guidance from those mental ruminations on the mountain than was justified.

I now believe that God did indeed guide me during that time on the mountain. The guidance, though, wasn't for the future but *for the present.* He was allowing me to get a better handle on some feelings that I hadn't previously understood.

He was letting me see that I was attracted to this woman, or at least intrigued with her. These feelings *might* indicate that I should take some steps to develop a friendship with her or even ask her for a date. Or they might simply be feelings and nothing more. In any case, they were in no remote way a promise from God about the years ahead. They were not a pledge from God that she would even accept a date, let alone agree to betrothal. They were merely light unto my path—the path of better understanding my emotional insides.

I mention this incident not just to air the gory details of my past but because I find this scenario to be so common. In fact, I've known a large number of Christian men and women who have had a similar experience of apparent divine enlightenment about a future mate which in time led to disappointment. Actually, it isn't hard to understand how this can happen in the romantic area, where emotions run so strong. It's only too tempting to think that God is giving you a forecast of the future through them.

Yet the problem often occurs with vocational choices as well. Not a few Christians, for instance, conclude that they've actually received a call to the mission field or to some area of pastoral service. If over time their impression coincides well with their gifts and aspirations and with the opportunities that open up, there may be no particular problem. But if it doesn't, disappointment and disillusionment often set in. "Why did the call fail?" one wonders. "Did I misunderstand it to begin with?" "Did I understand it correctly at the outset but miss some vital detail along the way?" "Did sin in my life keep it from working out?" "Has God changed his mind?"

Such an experience leaves some gun-shy about taking any more major steps of faith. It's typical, too, to feel angry at God for not carrying through on his "promise" to open doors.

Particular problems arise for the person who announces his or her apparent call to others. They may not be too quick to let their friend off the hook, if feelings or circumstances change. "Hasn't God *told* you to go to Africa?" they insist. "Didn't he clearly reveal that you're to enter the ministry?" And so this person's guilt and confusion are compounded.

Or take the person who at first successfully pursues a call but after some time wants to change directions. Such was the case with a man I know who served a missionary post in Asia for nine years. When he decided it would be best to return to the States and enter a different profession, associates were quick to let him know he was abandoning the call of God—even though the profession he wished to enter was the conventional pastoral ministry! The belief that he could be reneging on a call weighed on him for some time and made the vocational switch more agonizing than it should have been. Such problems arise because so many Christians believe that a call from God is usually a mandate given for life.

The internal and social pressures are enormous, then, to look for more guidance than we need and to read more into God's guidance than is there. To stay clearheaded in the midst of this, we need a solid biblical perspective to keep us anchored. Let's look more carefully at the scriptural evidence for step-by-step guidance. In the next chapter we'll explore a richly inspiring example from Paul's life, and note some other biblical data that's pertinent to the point as well.

For Personal Study:

1. Scripture provides a helpful picture of step-by-step guidance in the

example of Joseph, the father of Jesus, from the time when he heard about Mary's miraculous pregnancy until the time when he settled his family in Nazareth. Read Matthew 1:18—2:23 for the full context.

☐ Note each instance where Joseph made a change in direction, and the different ways in which he gained his understanding about what to do.

☐ Although Joseph received exceptional guidance at times, what evidence do we have that he was often surprised by the turn of events?

☐ What can we learn from his example for our own approach to guidance?

2. Read Exodus 33:12-14. Note the request Moses makes to God and the response God gives to Moses.

☐ How does God's answer differ from what Moses requested?

☐ How does Moses' request parallel the requests for guidance which we often make?

☐ What can we learn from God's response to Moses?

4
Step-by-Step Guidance in Scripture

Key Questions:

■ *In what ways is step-by-step guidance illustrated in the Bible?*
■ *What implications should I draw from this for my own search to know God's will?*

*W*hen we look closely at the examples in Scripture, it's surprising how seldom those who were guided by God actually received any insight into the future at all. There were exceptions; these always involved supernatural revelation, and there seem to be clear reasons why these exceptions occurred. We will look more directly at the matter of exceptional guidance in part three, and note occasions where it might occur today.

But in the great majority of instances in Scripture, God's guidance was experienced only incrementally, in the step-by-step, light-unto-one's-path fashion we've been suggesting is normative. While examples of this sort of guidance permeate both the Old and New Testaments, one of the most interesting and instructive comes from Paul's experience in Acts 16:6-40. The passage begins by relating two thwarted attempts by Paul and his friends to open doors for ministry:

> Paul and his companions traveled throughout the region of Phrygia and Galatia, having been kept by the Holy Spirit from preaching the word in the province of Asia. When they came to the border of Mysia, they tried to enter Bithynia, but the Spirit of Jesus would not allow them to. (NIV)

From everything that we know about Paul, we can assume that his attempts both to enter Asia and Bithynia were tenacious efforts, involving months of travel and strategizing. Yet both opportunities utterly failed to materialize. Though we're not told exactly how the Holy Spirit kept Paul and his associates from entering these areas, the Greek may imply that a physical prevention of some sort took place.

In any case, what's most obvious is that God didn't provide any advance revelation to Paul or his companions that these doors would be slammed shut. Certainly if they had known, they would have invested their efforts elsewhere. There's no indication, either, that these men were in any way out of God's will in moving toward Asia or Bithynia. The implication is that they were right in following the light they had at the time.

It's equally interesting that they didn't turn a hard heart to God at this point or decide to give up on future efforts. While they must have felt some disappointment, the resolve to keep seeking opportunities for ministry never left them. Which may be why God honored Paul at this point with an exceptional revelation. The passage continues:

> So they passed by Mysia and went down to Troas. During the night Paul had a vision of a man of Macedonia standing and begging him, "Come over to Macedonia and help us." After Paul had seen the vision, we got ready at once to leave for Macedonia, concluding that God had called us to preach the gospel to them. (NIV)

Here we do have an instance where Paul received dramatic guidance. Though such occurrences were the definite exception in his experience, they did happen. This is, too, the only occasion in the New Testament where anyone is referred to as being "called" to a particular geographical location to do ministry. In this case, while the call came through a direct, personal vision of Paul's, his companions inferred that they were likewise called to evangelize Macedonia.

We can scarcely imagine the relief which Paul and his party must have felt in finally receiving such definitive guidance after two major false starts. Yet just how definitive *does* the guidance turn out to be? Judging from our popular conception of a call today, we would expect these men to make several logical assumptions about the guidance Paul received:

1. The vision will transpire exactly as Paul received it. They'll go to Macedonia and find a man in a leadership position of ministry, desperate for their assistance.

2. Since the guidance has come so dramatically, further direction to carry out this call will probably come through supernatural means as well. As for knowing what to do, it should be smooth sailing from this point on.

3. The call must imply a mandate to stay and minister in Macedonia for a considerable period, perhaps for life.

Yet as we read on we find that *not one* of these expectations became reality.

Revision of the Vision
We look in vain, for instance, for any reference in the lengthy sixteenth chapter of Acts to a man in ministry leadership in Macedonia. Though we cannot prove from silence that Paul never found him, it would be unlike Luke, the highly detail-conscious author of Acts, to omit such a critical detail from his narrative. What we find instead is that shortly after their arrival in Macedonia, the attention of Paul's ministry shifts in a direction rather different from what they must have anticipated. We read on (Acts 16:13-15):

> On the Sabbath we went outside the city gate to the river, where we expected to find a place of prayer. We sat down and began to speak to the women who had gathered there. One of those listening was a woman named Lydia, a dealer in purple cloth from the city of Thyatira, who was a worshiper of God. The Lord opened her heart to respond to Paul's message. When she and the members of her household were baptized, she invited us to her home. "If you consider me a believer

in the Lord," she said, "come and stay at my house." And she persuaded us. (NIV)

The first recorded encounter of Paul's team with people in Macedonia is not with the man of Paul's vision nor with any men at all but with a group of women, and one remarkable woman in particular, Lydia. If we're right in assuming Paul hasn't yet encountered the man (and again, I think Luke would have mentioned it), then it's particularly striking that he takes the time to minister with these women. It would seem more natural for him to move on and look for the man. Especially when we remember the demeaning views held toward women during this time. Paul's team might have concluded they would better invest their time with men.

To the contrary, they stay and converse with these woman. It's of interest, too, that Paul had no dramatic guidance to do so, as he had experienced in his call to Macedonia in the first place. Here he takes a *circumstance*—the opportunity to minister to these women—as guidance. It is light unto his path, surprisingly adjusting his expectations and plans. Yet he respects this guidance and follows it, even though it doesn't fit perfectly with his initial vision.

The encounter of Paul's team with these women isn't a brief or superficial one. There's enough time and depth involved that Lydia gives her heart to Christ. To say the least, this was an enormous step for any Jewish person and most likely wouldn't have occurred without much dialog with Paul and his friends.

Then a greater surprise: Lydia offers accommodations to Paul's party and they accept. Here we have the most convincing evidence that Paul hadn't found the man in his dream, for if so he very likely would have been hosting Paul and his team himself. (Even at the end of Paul's stay in Macedonia, Lydia's home is still the locus of ministry—see v. 40.)

Again, it's noteworthy that Paul's team received no dramatic guidance to take up residence at Lydia's home. Their decision to stay there occurred simply because "she persuaded us." It's intriguing that they were willing to listen to the reasons she offered and to take her argument as light unto their path, even though it didn't coincide well with Paul's vision of a man. Indeed, the decision to stay at Lydia's home must have been a radical alteration to their plans.

More Surprises

As we read on in Acts 16, we encounter Paul and his team in several adventures. As they are en route to a prayer meeting, they are met by a slave girl whom Luke describes as having "a spirit by which she predicted the future" (v. 16 NIV). He tells us too that "she earned a great deal of money for her owners by fortune-telling" (v. 16). From this point on she follows Paul and his group, shouting "These men are servants of the Most High God, who are telling you the way to be saved" (v. 17). Far from being flattered by this accolade, Paul is annoyed with her chanting, which undoubtedly is loud and disruptive. Paul apparently ignores her at first, assuming she'll soon tire of the routine and go away.

But she persists "for many days" (v. 18). And her presence presents a dilemma for Paul. While he could use spiritual means to cast out her spirit of divination, this would anger her owners and perhaps jeopardize his ministry or even the lives of himself and his companions. There's no indication that God intervened and gave Paul special guidance about how to handle this delicate situation. Rather, when Paul "became so troubled" (v. 18)—that is when his irritation level reached the boiling point—he exorcised the spirit, and it left her immediately.

The immediate problem is solved; a much more threatening one is created. The owners of the slave girl are so enraged that their servant girl is no longer capable of divination that they drag Paul and Silas into the marketplace to face the town authorities, and publicly accuse them of insurrection against the Roman government. A crowd riotously joins in the accusation, and the magistrates have Paul and Silas beaten and imprisoned (vv. 19-24).

Now the excitement really begins. Paul and Silas respond to their imprisonment with unbelievable good nature, "praying and singing hymns to God" (v. 25). Luke notes too that the other prisoners take notice. But about midnight a fierce earthquake so violently shakes the prison foundation that the cell gates fly open and the prisoners' chains are loosened.

The jailer, assuming that the prisoners have fled into the darkness, draws his sword to kill himself, apparently fearing reprisal from his superiors. Paul intervenes in the nick of time, shouting to the jailer not to harm himself—because in fact no one is taking the liberty to escape. This prompts the severely traumatized jailer to seek spiritual counsel from Paul and Silas, and within an hour he and all his family receive Christ. We witness one of the great conversions of Scripture (vv. 25-34).

But surprisingly, it's not one of the great revivals. The conversion of the jailer's family doesn't lead to a city-wide evangelism explosion as we might expect. Instead, the magistrates, after discovering that Paul and Silas are Roman citizens, ask them to leave town. They comply, taking Timothy and leaving the city. The text reads, "After Paul and Silas came out of the prison, they went to Lydia's house, where they met with the brothers and encouraged them. Then they left" (vv. 35-40 NIV).

Here the passage throws us the biggest curve ball of all. Even though Paul had received a supernatural vision to go and minister in Macedonia, he still felt the freedom to leave after a brief stay of probably only a few months. And his decision to exit the city was not prompted by supernatural guidance at all, as the decision to come to Macedonia had been. It was merely a judgment call, based on what seemed to be the most spiritually expedient step to take at this time. The request of the town authorities that he leave, along with other factors at the moment, were light unto his path—guidance as significant as the vision in the night had been.

What we're beginning to see is that Paul's vision itself had merely been light unto his path. It was not the panacea of elaborate and infallible guidance which we might have expected it to be. It did little more than nudge Paul to move on to Macedonia. It told him nothing of what would happen once there or what would be expected of him. Paul felt free (indeed, compelled by responsibility) to continue to seek further light unto his path, even to renegotiate the original vision in view of further light he received. He didn't insist on seeking out a man in ministry but instead gave his attention to discipling a woman. And he felt the liberty to leave Macedonia after a surprisingly brief stay.

His decision to leave was not irresponsible; he had planted important seeds, and he left Luke behind for a time as well to nurture the developing ministry. Yet he didn't personally feel locked into a perpetual call to minister in Macedonia; the vision had a time limit.

The passage, then, provides a wealth of insight into guidance. There is a message of considerable encouragement for those who are eager to follow God's leading.

We are shown that God's guidance usually comes in a much more subtle and incremental way than we might be inclined to expect. His guidance is there in the ongoing details of life and in the ability he gives us to make wise assessment of these (a point we'll consider in much greater depth in the chapters ahead).

Our enlightenment, though, comes only step by step, and moving forward is always necessary before we will understand what direction to take next. The liberating side of this is that it's okay to take a step forward—even a major step—without a call or supernatural insight into the future.

Yes, Paul did receive a vision to go to Macedonia. Yet his experience does more to prove the point we're making about step-by-step guidance than to disprove it. The dream told him virtually nothing about the events ahead. Indeed, one major aspect of the dream—the vision of a man in ministry—apparently had to be adjusted as new light came unto Paul's path. And the dream did not leave Paul feeling constrained to stay in Macedonia indefinitely; after setting some ministry wheels in motion, he moved on.

Seeking Fresh Light

One thing we learn from Paul's experience with the vision is that no matter how definite or dramatic our sense of leading into a ministry or vocational situation might be, we're still free to seek further insight and even to reconsider our direction in view of new understanding we gain. Even if we should have the rare experience of a supernatural vision, our *perception* of that vision is processed through our own internal filters— as it very possibly was in Paul's visualization of the man. In other words, the vision may need some adjusting at points.

And Paul's experience shows us that ministry and vocational situations have their time limits as well. We're not necessarily locked in forever. This doesn't imply a license for unfaithfulness or irresponsibility. In every situation of life we are to invest ourselves responsibly, in a way that most clearly glorifies Christ, and commitments to others must always be honored. And situations need to be given a fair opportunity before we assess just how well we're fitting in. Yet when we're not breaking a pledge to anyone and when we're not clearly acting irresponsibly, we're free before God to consider a different direction. There's nothing inherent even to a supernatural call, in other words, which binds us to a course of direction perpetually.

But while there's significant encouragement in all of this, there is a warning here as well. For one thing, it shows us that we're not to wait indefinitely for dramatic or unmistakable guidance before taking important steps toward seizing ministry and vocational opportunities—and, for that matter, relationships. Points come where we need to move forward in light of the information we have, even though all the facts are not yet in, and further clarity about God's leading will only come as we do.

Just as important, we must not think that any guidance we receive, no matter how dramatic, ever gives us a purchase on our personal future— that is, a guarantee that events will transpire in a particular way. The moment we believe we've been told by God what's going to happen at some future point in our life, we set ourselves up for presumption and disappointment. We must learn to take the Lord's guidance for what it is—light unto our path—and not to assume that more enlightenment is being given at any time than wisdom to take the next step.

This matter is so critical, that it will help to note several other points of biblical evidence which reinforce it.

God's Plan vs. God's Wish

To begin with, whenever the New Testament refers to our responsibility for knowing or doing God's will, the Greek term used for *will* is always *thelēma*, which generally implies not God's resolute intention but simply his wish or desire, which requires our cooperation for its fulfillment.[1]

When Paul states, for instance, "this is the will of God, your sancti-fication: that you abstain from unchastity" (1 Thess 4:3), he's not talking about something God plans to do regardless of our cooperation. Rather, he's stating a *wish* God has for our behavior—one which we can choose to obey or not.

Another Greek term sometimes interpreted as *will, boulē,* indicates God's immutable plan which will be carried out regardless of our coop-eration.[2] Jesus was delivered up "by the deliberate will *[boulē]* and plan of God" (Acts 2:23 NEB). But nowhere does the New Testament suggest that we should seek knowledge of God's *boulē* in making personal deci-sions.[3]

Furthermore, nowhere else does the New Testament counsel us to seek any knowledge of our own future. It might be argued that Paul urges this when he encourages the spiritual gift of prophecy.[4] But it's most probable that this gift refers not to foretelling the future but to the capacity to clearly expound biblical truth.[5]

Even if it does indicate some capacity for prediction, I don't believe that Paul implies we should try to predict our *own* future through this gift. We'll note in chapter seventeen that Paul sees the gifts of the Spirit not for personal edification but rather for the benefit of the body of Christ. Whatever he means by prophecy, he means a gift through which we can minister to other Christians.

It would be wrong to see this gift as some sort of magical tool for simplifying our own decisions. This isn't in any way to discredit the importance of this or any spiritual gift (all of them are vital to Christ's ministry) but simply to try to understand it in a biblical context.

No Crystal Balls

While the New Testament gives no encouragement to seek knowledge of the future, the Old Testament vehemently warns against this activity. Statements are numerous throughout the Old Testament condemning fortunetelling.[6]

And when Saul, king of Israel, sought knowledge of his own future through a fortuneteller, that was one of the factors that led to his downfall and death. In 1 Chronicles 10:13-14 we are told, "So Saul died for his unfaithfulness; he was unfaithful to the LORD in that he did not keep the command of the LORD, and also consulted a medium, seeking guidance, and did not seek guidance from the LORD. Therefore the LORD slew him, and turned the kingdom over to David the son of Jesse." (Please understand I'm not implying that you have committed the unpardonable sin if you have consulted an astrology chart or in some other way sought clairvoyance of your future. The blood of Christ can cover this sin as well as others you commit. I suspect that God's severe punishment of Saul was due to this being the final straw in a long history of disobedience, particularly considering the unique position of trust in which he had been placed. But it does bring home the fact that we have no business as Christians attempting to divine our personal future.)

There is no denial that fortunetelling may sometimes provide reliable insight into the future. Thus Saul gets a correct prediction of his death through the witch (1 Sam 28:9) and Balaam the diviner gets an accurate notion of God's intention to bless Israel (Num 22:7-12). The point is that we have no business looking into the future; such knowledge can only be harmful.

In this same context we should remember that the spirit which Paul cast out of the slave girl in Acts 16, noted above, was a spirit of divination by which she foretold the future. Luke never denies that her clairvoyance may have been accurate. Yet the fact that Paul took steps to extinguish her capacity for fortunetelling seems to reinforce the Old Testament point that this ability is not one generally used to the glory of God.

Beyond this biblical evidence, we should note some purely practical reasons why knowledge of our own personal future could be harmful to us.

First, it could be paralyzing. This was precisely Saul's experience when he consulted the witch. He learned through her seance that his doom was near, and this knowledge was so frightening that it immobilized him (1 Sam 28:20).

And we can guess that in the large majority of situations into which

God leads us we would shrink back in fear if we had full knowledge of the difficulties ahead. How many, for instance, would willingly get married if they had a full preview of all the challenges awaiting them? It is axiomatic that God leads us as much by the information he withholds as by the information he gives!

Second, knowledge of the future could stifle our moment-by-moment obedience to God. If we knew for certain what God intended to do with our lives, we would begin to feel as though we had God "locked in"— that no disobedience on our part would prevent God from carrying out his plan.

Third, such knowledge could also stifle our moment-by-moment faith and trust in God. If we knew for certain what God was going to do in the future, we would have no opportunity for the kind of faith required when we're forced to trust him each moment for fresh guidance.

Fourth, knowledge of the future could stunt the growth of the intellectual faculties God has given us for decision making. Being spiritually "spoon-fed," we wouldn't develop our rational ability for responsible decision making.

Fifth, if it had no other detrimental effect upon us, such knowledge would probably add an unfortunate dimension of boredom to our lives. Knowing what the future held would cause us to lose the sense of curiosity which adds a continual element of anticipation and adventure to our existence. Being guided step by step is surely a much more exciting experience than having an elaborate blueprint of the future before us!

Sixth and finally—to return to the point with which we began chapter three—God has so created our minds that they best handle information not in large quantities but bit by bit. A revelation of the future would normally amount to a mental overload. Our minds are best able to process the enlightenment Christ gives us when it comes step by step. Praise God that he guides us in a way that is appropriate to the mental faculties he has put within us. Step-by-step guidance makes sense not only spiritually but psychologically.

It should be clear, then, that knowing God's future plan would not normally be good for us. Predicting the future should not be our concern as Christians, and we may be freed from the anxiety of thinking we need to know the future to understand God's will for the present.

We don't deny that there may be rare occasions when God wishes to reveal the future to someone, and we certainly don't question God's power to do so. But Scripture gives us no reason to expect this would happen frequently or that the average Christian would ever experience such knowledge. It never instructs us to pray for knowledge of the future. We should assume that, apart from God's giving an unsolicited revelation of the future, such knowledge would be harmful to us.

Not Losing Heart
Once we accept that God isn't likely to guide us through a dramatic call or revelation of the future, there's a danger—namely, that we lose heart and doubt that he's interested in guiding us at all. Actually the peril is twofold.

We may conclude that outside of moral areas God doesn't care what choices we make. This can diminish our sense of purpose and lessen our motivation to invest our lives in ways that can make a difference and that will please him.

Or we may start approaching our decisions in a purely human, rationalistic manner, without reliance on the Lord. Not only is our fruitfulness for Christ diminished when this happens, but also we miss an important part of the joy of a growing, intimate relationship with the Lord.

For these reasons we need to remind ourselves—and to do so constantly—that God does care about our decisions, that he does have a will for our choices. While his guidance is light unto our path—enlightenment only for the step in front of us—he does whatever needs to be done to see that we have this light and exactly the right insight needed for taking that step. He can be trusted fully to guide us, in a way that not only fits into his plan for all humanity but that reflects his very best for our own individual life as well.

In part two we'll begin to look at what our responsibility is for understanding the light which God throws on our path. First, though, it will help to give some attention to deepening our assurance that he will provide this light. In the next chapter we'll look more closely at biblical evidence that God promises to give us the guidance we need. Confidence in that promise will ensure that our study of guidance proceeds on the right foundation.

For Personal Study:

1. Read 1 Corinthians 16:5-9, where Paul tells the Corinthians of his desire to visit them. Does he give any indication that he had received a revelation that this visit should or would occur?

☐ Find as many words or phrases as you can in verses 5-7 which indicate that Paul's understanding of God's future guidance in this matter was in fact tentative at best.

☐ What can we learn from Paul's example here to help us in our own understanding of God's will and in our efforts to plan for the future?

2. While Scripture instructs us through direct statements, it teaches us in many symbolic ways as well. Read Exodus 16:13-21, Deuteronomy 33:25, and Matthew 6:25-34—passages which speak of God's promise to provide the daily needs of his people.

☐ In your own words, what general principle of God's provision is underlined by these passages?

☐ What human attitude of expectation is encouraged by them?

☐ In what ways do these passages symbolize and reinforce the points about step-by-step guidance which we have stressed in chapters three and four?

5
The Promise of Guidance

Key Questions:

■ *What sort of responsibility does God take to see that my decisions agree with his will?*

■ *In seeking God's will, should my attitude be chiefly one of confidence in God's determination to guide me or of concern over the possibility of missing God's will?*

*M*y son Nate and I went for a bike ride one evening and returned just as it was getting dark. As we were putting our bikes into our storage shed, Nate asked whether the shed was dark inside during the day. I remarked that it was fairly dark but that a small window in the back let in some light. He then asked, "Why doesn't the darkness flow out?"

Nate was not joking. He was genuinely intrigued with the fact that darkness doesn't affect light. Though I've often mused over this before (it's a favorite analogy of preachers), hearing the observation come unprompted from a child's mind made it seem very fresh to me. It *is* striking that darkness has no effect on light. If you open the door between a lighted room and a dark one, light spills into the one but not vice versa.

So often Scripture compares the power of Christ over Satan to that of light over darkness. By the same token it speaks of his power in our own lives as that of light dispelling darkness. Yet we don't grasp the impact of these parallels until we appreciate the *absolute power* light has over darkness. "The light shines in the darkness, and the darkness has not overcome it," John reminds us in the introduction to his gospel (Jn 1:5). Many Christians assume that light and darkness co-exist in about equal measure in our Christian experience. While they wouldn't deny that Christ's power is immense, they still assume that the power of evil exercises about an equal influence in their life—a perspective not greatly different from the oriental yin-yang philosophy. Scripture, however, puts matters on a much more triumphant note. "I am the light of the world; he who follows me will not walk in darkness, but will have the light of life," Jesus declared (Jn 8:12). His light within us *substantially* erases the darkness. His power is *immensely* greater than Satan's. The Christian life, in short, is to be lived in a spirit of victory, not defeat.

A Basis for Confidence

While this fact has implications for every aspect of our Christian experience, it is especially pertinent to the area of guidance. It brings home the fact that God's guidance triumphs over human factors that we fear might annul it. And since we have spoken of his guidance in terms of a light unto our path, it is appropriate now to say that this light is absolutely reliable in its appearance. "The light shines in the darkness, and the darkness has not overcome it." God takes uncanny initiative to see that we have the light needed for the decision in front of us. We may be assured that he'll take the responsibility necessary to move us forward.

The subject of guidance should really begin with God—what is his role in the whole process? Unfortunately, many popular discussions on guidance leave us feeling as though guidance depends on our ability to figure out God's will. We fail to realize that guidance ultimately is *God's* problem. We have reason to feel secure.

I don't in any way mean to imply that there is no responsibility on the human side in guidance. In fact, much of this book is devoted to looking at that responsibility. But first, we need to come to grips with the kind of attitude in which this responsibility is to be carried out—namely, one of tremendous assurance that *God himself takes the initiative in guiding the person who is open to being directed by him.* I cannot possibly emphasize this point strongly enough.

If we're really honest, we have to admit that we experience a lot of anxiety here. We fear that if we do not discern God's will carefully enough in some key part of our lives, we'll miss it. When I was single, for instance, I remember feeling as if I was walking a spiritual tightrope in various dating relationships. I would be on edge, wanting to know God's will for each relationship, fearing that if I missed a signal here or a sign there, I'd miss God's plan and forever forsake the chance to be married to the woman of his choice.

But the more I understand about the biblical teaching on guidance, the more I'm convinced that this sort of anxiety is largely misplaced. I see an overwhelming emphasis in the Bible on a God who *takes the responsibility to guide us* in spite of our confusion over his will.

Just Following Along

If we look at the many instances in Scripture where God gives supernatural guidance, we discover an intriguing fact. In most cases God intervenes unexpectedly and gives a person guidance *even when no request has been made for it.* In other words, God goes "out of his way" to make sure the person has adequate knowledge of his will in order to do it.

We see God doing this when he calls various great leaders in biblical history. Consider Moses, who was tending sheep for his father-in-law when God called him to deliver the people of Israel from slavery in Egypt (Ex 3). Or Saul, who in looking for some lost asses was led to Samuel who anointed him king (1 Sam 9—10). Or David, who was tending the flock and because of his age was not even included with his seven brothers when they were "interviewed" by Samuel for the position of king (1 Sam 16:1-13).

Samuel said, "None of these tall, handsome guys is the person God sent me to anoint. Jesse, are these all the sons you have?"

And Jesse said, "Well, there's young David, but he's out tending the sheep. He's not a likely candidate."

Samuel said, "Send for him." And he poured the oil on the shocked teen-ager, saying, "God wants you to be the king."

In none of these instances did any of these men have the slightest inkling that they were about to be commissioned for an extraordinary leadership task. They were simply doing their duty, carrying out their mundane responsibilities—not even seeking special guidance—when God broke through and revealed his will to them.

Beyond such examples, there are numerous statements throughout the Bible which point directly to God's sovereign initiative in guidance. But there is probably not a more profound and helpful picture of this role than that of God as a shepherd leading his sheep and tenderly caring for them.

The analogy of God's care for Israel to a shepherd's care for his sheep is a familiar one in the Old Testament.[1] In the New Testament Jesus is pictured as the Good Shepherd, who compassionately leads those who choose to follow him. We find this picture developed most extensively in John 10, one of the most inspiring New Testament statements on guidance:

"Truly, truly, I say to you, he who does not enter the sheepfold by the door but climbs in by another way, that man is a thief and a robber; but he who enters by the door is the shepherd of the sheep. To him the gatekeeper opens; the sheep hear his voice, and he calls his own sheep by name and leads them out. When he has brought out all his own, he goes before them, and the sheep follow him, for they know his voice. A stranger they will not follow, but they will flee from him, for they do not know the voice of strangers." This figure Jesus used with them, but they did not understand what he was saying to them.

So Jesus again said to them, "Truly, truly, I say to you, I am the door of the sheep. All who came before me are thieves and robbers; but the sheep did not heed them. I am the door; if any one enters by me, he will be saved, and will go in and out and find pasture. The thief comes only to steal and kill and destroy; I came that they may have life, and have it abundantly.

"My sheep hear my voice, and I know them, and they follow me; and I give them eternal life, and they shall never perish, and no one shall snatch them out of my hand." (Jn 10:1-10, 27-28; see also Heb 13:20; 1 Pet 2:25; 5:4; Mt 9:36)

Throughout this passage Jesus explicitly speaks of taking the sort of responsibility for his followers that a shepherd takes for his sheep. And this responsibility clearly involves guidance: "he calls his own sheep by name and leads them out" (v. 3); "he goes before them, and the sheep follow him, for they know his voice" (v. 4); "My sheep hear my voice, and I know them, and they follow me" (v. 27).

And Jesus further makes a key reference to guidance in verse 9: "If any one enters by me, he will be saved, and will go in and out and find pasture." The concept of eternal life and salvation which Jesus presents here implies much more than life after death; it indicates a quality of life brought on by the leadership of Christ, one which begins the moment one is born of Christ. The reference to going in and out and finding pasture is to a Jewish expression of the time: "To be able to come and go out unmolested was the Jewish way of describing a life that is absolutely secure and safe."[2] Here Jesus indicates the freedom and security a sheep could enjoy under the care of a conscientious shepherd.

There are really two factors that make this shepherd analogy a particularly encouraging one for us who are seeking the will of God.

The first is the nature of the shepherd.[3] The Palestinian shepherd was known, not only for his compassion toward his sheep, but also for his firm leadership of them. The shepherd was really an autocrat over his sheep, taking absolute responsibility to see that the sheep got from one pasture area to another.[4] And he would take whatever measures were necessary to ensure this, short of physically harming the sheep. If a sheep strayed from the fold, for instance, the shepherd might sling a rock toward the sheep, aimed carefully so that it would land directly in front of the sheep but not hit it. The sheep would be startled and would quickly return to the comfort of the fold.[5]

The second factor is the nature of the sheep. Of all animals, the sheep is known for being exceedingly dumb—a beast with little sense of direction, who can scarcely find its way anywhere without the shepherd. When Jesus wanted to describe the lostness of people, he called them sheep, for a sheep when lost is really lost.[6] The sheep is totally dependent upon the shepherd.

We are reminded, then, that God realizes we are like sheep who have little sense of where we should be going, who experience tremendous confusion over finding the right way. But God takes a phenomenal amount of initiative to guide us in spite of our confusion. Realizing this should bring us tremendous security as we seek to know and to do the will of God.

No Need to Fear

Realizing God's concern for me should free me from several common fears.

First, I can be free of the fear that *God may not give me the information I need to decide within his will.* It's easy to fall into the trap of thinking that God is too busy, or too far removed, to be concerned with giving me guidance. He would surely give guidance to the great saints and Christian heroes—those whom he uses to make an obvious mark on the course of history—but it's presumptuous for me to expect the same sort of leading from him. I'm simply not that important.

Yet to understand Jesus' language in John 10 is to realize that God's guidance is not something reserved only for the Christian "heroes" but a precious gift given to each and every believer. The picture of the sheep certainly depicts not a spiritual super-giant but an ordinary believer. Jesus talks about giving guidance to *all* his sheep (v. 4) and makes an explicit promise in verse 9: "I am the door; if *any one* enters by me, he will be saved, and will go in and out and find pasture" (emphasis added).

Second, I can be released from the fear that *I may not be able to understand God's will if he does convey it to me.* In other words, even if I believe God will give me guidance, I may doubt my ability to understand what he is saying. In my finite understanding I might miss a key signal which would throw me hopelessly off the course of God's will.

But when Jesus promises in John 10 that he will lead us, he is promising much more than simply the giving of information. He is promising a shepherd's guidance, which means he'll take the full responsibility to see that we get where he wants us to go when we're open to his leading. Where we lack understanding, he'll so arrange our circumstances that we still end up doing what he desires. He's simply too big to allow our lack of understanding to keep him from leading us in the path of his will.

Third, I can be free of the fear that *a past decision made in faith may later be found to be outside of God's will.* As Christians we are notorious for re-evaluating our past decisions. We may be convinced that a certain decision is God's will, but later we discover new information which would have caused us to decide differently, and we conclude that we must have misjudged God's leading.

A friend of mine recently told me that although he had felt strongly led by God to go to St. Louis, severe job frustrations were now making him think he had misunderstood God's direction in moving there. If we take God's sovereignty in guidance seriously, we must conclude that such rehashing of past decisions is really unnecessary. It is also impious. I must trust that God allowed me to have the information I needed at the time of the decision and likewise withheld information that might have discouraged me from going where he wanted.

Later information may signal a change in direction, but it cannot challenge my original understanding of God's will. It is axiomatic that *God leads as much by information he withholds from us as by information he gives.*

Fourth, I can be free of the fear that *my sin may ultimately cause me to miss God's plan for my life.* Now here I need to back up quickly and put some strong qualifications on what I'm saying. We're talking here about the person who is serious about wanting to do God's will in the first place. Among such persons there are some who have a deadly fear that their own sinfulness is interfering enormously with God's plan. They worry themselves sick that they will never find the person God wants them to marry or never end up in the profession in which God wants them, because their sin will cause God to reject them from his plan.

This sort of fear is quite unjustified in the person who has a heart toward doing God's will. I think the most beautiful aspect of the shepherd-sheep analogy is that it reminds us vividly that Christ guides us not only in spite of our confusion about his will but also in spite of our *waywardness*. Sheep in the Bible are pictured not only as confused animals but as wayward ones.

Here we immediately confront a host of theological questions about God's sovereignty versus human free will and responsibility. If dealt with thoroughly, these difficulties would take us considerably beyond the confines of this book. The minute we begin to deal in this realm, we must realize we are confronting a theological mystery which cannot be fully explained. Yet there are some very practical aspects to guidance.

On the one hand, it's clear from the Bible that we are to have a healthy fear about the possibility of our sin interfering with God's will—I'm not in any way denying this. It's abundantly clear from Scripture that our sin can and often does cause us to deviate from God's perfect plan. It's clear that our sin always causes us to miss blessings we would have known if we had followed God's will more perfectly. Christians who are indwelt by the Holy Spirit are going to be concerned about the sin in their lives and are going to carry on a lifetime battle with it.

But on the other hand, it's equally clear that we are not to be obsessed with a fear that loses sight of the fact that he who is in us is greater than he who is in the world (1 Jn 4:4). In fact, it can certainly be said that if we have a healthy concern about sin in our lives, there is no need for *extreme* fear. The biblical picture of guidance is one of God's taking the person who has a basic desire for his will and working out a plan in that person's life which is realized to an important extent in spite of his or her weakness and sin. While sin may cause a person to miss some of the blessings of God, it does not throw him or her hopelessly off the path of God's will. We see this illustrated in person after person among the great saints of the Bible in the Old and New Testaments.

What this boils down to is that if our basic disposition is to do God's will in the first place, we may be confident that he will take us to the key points in his plan, even though we may reach them in a wayward manner. While we need always to be doing battle with sin in our lives, the battle should be carried on in a spirit of victory, not one of defeat. Our search to know and do God's will should be carried out in an attitude of tremendous security, not of neurotic anxiety.

As we begin now to look at what *our* responsibility is in the process of discovering God's will for personal decisions, keep in mind what has been said about *God's* initiative. We must be careful not to lose sight of the forest for the trees. We must never forget that guidance is ultimately God's responsibility, that he is infinitely more concerned that we know and do his will than we could ever be, and that he is taking a most gracious initiative to guide us as we are seeking to respond to him.

Guidance for the consecrated believer is not merely a possibility, nor simply a good probability. It is a *promise*—one of the great promises of the Bible.

For Personal Study:

1. Read Psalm 139, which describes God's intimate involvement in our lives. Note ways in which this psalm reinforces our confidence that God will provide us with the guidance that we need.

2. Fundamental to our fear that God will not give us the guidance we need is the idea that our mistakes or sin might prevent him from doing so. The example of Jesus in his earthly ministry provides some significant encouragement at this point, for we often see him compensating in gracious ways for the blunders of his disciples and others. This is evident in both his first miracle and his final miracle (before his resurrection), for instance. Read John 2:1-11 and Luke 22:50-51 for descriptions of these two incidents.

☐ Note significant mistakes which individuals made and how Jesus bailed them out.

☐ What reassurance may we take from these incidents about his intention to provide for our needs? about his determination to guide us?

3. This question is for those who are familiar with the life of Joseph the patriarch in Genesis. If you are not, you might want to take the time to read the lengthy section in Genesis about him—especially chapters

37—50; it is one of the richest personal stories in Scripture.

☐ What major mistake did Joseph make, as a teenager, which resulted in extensive problems for him?

☐ Did this mistake prevent God from working out his ultimate plan for Joseph?

☐ In what critical ways did God use this mistake to further his plan for Joseph?

☐ What reassurance may we take from Joseph's life in the face of our own concern to carry out God's will?

Part **2**
My Responsibility for Knowing God's Will

6
The Call to Responsibility

Key Questions:

■ *How do God's responsibility for guidance and mine interrelate?*
■ *Does my experience of guidance change as I grow in Christ?*
■ *Should I expect to take more initiative for discerning God's will, or less, as I mature spiritually?*

W hile Scripture has much to say about God's initiative in guidance, it has plenty to say about our own role as well. And though its teaching on this is far-reaching, it boils down to one basic point: *We can—and should—take significant responsibility in the whole guidance process.*

This is a message of immensely good news, for it says that there are actually things we can do to better understand and follow God's will. We can invest our restless energies in constructive ways toward this end! By the same token, there are steps we can take to realize our potential for Christ more fully. While walking with Christ often means waiting in faith, it often means taking steps of faith as well.

If I want to be married, for instance, I don't have to merely sit passively and wait for my princess charming to arrive on my doorstep. I can take initiative toward finding a partner, or toward resolving the direction of a relationship I'm already in.

Or if I'm in a job or profession which doesn't adequately utilize my God-given gifts, I can take steps to find employment where I can better invest myself for Christ and be the person he has created me to be.

But while this is wonderfully liberating news, it lays a definite challenge on us as well. It brings home the fact that we must take responsibility if we're to properly understand and cooperate with God's leading. *He will most fully guide us as we take responsibility for knowing and doing his will.* There are exceptions to this pattern, to be sure. Yet they will most likely occur in the early stages of our Christian experience. As we mature in Christ, God will expect us to take greater responsibility for major life choices.

When It Was Simple
Let me share with you two experiences from my own life which help to underline the point.

The first major decision which I faced as a very young Christian was remarkably easy. It concerned my involvement with a rock band I directed, the Newports. When I gave my life to Christ as a third-year college student, I was spending a lot of time managing and booking this group, which played frequently for local dances and social events.

The question now was whether or not God wanted me to continue performing with the group. At first it was easiest just to follow the course of least resistance, so I stayed in. But after several months the resistance on that path got much stronger. In fact, in an instant.

I was studying in a dormitory room at Georgetown University when it suddenly became crystal clear to me that God wanted me to leave the Newports. At least this was my perception. While I didn't hear an audible voice, I did have an overwhelming sense that God was prompting me. I must hasten to say that this was not a philosophical conclusion about music, such as "rock music is of the devil." I wasn't mature enough in the Lord to deal with an issue of that sort (and for the record, I don't believe that any form of music is moral or immoral in itself). The conviction was simply a deep, intuitive one. I was certain God was speaking to me and nudging me to quit this group.

I didn't even question it. Within a day I spoke with practically everyone associated with the band—about ten people in all—and in the unsophisticated manner of a new Christian boldly asserted that God had spoken to me and told me to resign. Even though most of them questioned my lucidity, I had no doubt I had been led by God.

There is one factor, especially, which persuades me that this was an authentic experience of exceptional guidance and not just a grandiose delusion. Within about a week after making this decision, I simply stopped receiving phone calls from people wanting to hire the Newports. There was no clear explanation for this. The group's services had been in considerable demand up to this point, and most people wanting to hire the group wouldn't have known yet that I had quit. But for some reason the calls just stopped coming in. I've never known how to explain this apart from its being a dramatic confirmation from the Lord that I made the right choice.

Of course, my interpretation of these events is subjective. There's no way ultimately to prove any explanation for them. Yet the evidence leads me to believe that I did have an experience of special guidance.

If so, then the obvious question is why this experience proved genuine, when my "vision" on the mountain of my future mate (described in chapter three) turned out to be so much wishful thinking. Again, I can only offer a subjective answer.

The guidance to leave the Newports came at a time when I was very young in the faith and not ready to take responsibility for a major decision. God, I believe, was gracious to intervene and guide me in a direct manner. He even took care of the ramifications of that decision in a remarkable way.

The experience on the mountain, however, came several years later when I undoubtedly should have known better and the Lord undoubtedly wanted me to take a more mature approach to decisions. Again he was gracious—but this time not to let me get away with thinking I had a purchase on my own future. Had that vision worked out as I wished, I wouldn't have been challenged to grow in the way I approached my decisions.

The Normal Pattern
The fact is that I have never had another experience of guidance as direct and unmistakable as that one in the dormitory. Over time, in fact, my decisions have tended to become more challenging rather than less so.

When Evie and I had the opportunity in 1978 to move back to Washington, D.C., and begin Nehemiah Ministries, we wrestled with that option for several months. While there were many reasons to recommend it, there were also many reasons to think I shouldn't abandon my pastoral position in St. Louis. All in all, this was a most difficult decision. There was no dramatic guidance to simplify things, as when I left the Newports. Even up until the moment of resolving it, Evie and I had real questions about what the Lord wanted us to do.

We finally decided to make the move. In retrospect I have no doubt that this choice was as much in God's will as the decision to leave the band had been some thirteen years earlier. Yet these alternatives were arrived at in quite different ways.

I find that my experience parallels that of many Christians. Many discover that as they grow in Christ, they are compelled to take greater responsibility for important steps. Decisions become more complicated and require more personal involvement and initiative. Too often this is interpreted negatively. One may assume it is a sign of poor spirituality or of indifference on the Lord's part. "If I were only closer to Christ," one thinks, "or if he were only more concerned about guiding me, I wouldn't be forced to spend so much effort working through this decision."

Yet there is much in Scripture to suggest that as we grow in Christ, God *expects* us to take greater responsibility for our major choices. There are certain important reasons, too, why it makes sense that he would call us to do this.

One reason is certainly to encourage us to grow. Through tackling more challenging decisions we develop our rational faculties in a way that would never occur if God always intervened and told us instantaneously what to do. We grow, too, in our ability to handle responsibility, a benefit which has positive impact in all areas of life.

He does this also, I suspect, to bring a greater element of adventure into our experience. As Paul Tournier points out in his classic book *The Adventure of Living,* adventure is at the heart of God's intention for the Christian life.[1] He has placed an intense instinct for adventure deep within each of us. Though we tend to repress this instinct in favor of our security needs, God is even more concerned to bring adventure into our lives than security and comfort. Adventure comes close to what Christ meant by "abundant life" (Jn 10:10) and is fundamental to living a life which is both fulfilled and fruitful.

When we stop and think about it, some of our most meaningful times of adventure are the periods of working through major decisions. Once we accept that the element of challenge *should* be there, the decision process becomes more stimulating and enjoyable. Indeed, these are often the times when we feel most fully alive.

Partners with Christ

There is another reason, though, that I believe God allows us to face challenging decisions, and that is to increase our sense of purpose and personal worth. It's to give us a role in the work he's doing, to be a participant with Christ in his mission. St. Paul, in fact, comes close to calling serious followers of Christ *partners* with God in his ministry. He refers to his readers as "ambassadors for Christ" in 2 Corinthians 5:20, then several verses later speaks of them being "God's fellow workers" (2 Cor 6:1).

Jesus implied the notion of partnership even more directly in his last discourse when he declared his disciples to be his "friends" (Jn 15:14). To be a friend with him, Jesus said, is a step beyond being merely a servant who "does not know his master's business." The friend, by contrast, is familiar with the strategies of God. Jesus' implication, I believe, is that the friend is now capable of making good decisions—choices which reflect the mind and heart of God. By this Jesus was undoubtedly saying that he expected his disciples to take more initiative in the decision making process. While he didn't mean he would no longer be guiding them, he did mean that his guidance would now come as they took initiative.

It's interesting that Jesus didn't declare his disciples friends when they first began walking with him but only after a significant period of growth and discipleship. Again, this seems to underline the fact that as we grow in Christ, he expects us to take greater responsibility for decisions.

Where We're Heading

Our purpose from this point on in this book will be to consider how we can take this responsibility for decision making in the most mature and wholesome way. We will build up to the point that much of this responsibility involves carefully thinking through the options before us. But there are more foundational steps which must first be taken to reach the point where our judgment is reliable.

Most important is our need to become willing to accept God's will in a decision, even before we know what it is. It's in an attitude of willingness that we're best able to understand and respond to the Lord's leading. Also critical is the need for serious prayer with respect to decisions we're facing. Prayer not only helps to clarify our thinking but is often the most significant step toward becoming more open to God's will. In addition, our personal study of Scripture serves in vital ways both to draw us into a more pliable relationship with Christ and to help us more clearly understand his guidance.

We will devote the next three chapters to looking carefully at each of these basic needs. Then in chapters ten and following we'll consider the need for sound thinking, look at a number of examples of a reasoned approach to guidance in Scripture, and explore some specific areas.

For Personal Study:

1. Read 1 Corinthians 7:1-7, where Paul gives straightforward advice about deciding whether to marry (if you wish, read all of 1 Corinthians

7 to understand the fuller context).

☐ Does Paul say anything about waiting for special guidance in the marriage decision?

☐ Note different ways he addresses personal responsibility in this issue.

☐ What application can I make to a marriage decision which I or someone else would face today?

2. Read 2 Thessalonians 3:6-13. Paul exhorts believers in this passage to be gainfully employed and not to presume unfairly on others for help. Laziness is one factor which could keep us from carrying out Paul's command.

☐ How could a view of guidance which requires us to wait for special leading also hinder us here? Does Paul make any allowance for such a view in his teaching in this passage?

☐ How would you characterize the view of guidance which underlies what Paul says here?

☐ What application may we make to our own vocational decisions today?

3. This question is for advanced students of Scripture. We've suggested in this chapter that experiences of special guidance seem more typical to the early period of our Christian walk, and that as we grow in Christ, he calls us to take greater responsibility for our personal choices. Can you think of one or more examples of individuals in Scripture who illustrate this pattern?

☐ Note specifics from these individuals' lives which suggest that their experience of guidance changed with age or spiritual growth.

7

Are You Willing?

Key Questions:

■ *What sort of attitude do I need in order to understand God's guidance?*
■ *Must my motives be perfectly pure?*

A woman whom I know, Sarah, struggled with crippling stage fright. The problem began when she was twelve and became tongue-tied giving an announcement at a church service. Her humiliation was so extreme that she went to any lengths after that to avoid any situation where she would have to speak in front of a group.

In her thirties she became involved with a large Bible study for women. As these women came to know her, they perceived that she had gifts for leadership and teaching. They saw her potential more clearly than she did. Through much prodding and encouragement they finally persuaded her to try teaching at one of their weekly meetings. This was not a trivial task, as it involved giving a forty-minute lecture.

Though she was quite apprehensive as she began her talk, she was surprised to find that she quickly relaxed and was able to present her material coherently. Her presentation was very well received.

Most interesting is the observation she shared with me about the experience: "You know, I found I was putting as much energy into looking for ways to avoid public speaking as it took to finally go ahead and face the challenge."

I find Sarah's experience especially instructive for us as we begin to look at willingness to do God's will. The fact is that we spend much of our energy in life trying to avoid the things that would be best for us to do. Ironically, as Sarah's example reminds us, it often requires no more effort to go ahead and face a challenge than to avoid it. And the serendipities that follow are often considerable.

Sarah's experience brings to mind, too, that until we reach the point of being willing to do the difficult thing, our minds are often not able to think clearly about our options. Sarah had spent many years trying to convince herself that she wasn't cut out for public speaking. Only when she crossed that magical line and became willing to try did she begin to see her potential in a more positive light. The simple act of becoming willing opened up a whole new horizon for her.

Willingness, then, is a critical first step toward understanding our potential and the options that are before us. Beyond this psychological truth is a vital spiritual truth as well. Scripture shows that God is often unwilling to make his will clear to us until he knows that we're willing to accept it. While this fact should concern us, there's a wonderfully positive side to it as well: As we become willing to accept God's will, our understanding of what he wants us to do usually deepens. In addition, we gain a remarkable basis for confidence that our decision process is being guided by him and that what we decide reflects his will.

Being Open to Suggestion

It's often thought that our main role in guidance is to try to figure out what God's will is. But without in any way belittling our responsibility in that area, it must be stressed that biblically our primary responsibility isn't an intellectual but *volitional* one. Before all else we are to strive for an attitude of willingness to do God's will; it's only in the context of such an attitude that we can truly see clearly what God's will is. I'm convinced that in the majority of cases when Christians experience long-term confusion over God's will, the problem isn't that his will isn't clear enough but that they simply don't want to accept it.

Throughout the Bible, for instance, where we see God giving special calls to various people, in almost every case it seems the person was willing to do God's will before it was ever revealed.[1] We conclude this simply from the fact that most of them responded quickly and obediently to God's leading. While there are cases where great leaders felt ambivalence about their ability to carry out an assignment (for example, Moses or Jeremiah), we seldom sense that underneath they were resistant to doing God's will. And it was certainly this underlying attitude of heart which had much to do with God's choosing them for extraordinary tasks.

I don't know of a passage in Scripture that sums up this condition of willingness and its results more succinctly than Romans 12:1-2:

I appeal to you therefore, brethren, by the mercies of God, to present your bodies as a living sacrifice, holy and acceptable to God, which is your spiritual worship. Do not be conformed to this world but be transformed by the renewal of your mind, that you may prove what is the will of God, what is good and acceptable and perfect.

This passage makes a tremendous promise about the will of God—that we can *prove* his will ("what is good and acceptable and perfect" is a modifying clause). The word *prove* in the Greek is a pregnant term for which we really have no good English equivalent. It's the same word used of the process of purifying precious metal in a furnace and testing its strength.[2]

In the context of our passage it means that we'll live out God's will and discover it through experience. In plain and practical terms, it means we'll both know God's will and do it at the same time. We'll have the knowledge of his will that we need along with the spiritual strength to carry it out. This is the remarkable promise of guidance we saw in chapter five.

But the passage also states two conditions to the promise. The first is given by "present your bodies as a living sacrifice." Paul sees this as a commitment of one's entire being to Jesus Christ, like the commitment made to your spouse once and for all in a wedding ceremony. This is beautifully implied by the Greek verb *present*, which is in a tense indicating a one-time action which affects your life from that point on.[3]

Paul is saying, then, that the most essential condition for knowing God's will is to become a Christian—to give one's life once and for all to Jesus Christ. I cannot know God's will unless I first know God through Jesus Christ. This is where it begins.

Yet it does not end here. Paul sets forth a second condition that must be fulfilled on an ongoing basis once one becomes a believer. It's indicated by "do not be conformed to this world but be transformed by the renewal of your mind." These verbs in the Greek, interestingly, are in a tense which indicates *repeated* action, in other words, something that we must do continually.[4]

The negative side of this condition ("do not be conformed to this world") suggests that we must strive to avoid doing those things we clearly know are against the will of God. The positive side ("but be transformed by the renewal of your mind") tells us that we must be constantly yielding our minds to the control of the Holy Spirit. Here, however, it's important to understand that the word *mind* in Greek is *nous*, which means not just intellect but the whole "inner direction of one's thought and will and the orientation of one's moral consciousness,"[5] with a special emphasis upon the will.[6]

Paul, more than anything, is telling us that we must constantly strive for an attitude of yieldedness, an attitude of openness to the will of God. If we have that attitude, then, Paul makes it clear that we will both know and do God's will.

In short, then, Romans 12:1-2 makes an extraordinary statement: *If I'm willing to do God's will, I will do it.* This is really the most important point of our study.

Practical Implications

In practical terms I believe this willingness really amounts to two things. First of all, I must do what I already know to be God's will. And second, I must be willing in advance to accept whatever alternative God might show to be his will, even before I know what it might be. It's like giving God a blank contract with my name signed at the bottom, with the freedom to fill it out any way he chooses.

But how do I determine whether I'm really willing to do God's will? The most effective way is to imagine all the alternatives which could be logical options in a decision. If I know that I would accept any of these if God said to, then I may be confident that I'm willing to follow his will. This doesn't mean that God will necessarily lead me to choose the least appealing alternative (we'll discuss the problem of understanding our desires in chapter fifteen), but it does mean that I must be willing to accept that option if it's clear God wishes me to.

Unfortunately, this is where we too often run into problems. So often we're intensely curious about God's will yet have already made up our minds what we're going to do; we seek to know God's will simply to find out whether his choice coincides with ours. We're hoping he'll rubber-stamp the decision we have already made! Or, while we may be open to certain alternatives, we remain closed to others.

A young woman came to me for vocational counseling. She desperately wanted to find employment in a particular artistic field which would give her a unique chance to witness for the Lord. I immediately thought of an opportunity she could pursue in California and suggested it to her.

Her reply, however, was most revealing. She was certain God wouldn't want her to go to California. It would be too far away from family and friends; she was sure God would want to give her a job in the eastern part of the U.S. As we talked, she finally admitted that even if God wanted her in California, she wasn't willing to go.

When this is our attitude, it's really beside the point to expect God to show us anything. *Only when we're willing in advance to accept whatever God might want are we in a position where we can hope to prove his will.*

What about Motives?

In talking about willingness I must clarify that I'm not referring to absolute purity of motives. This is an area where many Christians do get confused. Popular writings on guidance sometimes imply that it's impossible to know the will of God until your motives are perfectly pure. Consider, for instance, the following statement by F. B. Meyer:

So long as there is some thought of personal advantage, some idea of acquiring the praise and commendation of men, some aim at self-aggrandizement, it will be simply impossible to find out God's purpose concerning us. The door must be resolutely shut against all these if we would hear the still small voice. All cross-lights must be excluded if we would see the Urim and Thummin stone brighten with God's "yes," or darken with His "no."[7]

While I have the very highest respect for F. B. Meyer, I am troubled by his language here. Undoubtedly he's trying to prod Christians toward a healthy sort of willingness to do God's will. But the language speaks more to the need for complete purity of motives. I must confess that if I truly believed that the requirement he speaks of were laid upon me, I'd never get up in front of a group again to speak, nor would I ever set my fingers to a typewriter.

There's never a time when I make the effort to communicate, publicly or through writing, when my motives are perfect. There's always the hope that others will appreciate what I'm saying and affirm me for it. I must be honest in saying, too, that it isn't always easy to take my spiritual temperature and know whether such motives are good or bad. I do know, for instance, that without some desire to be accepted by others, I would never make the effort to communicate effectively. It seems to be more a question of balance than anything.

I'm certain that perfect pristine purity of motives in any action we take is a psychological impossibility. Even as Christians, it's not possible to do anything where there's not at least some selfishness of motive involved; this is simply part of the plague of always having the old nature to deal with this side of eternity.

In addition, it's axiomatic that when Christ leads us to do something, we'll almost immediately begin to experience selfish motives about it. The person called to be a missionary, for instance, will almost unavoidably begin to imagine all the praise and honor this sacrificial service will bring from folks back home. This is an impossible psychological syndrome out of which to break.

It's precisely here that many Christians with sensitive consciences get paralyzed. At first they're convinced about a course of direction Christ wants them to take. But then they begin to experience selfish motives, and, try as they may, they cannot get rid of these. So they reach the fateful conclusion: "Christ must not be leading me in this direction at all!" Satan, I believe, has a field day immobilizing Christians through this sort of introspection.

I find this a common problem among musicians and artists as well as with those in various areas of leadership and teaching ministry. A man I know who attends a church in New England has had a most effective ministry giving children's messages in the services of that church for many years. Yet tears came to his eyes when he told me that he wondered if God really wanted him in this role. His concern, he said, was that *he enjoyed it so much;* this led him to question whether his motives were really right in doing it.

I doubt anyone at this church is the least bit troubled by this man's motives. From what I can see, all are exceedingly grateful for his ministry. Knowing the difficulty most pastors have in formulating children's messages, I'm certain the minister is especially indebted to him. The fact is that this man is effective—both with the children and with the adults who hear his weekly homilies—precisely *because* he enjoys the responsibility as much as he does.

Gifts and Motives

It's striking that in his extensive teaching on spiritual gifts, Paul says hardly anything about refraining from using them because of motives. He does command "Never be in a hurry to ordain a man" in 1 Timothy 5:22, apparently cautioning against putting a new believer in a position of honor who hasn't yet developed the maturity in Christ to handle it. Yet beyond this one caution, the overwhelming emphasis in Paul's teaching is upon using our gifts and employing them in the service of Christ. Very little is said about the occasional situation where God might ask us to hold back. Rather we're told in strong language in various places to get about the business of using the gifts God has given us and to give our full attention to developing them.

Consider Paul's exhortation in Romans 12, for instance, which immediately follows the instruction about proving God's will which we've just examined:

As your spiritual teacher I . . . give this advice to each one of you. Don't cherish exaggerated ideas of yourself or your importance, but try to have a sane estimate of your capabilities by the light of the faith that God has given to you all. For just as you have many members in one physical body and those members differ in their functions, so we, though many in number, compose one body in Christ and are all members [of] one another.

Through the grace of God we have different gifts. If our gift is preaching, let us preach to the limit of our vision. If it is serving others let us concentrate on our service; if it is teaching let us give all we have to our teaching; and if our gift be the stimulating of the faith of others let us set ourselves to it. Let the man who is called to give, give freely; let the man in authority work with enthusiasm; and let the man who feels sympathy for his fellows in distress help them cheerfully. (Rom 12:3-8 Phillips)

In this passage Paul certainly condemns the bloated ego ("Don't cherish exaggerated ideas of yourself or your importance"). But he likewise discourages the sort of self-deprecation we too easily fall into regarding our gifts, often due to obsessive concern over motives. "Have a sane estimate of your capabilities," Paul insists. He clearly says that as a general principle God wants us to pursue our areas of potential earnestly. He then gives a solid exhortation about using specific gifts which we clearly have.

Paul was certainly aware that some of these young believers had motives which were less than perfect. Yet he says nothing to them about holding back on that account. To the contrary, he indicates that the road to sanctification is more likely *through* using one's gifts. There's considerable liberation and encouragement in this thought.

"I Don't Deserve Marriage"

Christians obsess about motives in decisions about marriage as well. As I note in *Should I Get Married?*, some who would truly like to be married are convinced they don't deserve this benefit. While they reach this conclusion for different reasons, concern about motives is one of the primary factors. Some serious Christians are convinced that their fantasies about sex or even their desire for fulfillment through marriage itself disqualifies them from God's provision of marriage. The fact that their level of self-interest in getting married is so strong convinces them that the urge to marry is not from the Lord.

Again, Paul's teaching on this matter is surprisingly consoling and liberating. He begins a lengthy excursion on the marriage decision in 1 Corinthians 7 declaring, "It is good for a man not to marry. But since there is so much immorality, each man should have his own wife and each woman her own husband" (v. 2 NIV).

We might expect Paul to have said "since there is so much immorality, first prove yourself morally worthy, then marry." But he says practically the opposite. He indicates that our struggles with sexual temptation are a primary reason to *consider* marriage. Marriage, in short, is given not because we deserve it but because we *need* it. It's a fundamental answer God provides for the problem of lust and the need for marital fulfillment.

Paul does balance this teaching with that of 1 Thessalonians 4:3-5: "For this is the will of God, your sanctification: that you abstain from unchastity; that each one of you know how to take a wife for himself in holiness and honor not in the passion of lust like heathen who do not know God." But he stops far short of saying that our motives must be perfectly pure before God would want us to go ahead with marriage. To the contrary, Paul understands marriage as an *antidote* to the problem of sexual temptation. It's a station of life where we learn to focus our sexual energies toward one individual—our spouse—and thus are helped to resist the lures of involvement outside the bounds of marriage. Those who feel compelled not to marry because of personal unworthiness may in effect be trying to atone for their own sin rather than fully accepting the forgiveness of Christ. And they may render themselves vulnerable to living this part of the Christian life in their own strength rather than in that which the Lord might provide through marriage. Please understand I'm not suggesting that all or even most who stay single do so over concern about motives. But this is a factor with some. Fortunately, Scripture relieves us of the need for obsessive concern at this point.

Balancing the Thought
This isn't to say that we shouldn't be concerned with improving our motives. Indeed, we must make every effort to purify them, and this is an ongoing battle to which we must be committed until we go to be with Christ.

Yet we must not allow our concern to paralyze us from action that would otherwise be to the glory of God. We should consider our disposition toward God's will more from the standpoint of whether we are willing to do his will than from the standpoint of what our motives are. Here Oliver Barclay gives some helpful counsel:

If we are honest we shall never be certain that our motives are absolutely pure. We know our own hearts too well. In such a decision we must pray for a true objectivity and ask God to give us such an overriding desire for his honor and glory that we are able to judge aright.

But it is no good indulging in endless introspection. We must make allowance for our own selfishness and get on. By all means we must pray about it and ask to be given a willingness which does not come naturally to us and a fresh love for him which makes selfish considerations small. But then we must turn to the objective task of seeking out the divine wisdom of the matter, determined that, by God's grace, we will obey whatever is right.[8]

In short, then, being willing to do God's will is more a matter of will than a matter of motive. It's giving God the blank contract and saying, "Lord, please fill it in as you choose." It's opening myself to following any alternative he would have for me, even before I know what it is.

No matter what alternative he *does* choose for me, inappropriate motives will still arise as I follow it. These will need to be confronted. But they shouldn't be the basis for concluding God doesn't want me to pursue this option. God, indeed, is usually better able to deal with our bad motives when we are active than passive. Getting in front of a group and using my gift for teaching, for instance, puts me in a much better position for God to bring experiences which will cleanse my motives than if I merely sit at home and think, "What a wretch I am!"

The Problem Remains

Yet, when all is said and done, willingness to do God's will can still be a real problem. We face two possible roadblocks here. Sometimes we just don't want God's will in some area and are quite aware of it. The young woman who was unwilling to go to California is a case in point. But there's also a more subtle dynamic, and that's when we think we really are open to God's will yet underneath have reservations. The classic biblical example is certainly Peter, who was firmly convinced he would never betray Christ but then denied him three times.

Because of this possibility I believe it's a good rule of thumb simply to assume in beginning any major decision that there is some unwillingness—either conscious or unconscious—to be dealt with. That is generally a safe assumption—and the Lord knows all about it and will help us deal with it.

The big question, then, is, *How do we deal with unwillingness?* Either when it's an obvious problem, or when we want to guard against the possibility of being unwilling when the chips are finally down, how do we handle it? Here we raise the most critical question of our study.

And we must not minimize the problem here. Overcoming resistance to God's will is tantamount to changing the will, a most difficult task, as anyone who has tried to renounce a habit will testify. We might even go farther and argue that theologically it's impossible for any of us to change our wills merely through our own strength.

Fortunately, we'll see that there is a practical solution to this problem in the right use of prayer. It's through prayer that we can successfully do battle with an unwilling disposition, to the point of being confident that we're ready to do God's will. We'll see that the role of prayer in guidance is rather different from what we may have supposed.

For Personal Study:

1. Read Matthew 12:38-39 and John 20:24-28. In both of these passages, individuals seek special evidence to validate the claims Jesus makes about himself—the Pharisees in the first passage and Thomas in the second.

☐ How does Jesus' response to Thomas's request for evidence differ markedly from his response to the Pharisees?

☐ Why did Jesus grant Thomas's request but not that of the Pharisees?

☐ What lesson do these incidents teach us about what our attitude needs to be in seeking insight from Christ?

2. Read Ruth 3 and 4, which describe Boaz's decision to marry Ruth. Note especially his effort to find out if his next of kin would be entitled to marry her.

☐ What does this suggest about Boaz's attitude before God concerning the possibility of marrying Ruth?

☐ What lesson do we learn from his example?

3. Read Galatians 2:11-14, which describes a time when Peter responded to improper motives in deciding not to eat publicly with Gentiles. What motives do you think led Peter to this unfortunate decision?

☐ How did God (through Paul) deal with Peter's motives in this incident?

☐ What action was *not* taken toward Peter (by God or Paul) in light of his inappropriate motives? (Is there any indication here or elsewhere that Peter was not allowed after this to use his gifts for teaching or leadership?)

☐ What can we learn from this incident to help us, both in dealing with our own motives and in putting them in right context in seeking God's will?

8
The Unique Role of Prayer

Key Questions:

■ *How should I pray for guidance?*
■ *Are there unhealthy patterns of prayer which I should avoid in seeking God's will?*
■ *How does prayer help me to understand God's will?*

*I*t was early Christmas morning. Before the first shred of torn wrapping paper graced our family-room floor, I had my camera ready.

Keeping in mind my wife's reminder that most photos I shoot look as if they were taken on the San Andreas fault during a tremor, I carefully framed each pose. With the most extraordinary care, I captured the ecstatic faces of our boys as they discovered long-awaited treasures in mysterious boxes. I later repeated the ritual at both grandparents' homes. As the typical doting parent, I was determined to preserve as many joyful images from the day as possible.

With all this effort, about fifteen exposures remained on the roll of film at the end of the day, so I set the camera aside for a further photo opportunity. I toted it along to a retreat following the holidays and asked a man attending to take some shots during my talks. At one point I asked him to come up front and photograph the audience. I told them to pose carefully for the picture, which I hoped to feature in my personal newsletter. A few days later I went to retrieve the film from the camera for processing. I pushed the release button, then turned the small crank that rewinds the film on its original spindle. Yet the familiar tension was not there; the film clearly wasn't rewinding. I studied the camera manual, pushed other buttons and tried the crank again and again, but with no success.

I concluded the camera must be broken. The only solution would be to remove the film and rewind it by hand. I went into a windowless bathroom, turned off the light and opened the back of the camera. I carefully stuck a finger in, not wanting to damage the film, which I suspected was still stretched across the back. To my surprise I found vacant space; the film must have somehow rewound, I assumed. Yet as I poked at either side of the camera, I found only empty spindles. . . .

Then reality struck.

Mortified, I realized I had never loaded any film in the first place!

Getting the Picture

That incident is one of those memories I wish could forget. But it still comes to mind, several years later, and probably for good reason, for it brings home one of those basic principles of life which you can scarcely be reminded of too often. The fact is that it's possible to give great effort to a task yet miss some fundamental part of the process which renders success unlikely or impossible.

Frankly, this is the perennial possibility we face as children of Christ. We may expend our energies on a project, a goal or relationship, even with some conviction that we're doing the Lord's bidding, yet in reality be following a course that is less than his best intention for us. Christ may be trying to get our attention to change directions but we're too preoccupied to hear. This is the warning from one of the most familiar psalms: "Unless the LORD builds the house, its builders labor in vain.

Unless the LORD watches over the city, the watchmen stand guard in vain" (Ps 127:1 NIV).

I say this cautiously, for I understand the biblical message to be fundamentally one of grace. God mercifully forgives our transgressions and with magnificent creativity works even our mistakes into his plan. Beyond this, he exercises such providential initiative in our lives that even if we belligerently attempt to rebel against his will, we face remarkable constraints, as the example of Jonah dramatically reminds us.

Within certain boundaries, however, God allows us the adventure of seeking his will, the privilege of being partners with Christ in his work, and the possibility of success or failure in the whole process. One of the critical steps we must take toward moving within God's will is to become willing to accept his will—the point stressed in the last chapter. We need to reach the point of being open to doing whatever God wishes even before we know what it is.

Yet it's here that we too easily overlook the obvious—a basic and indispensable need: prayer. In this matter of willingness, as in most other areas of the Christian life, we too often try to approach things in our own strength, rather than in the strength which Christ provides. It is through prayer that we best put ourselves in position for God to make us willing. The prospect of changing the will apart from prayer is about as good as taking a picture with an empty camera.

Though you have probably heard it said many times, there can be little question that Satan majors in trying to keep Christians from giving attention to prayer. I'm certain he directs his attention more to this area than any other. I experience the reality of this almost daily.

For many years I've had a regular devotional time in the morning. Yet there are few mornings when I'm not tempted to forgo it. It always seems to be a diversion from the other responsibilities of the day, at least at first. I have to remind myself practically every morning that this is a lie of the devil. While there is a sacrifice involved in taking time to be alone with Christ, the tradeoff is much more than worth it. The benefits that come through time set aside for prayer are immense.

It has become somewhat easier for me to win this mental battle in recent years. Yet the struggle continues and I'm sure always will until I go to be with Christ. It takes mental discipline, not only to set aside time for prayer but to keep the benefits of prayer in the forefront of my thinking.

The Mystery and Necessity of Prayer

It is always something of a mystery to explain exactly why prayer should be necessary in the Christian life, and theologians throughout the ages have attempted to do this. If God is sovereign, and if he knows our needs before we even express them to him (as Mt 6:8 clearly says), then why the need for prayer?

C. S. Lewis probably gave the most succinct answer when he said that God could have chosen to do his work on this earth in any fashion he wanted, but he chose in his sovereignty to do it, to an important extent, in response to prayer.[1]

Prayer is really for our sake; it's through prayer that God allows us to take responsibility for his work in the most mature and wholesome sense, and through it we're allowed the privilege of spiritual growth which can come no other way.

Regardless what we would say about the "why" of prayer, its necessity cannot be denied. The importance of prayer is underlined throughout every portion of Scripture—so much so that John Calvin, in spite of his great stress upon God's sovereignty, devoted a healthy portion of his *Institutes of the Christian Religion* to prayer. He stated, "We see that to us nothing is promised to be expected from the Lord, which we are not also bidden to ask of him in prayers."[2]

Andrew Murray put it even more strongly:

It is in very deed God's purpose that the fulfillment of His eternal purpose, and the coming of His kingdom, should depend on those of His people who, abiding in Christ, are ready to take up their position in Him their Head, the great Priest-King, and in their prayers are bold enough to say what they will that their God should do. As image-bearer and representative of God on earth, redeemed man has by his prayers to determine the history of this earth.[3]

Did you catch that? Murray is saying that the results of prayer are earth-shaking! They affect the future of life on this planet! Don't listen to Satan when he whispers, "What difference are your small prayers going to make, really? Another half-hour of sleep would be a better investment."

Praying to Know God's Will
When it comes to knowing God's will, the Bible makes it clear that we should not presumptuously *expect* God to reveal it to us. Rather, we have a responsibility to *ask* him to make his will known.

In Joshua 9 we're given a most instructive picture of what can happen when this isn't done. The Israelites had experienced recent victories of incredible magnitude crossing the Jordan, destroying Jericho and Ai. They had been commanded to destroy the inhabitants of Canaan and were well about the task. But the people of Gibeon, a city near the Israelites' camp, were determined to avoid annihilation.

As a desperate move, they devised a cunning plot to deceive the Israelites into sparing them. Dressing up in tattered clothing and carrying dusty, worn-out provisions, they approached the Israelite camp, saying they were from a faraway nation. They persuaded the Israelites to make a treaty of peace with them. Their plot succeeded magnificently; the Israelites were completely beguiled.

Scripture makes it clear that there was a plain and simple reason why God allowed the Israelites to be tricked—the fact that *they didn't make the effort to ask* for divine guidance in the matter. "So the men partook of their provisions, and did not ask direction from the LORD" (Josh 9:14). The incident stands for all time as a warning against rushing into major decisions without first praying for guidance.

In the New Testament the most explicit command to pray for a knowledge of God's will is given in James 1:5-6: "If any of you lacks wisdom, let him ask God, who gives to all men generously and without reproaching, and it will be given him. But let him ask in faith, with no doubting." James here tells the believer to pray for wisdom—that is, for God's perspective on things. Although in the context of the passage James is talking about the need for wisdom in the face of trials (see vv. 2-4), scholars note that "the language employed is so general, that what is here said may be applied to the need for wisdom in all respects."[4] "If any of you lack wisdom," is certainly an ironic statement; of course we all lack wisdom and are in constant need of it.

James, then, tells us that when we lack understanding of God's will we have a responsibility to ask him to clarify it.

There's no question that many Christians don't begin to take this responsibility seriously enough. In his classic booklet *Affirming the Will of God* Paul Little recalls his own experience:

At the Urbana Convention in 1948, Dr. Norton Sterrett asked, "How many of you who are concerned about the will of God spend five minutes a day asking him to show you his will?" It was as if somebody had grabbed me by the throat. At that time I was an undergraduate, concerned about what I should do when I graduated from the university. I was running around campus—going to this meeting, reading that book, trying to find somebody's little formula—1, 2, 3, 4 and a bell rings—and I was frustrated out of my mind trying to figure out the will of God. I was doing everything but getting into the presence of God and asking him to show me.[5]

Then Little adds,

May I ask you the same question: Do you spend even five minutes a day specifically asking God to show you? All of us as Christians would do well to take this question to heart. Praying for God's will is a daily responsibility, and one for which the serious Christian must simply make time.

On the other hand I may surprise you in saying that I believe there are Christians who actually take this responsibility *too* seriously. There are those, for instance, who pray incessantly for guidance on mundane matters. If we are to live our lives fruitfully and efficiently for the Lord, it's simply a bad investment to spend much time in prayer over a simple decision. Paul Little again has an apt comment:

God really does not have a great preference whether you have steak or chicken. He is not desperately concerned about whether you wear a green shirt or a blue shirt. In many areas of life, God invites us to consult our own sanctified preferences. When we are pleased, God is pleased.[6]

This doesn't mean there's anything wrong in asking the Lord briefly for guidance even in small decisions as part of continually practicing his presence. But to spend much time in prayer over them really shows a lack of faith in his capacity to guide. It's a much healthier approach merely to spend a few minutes in prayer each day asking God to guide all the minor decisions of that day. Then go ahead and apply yourself to the day's decisions in the faith and confidence that God is answering your prayer.

I also believe there are Christians who spend too much time praying for God's will in major decisions. Such praying can all too easily become a cop-out from doing what is very obviously God's will. Or else it can be a sign that we lack faith that God will show us his will. As one friend of mine put it, "I sometimes pray to God to show me his will to the point of unbelief!"

In the passage from James quoted above, James says that praying for wisdom must be done *in faith,* and this means believing that God will give wisdom once we have prayed for it. To pray importunately for a knowledge of God's will (the word *importunate* means "stubbornly or unreasonably persistent in request or demand"—American Heritage Dictionary) can indicate a lack of faith.

It's most interesting that beyond this passage in James, there's no other direct statement in the New Testament telling us to pray for a knowledge of God's will, in spite of the extensive emphasis on prayer in general. Likewise, in the book of Acts, where we have many examples of prayers, there's only one clear instance of a prayer for God to reveal his will.[7] We must conclude from this that while praying in this way is important, it shouldn't be the burden of our prayer life.

Asking God for wisdom to make decisions *is* vital, but it should be done in the context of a broader devotional time, where we thank God for his blessings, make requests for the needs of others, confess our sins and spend time in his Word. When we're faced with a major decision, we should spend a concentrated period in prayer for guidance. Some of this time should be spent petitioning God to make his will clear, but even more time should be spent asking the Lord to give us a heart that desires his will and the spiritual strength to do it. This is the most essential function of prayer in guidance.

Praying for Willingness

It is usually the most overlooked function of prayer in guidance as well. Most Christians think of praying for guidance purely in terms of asking God to reveal his will. In fact the Scriptures put far more emphasis on our need to pray for willingness. Understanding and applying this principle unlocks a critical principle for keeping in step with the guidance of the Lord.

There is no place where Scripture makes this point more clearly and helpfully than in the Gethsemane passage, where Jesus prays for strength to face his crucifixion. This is one of the most instructive examples of prayer found anywhere in Scripture. Let's look at Matthew's account of the event:

> He began to be sorrowful and troubled. Then he said to them [Peter, James and John], "My soul is very sorrowful, even to death; remain here, and watch with me." And going a little farther he fell on his face and prayed, "My Father, if it be possible, let this cup pass from me; nevertheless, not as I will, but as thou wilt."
>
> And he came to the disciples and found them sleeping; and he said to Peter, "So, could you not watch with me one hour? Watch and pray that you may not enter into temptation; the spirit indeed is willing, but the flesh is weak." Again, for the second time, he went away and prayed, "My Father, if this cannot pass unless I drink it, thy will be done."
>
> And again he came and found them sleeping, for their eyes were heavy. So, leaving them again, he went away and prayed for the third time, saying the same words. (Mt 26:37-44)

In this passage we observe a most intriguing fact. Jesus, the Son of God, experiences a human will different from God's. He has difficulty being willing to do God's will—the very problem we have talked about. As he contemplates the torture of the crucifixion and the agony of bearing the cup of human sin, his human will is understandably resistant. His desire is that he could somehow be spared the agony of the cross. This fact alone—that Jesus experienced emotional difficulty in yielding to God's will—should be tremendously reassuring to us and should encourage us not to be unduly harsh with ourselves when we have a similar problem. But the passage also shows how Jesus dealt with the problem. It is through prayer that Jesus successfully overcomes the dichotomy between his will and God's. And *how* he prays is most significant. He begins by confessing his true desires to God: "My Father, if it be possible, let this cup pass from me." This certainly shows us the freedom we have—even the mandate—to be brutally honest before God about our feelings.

But Jesus then goes a step further and prays, "nevertheless, not as I will, but as thou wilt." In effect, by praying in this way he was asking God to grant him the willingness to yield to the Father's will above his own. The essence of Jesus' prayer, then, was, "God, grant me the strength to do your will."

It's striking to note that nowhere in the Gospels do we discover Jesus, for all his emphasis upon prayer, ever praying for a knowledge of God's will. Because Jesus was God, he apparently didn't need to pray in this way. But he did find it necessary to pray for willingness to obey; and if Jesus needed to pray in this fashion, it forcibly underlines the need for this kind of prayer in our own lives. When facing a major decision it is critically important to spend concentrated time praying for the strength to do God's will—even *more* important than praying for a knowledge of God's will.

Again, this isn't to imply that praying for a knowledge of God's will is unimportant. Unlike us, Jesus knew clearly what God's will was simply by virtue of being God, and he prayed for yieldedness in light of that clear understanding. Our responsibility is different in that we must also pray for enlightenment. But I believe his example tells us where the *emphasis* should be in our prayer life.

Notice the advice Jesus gives his disciples in this passage. He instructs them to make the same type of prayer that he was making, saying, "Watch and pray that you may not enter into temptation; the spirit indeed is willing, but the flesh is weak." He is, in effect, telling them that apart from praying in this way they will lack the spiritual power which they need.

Now what is significant is that the disciples, unlike Jesus, don't know exactly what is ahead; they are expecting a crisis situation but are uncertain what choices they will have to make. Yet note that Jesus doesn't tell them to pray for the knowledge of what God would have them do, but rather for the strength to do it.

He knows that their greatest problem won't be knowing what to do but having the strength to carry it out.

And the results, of course, bear Jesus out in a most convincing way. The disciples don't pray but go to sleep. Then when Jesus is betrayed, they find themselves completely lacking the fortitude to stick with him (Mt 26:56), even though they have sworn they will never deny him (Mt 26:35).

The Gethsemane passage, then, strongly suggests that prayer for the willingness to do God's will is necessary in the Christian life. We should pray earnestly for willingness before facing a crisis situation or a major decision, and our prayers for guidance should concentrate more on willingness than on knowledge.

We should also note that in the Lord's Prayer, which Jesus gave us as a model for our daily prayer life, there are actually two petitions which amount to requests for the ability to do God's will: the third petition ("thy will be done") and the sixth ("lead us not into temptation"). Interestingly, these correspond to Jesus' prayer in the Garden and the one he told his disciples to make. Thus it is most significant that Christ's model prayer, while including no petition for a knowledge of God's will, exhorts us to pray for yieldedness.

It's clear that this sort of praying is a necessity for serious Christians. It is central to guidance and basic to gaining the willingness to do God's will. Through praying for yieldedness, we may be confident our decisions are in the will of God.

How Much Prayer Is Enough?
At this point, a practical question arises: Just how much time should we spend praying in this way before making a big decision?

In the last chapter we said that willingness to do God's will is a preface to being able to know his will and to having the spiritual capacity to carry it out. And now we're saying that prayer is the key to gaining this willingness. Yet at what point do we know we have prayed enough to be sufficiently willing?

Here it's impossible to give a precise formula. I believe the only really helpful answer is to say that we must pray until we have reached the point of being reasonably assured that we're open to God's will. Here I stress *reasonably*. In most cases it's impossible to know with absolute certainty just how yielded we actually are; even a man with the remarkable maturity of the apostle Paul claimed, "I do not even judge myself" (1 Cor 4:3). We may have the problem of thinking we're more yielded than we really are, the same delusion Peter and the other apostles experienced in the Garden.

Or we may have the opposite problem. Because the Holy Spirit is working in us, convicting us, we may have an intense awareness of our sinfulness to the point of thinking of ourselves as more resistant to God's will than we really are.

During the past two years a friend of mine has lost over two hundred pounds in a demanding weight loss program, going from obesity to a very trim figure. Yet she still thinks of herself as fat. In the same way, as we grow in Christ, we may have difficulty shaking off old self-images. The Christian with a scrupulous conscience may pray endlessly for willingness to do God's will yet never feel fully assured that he or she has attained it.

There are, of course, those times when we're well aware of areas of resistance in a decision. If I'm considering several professional options, and I've closed my mind to the possibility of teaching even though there's reason to believe God could want me there, I can bet there's some real unwillingness to deal with. But if it's merely a case of some vague, nagging doubts about my yieldedness, then I should probably go ahead and make my decision, realizing these are likely more a sign of spiritual health than anything else.

Whatever the case, we should certainly spend a concentrated period praying for guidance before proceeding with a major decision. Just how long that time should be cannot be set down in a rigid formula; it might be fifteen minutes in one case, a day or more in another. There should obviously be some relation to the dimension of the decision and to our ability to concentrate in prayer.

But ultimately the time comes when we have to stop praying and go ahead with the decision, trusting that God is answering our prayers and giving us the willingness and wisdom for which we've prayed. This involves a risk; yet the element of risk can never be removed from living a life for Christ on the growing edge.

The wonderful fact is that we can take this risk with the confidence that we follow a forgiving God who promises to give us the sort of shepherd's guidance we talked about in chapter five. He is able to work even our mistakes into his plan.

Retreat or Advance?—A Personal Example

Several years ago a retreat center near where I live offered me the chance to plan and direct a major adult conference during an Easter vacation. It was in many ways a *carte blanche* opportunity, for the conference center would fund the entire event including the honorarium for a major national speaker. The facility itself was a beautiful, inspiring setting, excellent for an activity of this sort. And there was about ten months' time to plan the event.

But for several reasons I was hesitant to assume this responsibility. I knew that the work involved in planning would be immense, taking several months of my time. I worried, too, about the feasibility of so many details falling into place. Not the least of these was the weather. Easter vacation would be the first week of April that year, a time when the weather in our area is unpredictable and often dank. While part of me wanted to go ahead, a big part resisted.

I was on the verge of saying no when it occurred to me that I hadn't spent any serious time praying about it.

Finally doing what I should have done in the first place, I set aside several hours on a Saturday afternoon to pray and consider this option, even though it seemed an intrusion into my busy schedule.

During this time I gave particular attention to asking God to make me willing to do what he wanted. By the end of the afternoon I was beginning to feel some unexpected motivation for the project. I spoke with Evie (my most significant earthly counselor); she felt it was probably best to go ahead with the conference. I decided to do it. The key would be to look to Christ in prayer at each point in the planning, to pace myself and delegate wherever possible.

The work involved was indeed considerable. Yet by God's grace the pieces came together more smoothly than I expected, none of the calamities I feared occurred, and much of the task was frankly a sheer pleasure. The event itself came off marvelously and many people expressed appreciation for the Lord's blessing during the time. The most surprising serendipity of all was the weather, which remained resort-quality, warm and sunny in the seventies throughout the week—highly unusual for this part of the country in early April.

In thinking back on the decision to organize that conference, I have little question now that it was the Lord's leading and the right step to take at that time. Yet I remember only too well how I came close to declining the opportunity. It was through prayer that the Lord's direction became clarified. And praying for willingness, especially, seemed to make the difference. Again, I'm convinced that praying in this fashion holds an important key to keeping our lives in line with God's best.

Listening

We've stressed in this chapter that praying for guidance is tremendously important for those of us who wish to know and do the will of God. We've noted that we're expected to ask God to show us his will, but not to the point of becoming obsessed with this concern in prayer. And we've emphasized that in praying for guidance we need especially to petition God to grant us a desire for his will and the spiritual strength to yield to his will above our own.

You may wonder at this point why our whole stress in this chapter has been on making requests to God. Why has nothing been said about the important matter of *listening* to God in prayer? Is not prayer communication with God, a time when more than anything we quietly listen and gain an understanding of his will? I would hope that you are raising this question.

Actually the remainder of the book will be devoted to this question—in effect, to what it means to listen to God. While we will not talk so much about prayer during the rest of our study, everything we will say touches on communication with God. Keep in mind that any serious effort to discern God's will should always be undertaken in a spirit of prayer or closeness to God. What we will be concerned with from this point on is how to listen to God in the most mature and responsible sense.

For Personal Study:
1. Read Mark 1:32-39 and Luke 5:15-16. While the Garden of Gethsemane incident shows Jesus in prayer at a crisis point, these two passages give us more of a glimpse of his *daily* prayer experience. Judging from the context of these two passages, what significant hindrance to fulfilling God's special will for him did Jesus often face?
☐ How did prayer help him to deal with this hindrance and to stay on course with God's will?
☐ What can we learn from Jesus' example here?
2. Read about Isaiah's experience in the temple in Isaiah 6:1-8. Note specific ways in which Isaiah's attitude or perspective changed through this time of prayer and communion with God.
☐ In what ways does Isaiah's experience reinforce points which we have considered in this chapter?
☐ Does his experience show us anything new about the role of prayer in understanding and responding to God's will?
3. Read 2 Corinthians 7-10, which tells of Paul's praying for removal of "a thorn in my flesh." Note ways in which Paul's experience in prayer parallels Jesus' experience in the Garden of Gethsemane.
☐ What does Paul's experience teach us about (a) our freedom to be honest with our feelings before God; (b) how we can better reach the point of being *joyfully* willing to accept God's will, even when it is different from what we have desired?

4. Is there a decision facing you where you are not fully open to God's will? Pray, asking God to give you willingness to do his will in that decision.

9

Searching the Scriptures

Key Questions:

■ *How can the Scriptures help me in resolving a complex decision, such as a job choice or whom to marry?*
■ *Are there unhealthy practices to avoid in seeking God's will through the Bible?*
■ *How important is a daily devotional time?*

*U*p to this point we've stressed that God takes the initiative in guidance and that our main responsibility is to be in close communion with him. If we're willing to do his will, we may be confident that he will ensure we walk in it, even though we may be confused. We've stressed that prayer, more than anything, is the channel through which we develop and maintain an openness to the will of God.

Use Your Head
This isn't meant to suggest that we should send our minds on vacation while seeking God's will. Someone might logically conclude, "If God will

guide us if we're submitted to him even though we're confused about his will, then there's really no point in making a mental effort to discern his will. Why bother?"

The answer is simple: Scripture clearly tells us that we have a responsibility to seek to understand God's will. Consider God's instruction to us in Psalm 32: "I will instruct you and teach you the way you should go; I will counsel you with my eye upon you. Be not like a horse or a mule, *without understanding,* which must be curbed with bit and bridle, else it will not keep with you" (Ps 32:8-9, emphasis added). Here God's promise of guidance is coupled with a clear command to use our minds to discern it. While God will guide us with the bit and bridle if necessary, this is not the ideal way he would have us proceed.

We are told in Scripture, then, to use our understanding to discern God's will. It would be hypocritical to claim to be willing to do God's will but not to be willing to follow this clear command of his. The person who is being empowered by God's Spirit to want to do God's will is going to have a natural desire to use his or her mind in seeking it.

It's important not only to understand the *requirements* that are laid upon us in knowing God's will but also to appreciate the *benefits* that come from fulfilling those requirements. In chapter six we suggested three marvelous benefits that result from taking responsibility for knowing God's will: personal growth, a greater sense of adventure and a deeper sense of purpose. To these we can add two more that come especially from taking the further step of using our minds to understand God's will:

1. *Deeper intimacy with Christ.* Even though it's greatly reassuring to know that Christ guides us in spite of our confusion, there's no denying that our confusion often causes us to feel distant from him. The more clearly we understand his leading, the more deeply we feel communion with him. This sense of intimacy has a positive impact in all areas of our Christian experience.

2. *A contribution to our mental health.* If we do not use our intellects to discern God's will, we may become vulnerable to unhealthy approaches to guidance which can result in emotional problems. We'll look at some of these unbalanced approaches in part three.

If we grant, then, that using our minds is important in guidance, we need to go further and say what, exactly, this means. Here our responsibility is actually twofold. First, we should study Scripture, coming to understand as fully as possible the guidance God has already given. Then we have a responsibility to use our reason to make a logical choice about God's will, as opposed to looking for supernatural indications or purely intuitive impressions of his guidance. We'll look at the role of Scripture in this chapter and then at the place of practical thinking in the next.

Understanding the Role of Scripture

One foggy night the captain of a ship saw what appeared to be another ship's running lights approaching in the distance. The oncoming vessel was evidently on a direct collision course with his own boat. The captain frantically signaled to it, "Please change your course ten degrees to the east."

The reply came back, blinking through the fog, "You change your course ten degrees to the west."

Furious, the captain shot another message: "I'm a sea captain with thirty-five years' experience. Change your course ten degrees to the east!"

And without delay the signal flashed back, "I'm a seaman fourth class. Change your course ten degrees west."

The captain, enraged, knowing they were destined for a terrible crash, beamed another message: "I'm a fifty-ton freighter. *Change course.*"

The simple message flashed back, "I'm a lighthouse. *You* change course."[1]

Chief among the means of guidance God has provided for us is a lighthouse: his Word.

He has blessed us with the Scriptures as a rock-solid, immutable testimony to his will and purpose for human life. The revelation of Scripture is as unchangeable as the nature of God himself, and its guidance is as non-negotiable as the beam of illumination from a lighthouse. Our ongoing challenge in the Christian life is to discern the extensive guidance which God has already given us in Scripture and—as that venerable sea captain was obliged to do upon realizing that the impending light had an unmovable source—adjust our course accordingly.

This is not to say that there is no interactive aspect to our study of the Bible. The most remarkable part of studying Scripture is that God influences us and works within us as we read. Yet it's important to understand how this does and does not happen.

In chapter two we noted that personal decisions cannot normally be fully resolved simply through reference to biblical principles. Thus, I shouldn't expect to find a principle in Scripture which tells me once and for all to marry Valerie Johnson or to become a biologist. We should, in short, avoid thinking that we'll find the specific answer to a complex personal decision in the pages of the Bible.

Likewise, we must constantly avoid the all-too-natural temptation of thinking that particulars in biblical passages are revealing God's will to us. I live in Damascus, Maryland. Near my home is a country highway aptly named "Damascus Road." Suppose one morning in reading through the book of Acts I come upon Paul's conversion experience and conclude that God is telling me to go out on Damascus Road and wait to be struck by a flash of light. That would be a wrong use of Scripture.

While this may sound far-fetched, the fact is that many Christians are inclined to apply Scripture in exactly this way. In reality, this amounts to making the Bible a crystal ball, taking a superstitious approach to its teaching.

But this doesn't mean that the Bible should play no role in complex decision making. Indeed, it has a most significant role. And the person who is serious about doing God's will needs to make a regular and frequent practice of studying Scripture. Here we find Psalm 1:1-3 most instructive:

> Blessed is the man who walks not in the counsel of the wicked, nor stands in the way of sinners, nor sits in the seat of scoffers; but his delight is in the law of the LORD, and on his law he meditates day and night. He is like a tree planted by streams of water, that yields its fruit in its season, and its leaf does not wither. In all that he does, he prospers.

In this beautiful passage the psalmist gives a promise to the person who meditates on the law of the Lord—that is, the one who is giving constant and close attention to God's teaching. In referring to *the law of the Lord,* the psalmist means especially the written teaching of God—the Pentateuch at the time the psalm was written, but today the entire canon of Scripture.

The promise he makes is twofold. First, the person who meditates on God's written Word will be *fulfilled* (this is the meaning of the word *blessed* that begins the psalm). Second, this person will be *fruitful.* The psalmist pictures him enjoying a prosperous life, bearing fruit as naturally as a tree that receives abundant nourishment.

The psalmist is not implying that the Christian will necessarily enjoy material wealth or success in worldly terms. The psalms which follow show again and again that the godly person may experience adversity and won't necessarily enjoy prosperity by the world's standards. But the psalm does assure us of success by *God's* standards and of a life that will be fruitful for Christ because it is lived in line with his will. The person who meditates on God's Word, in short, will be the one who is empowered to live a life reflective of his will.

The writer of the psalm doesn't go on to explain precisely how studying Scripture functions to keep us in the will of God; he simply indicates that this will be the case. But if we look closely, we can see at least five logical ways in which the Scriptures help us at this point.

1. Studying Scripture *deepens our consciousness of God.* This is the most basic and obvious advantage of Bible study. It's a simple fact that most of what goes on in our lives tends to divert our attention from God. We need disciplines in life which turn our attention back to him, for it's impossible to give any serious consideration to his will if our thoughts aren't focused on him in the first place. Because the Bible is most basically a book about God, it is an invaluable aid in helping us to concentrate on him.

2. Studying Scripture also *brings us into contact with God.* When we study the Bible with a prayerful spirit, there's a mystical sense in which our reading actually brings us closer to God. Yes, Scripture can be read in a purely academic way. But the fact is that when we approach the Bible we're approaching words which God himself authored through his Holy

Spirit; thus as we allow his Spirit to guide us in our study, we're doing more than reading facts—we're allowing ourselves to hear God speak.

As we allow the Spirit and the Word to work together, our desire for his will often deepens and we find ourselves more capable of understanding his guidance. Our minds and hearts are brought into communion with God in a way that enables him to influence us and guide us.

3. Furthermore, the Scriptures *inform us of God's principles.* While our complex decisions are not usually resolved through the mechanical application of some biblical principle, there are usually principles which apply to our decisions and should influence them. These include principles of morality and Christian lifestyle, which we must be careful not to transgress in our decisions. We must be constantly learning and reviewing these, as there is virtually never a decision we face which doesn't require some knowledge of these norms. In addition there are the principles of guidance, which we are looking at throughout this book. These also need to be reviewed often, as we too easily revert to our former and less adequate ways of approaching decisions.

4. Biblical passages may also *inspire or confirm a particular decision.* On occasion we may find in reading Scripture that we experience a sense of inspiration to do what the passage is talking about, and thereafter the passage serves as a constant encouragement and reminder of God's leading. I stress *on occasion,* for this will probably not happen frequently. Yet when it does, the impact can be significant and far-reaching. In a study question at the end of this chapter, we'll note how certain Old Testament passages influenced Paul's understanding of what God wanted him to do.

We are not talking here about applying Scripture to irrelevant situations, but about taking a passage in context and being moved by the Spirit to do what it says. A person reading about the great revival that followed Nehemiah's leading the Israelites to rebuild the wall of Jerusalem, for example, might catch a vision for bringing new life to a church through motivating the members to work together on a certain project.

It is important to stress that guidance in this sense should never be taken from Scripture alone; in all cases, one's inspiration should be carefully checked against other factors. The person who is visionary by nature is likely to experience many more inspirations than could ever be practically carried out. Yet there's no denying that the Holy Spirit will sometimes use a passage of Scripture to give a unique sense of inspiration which will stand the test of other logical considerations. When this happens, it is a special gift from God which thereafter serves as a confirmation of his guidance.

My own study of the book of Nehemiah had an influence on my decision to enter the ministry I've been involved in for the past twelve years. The influence came, though, not from the main part of the book where Nehemiah directs the rebuilding of the Jerusalem wall but from a lesser known aspect of his work, spoken of in the last two chapters of the book of Nehemiah.

After restoring and repopulating Jerusalem, Nehemiah reestablished the musicians and singers in a central role in the worship life of the community. He saw to it that people contributed part of their offerings to the musicians, so that they could devote their full-time energies to the ministry of music (see especially Neh 12:45-47).

I came across these chapters during a study of Nehemiah while in St. Louis. Having spent so much of my life in music, I was only too well aware of how the church typically fails to support and encourage artistic persons. Nehemiah's example helped motivate me to think about beginning a ministry which would give special help to creative Christians.

God has his own designs, and as Nehemiah Ministries has developed, our concern has been less directed toward the artist specifically and more toward helping Christians in general find their creative niches. Still, it seems that God used this portion of Scripture to help steer me in this direction. It was, to be sure, far short of a revelation or absolute confirmation of my decision, which was a difficult one involving the weighing of many factors. Yet Nehemiah's example was part of the inspirational process. And it has continued to be a confirmation—reminding me that our efforts to help Christians discover and use their potential are in line with one of God's basic concerns.

Just recently a friend, Janet, shared with me how a passage of Scripture helped in her decision to marry her husband. At the time Bob proposed, she had known him for two years and had excellent reasons for thinking she should marry him. Yet she was involved with a ministry organization which tended to dictate personal decisions to its members. Because of her lack of experience in making important decisions for herself, she was fearful of trusting her own judgment in deciding to marry Bob.

Then in a study of Proverbs she came across this statement: "Even a child makes himself known by his acts, whether what he does is pure and right. The hearing ear and the seeing eye, the LORD has made them both" (Prov 20:11-12).

The passage—especially the second sentence—spoke to her of God giving us the capacity to make good judgments. It helped to give her the courage to go ahead and make what seemed to be the best decision (and in fourteen years of happy and fruitful marriage, the wisdom of that decision has been confirmed many times).

What is important to note, in both Janet's experience and my own, is that these insights came simply as part of the process of studying Scripture in a daily quiet time. I wasn't looking for special guidance when I came across Nehemiah 12 and 13, and I don't believe that Janet was either. I strongly suspect that most of our experiences of gaining enlightenment for personal decisions from Scripture occur in this way—that is, in the context of a regular, disciplined devotional time. I'll return to this point in a moment.

5. Finally, the Bible can be *an invaluable aid in praying for guidance.* In the psalms we find quite a few prayers for guidance which can be read as our own prayer when seeking God's will. Psalm 143:8, 10 is one of these: "Teach me the way I should go, for to thee I lift up my soul. . . . Teach me to do thy will, for thou art my God! Let thy good spirit lead me on a level path!"

There are also prayers for a willing spirit, such as Psalm 51:10-12: "Create in me a clean heart, O God, and put a new and right spirit within me. Cast me not away from thy presence, and take not thy holy Spirit from me. Restore to me the joy of thy salvation, and uphold me with a willing spirit." Other prayers for guidance can be found in Psalm 5:8; 19:12-14; 25:4-5, 21; 27:11; 31:3-4; 86:11; 119:5, 10, 35-36, 80, 133, 176; 141:3-4.

The Nitty-Gritty

The Bible, then, helps us in a variety of ways in our search to know God's will. As John White says:

God does not desire to guide us magically. He wants us to know his mind. He wants us to grasp his very heart. We need minds so soaked with the content of Scripture, so imbued with biblical outlooks and principles, so sensitive to the Holy Spirit's prompting that we will know instinctively the upright step to take in any circumstance, small or great. . . .

Through the study of [Scripture] you may become acquainted with the ways and thoughts of God.[2]

But understanding all this is of no use unless we put it into practice. Each of us needs a time of daily Bible study, in the context of a regular devotional time. Psalm 1 speaks of the importance of meditating upon God's Word day and night, and while this doesn't mean that every waking thought has to be about Scripture, it does suggest that we should very frequently be thinking about teachings of Scripture and considering their relevance to the situations in which we find ourselves.

From a practical standpoint, that just won't happen unless we have a daily discipline of Bible reading. The regularity may be far more important than the actual amount of time spent. It is much more valuable to spend ten minutes a day reading the Bible than to spend two hours once a week, for the daily habit will keep the Scriptures in the forefront of our thinking. And I believe that faithfulness in this area gives the Holy Spirit maximum freedom to use the Scriptures in guiding us in God's will.

Often the best approach is to work through the entire Bible, either chronologically from front to back or according to the methodology of a particular daily study program. In addition, it is helpful to read a psalm or two, as the psalms often direct our attention to prayer.

Beyond this, in making a major decision we should spend some additional time reading any portions of Scripture that relate directly to that decision. Anyone considering the pastorate, for instance, should become intimately acquainted with the biblical teaching on the role of the pastor and the church. Here the help of a minister or someone else with a thorough knowledge of the Bible is invaluable in helping us know what sections of Scripture to study. Under normal circumstances, however, I believe it is best to study from the standpoint of gaining a greater understanding of the entire Bible, as opposed to studying for a particular decision.

In giving this advice I am, to be sure, speaking from my own experience. Each of us must find what works best for herself or himself. But in the absence of other ideas, it's often best to begin with what has worked well for others and then to change it as we begin to sense what disciplines are most beneficial to our own growth in Christ.

For Personal Study:

1. Read the following verses or brief passages: Romans 15:14-16, 1 Corinthians 15:1, 2 Peter 1:12, 2 Peter 3:1-2, Jude 1:5, John 14:26. What critical principle of human learning is underlined by these passages?

☐ What does this principle suggest about our own needs in studying Scripture, and how should we plan our study of Scripture in light of it?

2. We have noted five ways in which the Scriptures benefit us in seeking to know God's will. Read the following verses or brief passages, noting the particular benefits of studying Scripture underscored by each.

Matthew 22:29
John 20:30-31
Luke 24:32
Luke 24:45
Romans 15:4
1 Corinthians 10:11
Ephesians 3:4-5
Ephesians 6:17-18
2 Timothy 3:14-17
2 Peter 1:19-21
James 1:25

☐ Can you find each of the benefits we mentioned alluded to in one or more of these passages?

☐ Can you find additional benefits of studying Scripture beyond the ones we mentioned?

3. Read Romans 15:8-22. Note two or three ways in which Paul's study of the Old Testament influenced (or reinforced) his decision to give priority to ministering to the Gentiles.

☐ Note how Scripture functioned along with other factors in leading Paul to this perspective.

☐ What inspiration can we take from Paul's example for our own study of Scripture?

4. Do you have a regular devotional time (or "quiet time")? If not, why not resolve right now to include this as part of your daily schedule. Put your decision in writing. Then experiment, adjusting the time and place as needed.

10
Thinking Things Through

Key Questions:

■ *Does God expect me to think through a complex decision, or should I wait for him to impress his will upon me in a more direct manner?*
■ *How did New Testament Christians typically approach their personal decisions?*

*W*e come now to the point toward which we've been building so far in this book.

We've stressed that while God takes extraordinary initiative in guidance, he graciously allows us the privilege of taking important responsibility as well. We've emphasized our need for being willing to do God's will and noted how prayer plays a central role in gaining this openness. We've also looked at the role of Scripture, noting how our study of it both conforms our heart to God's will and gives us vital practical insights for our decisions.

But at different points in our study we've suggested that the time finally comes in a personal decision where God—to say it simply—expects us to think. We're called upon to use the rational faculties he has given us and *make a sound, logical decision*—one which would seem most obviously glorifying to Christ. While we've made many passing references to this point, it's time now to look at some solid biblical evidence for it.

I know that for many readers this will be the most liberating insight of the book. I remember how terribly confusing this area was for me as a young Christian. It was puzzling to understand what role God wanted me to play in major decisions. Was I to wait for special guidance? Or was I expected to take some initiative to think things through? Where was my brain to fit into this whole process?

At one point I was attracted to the idea of beginning a radio ministry. I had excellent reasons to think this was a good step to take and a logical channel for my gifts. Yet no one was beckoning me to do this. And there was no direct guidance from the Lord to do so. I felt painfully guilty about taking any initiative myself in the face of such silence. I feared usurping the Lord's prerogative.

I shared my confusion with a woman on the staff of the church I attended who had the sense to challenge my assumptions about remaining passive. She noted that God's leading might come *through* my inner deliberations rather than in some exterior way apart from them. She advised that I should feel free before Christ to take the responsibility to think through this idea and to go ahead with it if it made sense. Because I respected her greatly, I assumed that her understanding of guidance must be more developed than my own. Her counsel helped free me up to take initiative for this decision and some others as well.

Yet the freedom I was beginning to feel to be a decision-maker sprang more from confidence in her counsel than from clear biblical insight. Because of this, I continued to wrestle with whether it was really okay to take more than token initiative in major life decisions. It was not until several years later that I finally took the time to study the Scriptures in some depth on the point. It was through that study that I realized it's not only okay to take initiative but that this is actually *expected* of me as a follower of Christ.

Differences and Similarities

We naturally think that as Christians our experience of resolving decisions will be different—perhaps dramatically so—from the process we went through as nonbelievers. Though we may not be certain exactly *how* it will be different, we expect it to be different nonetheless. The whole idea of receiving *guidance* conveys the thought of having a mystical or obviously supernatural experience. It implies the idea of instantaneous direction which removes the need for thinking through a decision.

In reality, Scripture gives little basis for this all-too-understandable assumption. In fact, the differences between Christian and non-Christian decision making are not as great as might first be thought.

On one level there are some critical differences, and we've given much attention to these. As a Christian I operate with a radically different set of priorities than I followed as a nonbeliever. My objective now is to follow the will of God rather than my own inclinations, and this has a far-reaching impact on the choices I make. I'm now responsible to be open to God's will in any personal choice, and I'm called on to give serious attention to prayer in the process. I'm also expected to have a good understanding of the extensive guidance God has already given in Scripture. All in all, then, I am to approach my life decisions with a very different attitude and spiritual foundation.

But when it comes to actually thinking through these decisions, the *cognitive* experience is identical to what I went through as a nonbeliever. I am still using the same brain and going through the same mental process of evaluating options. While this process is now being directed by Christ, it's still the same psychological process nonetheless. I'm not likely to *feel* any different as I go about making decisions as a Christian, and there probably won't be any special spiritual or mystical sensation as I do. Yet while my experiential sense is the same, I can know as a matter of faith that Christ is now guiding my decision process. And that makes all the difference in the world.

Paul's Surprising Example

When we look carefully at examples of decision making in the New Testament, we find pervasive evidence for this perspective. In fact, in the overwhelming majority of personal decisions noted in the New Testament,

God's will was discerned simply through a reasoned decision. Human reason was the channel through which God's will was normally known. In most cases discerning his will boiled down to a matter of making a sound, logical choice.

While this can be documented from various places in the New Testament, it comes across most obviously in the example of the apostle Paul. Although Paul is popularly imagined as one who received frequent supernatural guidance, the dramatic instances recorded for us are few. Most of the time Paul merely followed the dictates of his sanctified reason—that is, reason dedicated to serving God. Let's look at some examples.

Choosing a Path

Paul's travel itinerary seems to have been based primarily on logical considerations. In Romans 15:18-24, for instance, Paul discloses how he determined where he would evangelize:

> For I will not venture to speak of anything except what Christ has wrought through me to win obedience from the Gentiles, by word and deed, by the power of signs and wonders, by the power of the Holy Spirit, so that from Jerusalem and as far round as Illyricum I have fully preached the gospel of Christ, thus making it my ambition to preach the gospel, not where Christ has already been named, lest I build on another man's foundation, but as it is written, "They shall see who have never been told of him, and they shall understand who have never heard of him."
>
> This is the reason why I have so often been hindered from coming to you. But now, since I no longer have any room for work in these regions, and since I have longed for many years to come to you, I hope to see you in passing as I go to Spain, and to be sped on my journey there by you, once I have enjoyed your company for a little.

It is interesting that in this passage Paul makes no reference to supernatural guidance in planning his missionary travels. While he does refer to supernatural events occurring in his ministry ("by the power of signs and wonders"), he says nothing about supernatural *guidance* dictating his travel plans. His language indicates, rather, that he made logical decisions about where to go, in light of which areas were most in need of his service.

Paramount in his thinking was the strategy of visiting unevangelized territory; he speaks of "making it my ambition to preach the gospel, not where Christ has already been named." Paul felt he would lay the broadest foundation by breaking fresh ground. Though he never claimed this would have to be the strategy all disciples followed, he did regard it as the right priority for his gifts. We are given the impression that in light of this priority Paul simply sat down with a map and looked for the most expedient geographical spot to visit next.

His reference to "making it my *ambition*" is especially interesting, for it suggests that he not only made logical decisions about where to travel but even took considerable personal initiative in the process. Unlike some modern Christians who feel uneasy being assertive and assume they must wait with hands folded for the Lord to open any doors, Paul had no qualms about knocking on them. He aggressively looked for places to invest his gifts and didn't hesitate to ask others for the opportunity to minister.

Paul's practice of looking for open doors is well illustrated in 1 Corinthians 16:5-9. Here he writes to the Corinthians, telling them of his desire to visit them eventually and of his understanding of what God wants him to do at the present time.

> I will visit you after passing through Macedonia, for I intend to pass through Macedonia, and perhaps I will stay with you or even spend the winter, so that you may speed me on my journey, wherever I go. For I do not want to see you now just in passing; I hope to spend some time with you, if the Lord permits. But I will stay in Ephesus until Pentecost, for a wide door for effective work has opened to me, and there are many adversaries.

In this passage Paul clearly wants to reassure the Corinthians of his determination to visit them but also to justify to them his decision to remain in Ephesus for a while. If he had received supernatural guidance to stay there, he certainly would have said so, for he wanted to provide the Corinthians with all the evidence he could that he shouldn't come immediately to see them. But he says nothing of special guidance. He merely notes that an *opportunity* is available to him: "a wide door for effective work has opened to me." A logical decision on the basis of circumstantial evidence led Paul to this conclusion about God's will.

Two other points are of particular interest in this passage. For one thing, Paul refers not only to an open door in Ephesus but also to the fact that "there are many adversaries" there. Paul saw a prime opportunity for ministry—and with the open door came an open challenge.

Paul's perception of an open door, interestingly, challenges the supposition of many Christians that when God opens a door it means smooth sailing. Many Christians wouldn't perceive the open door which Paul did; they would take the adversaries as circumstantial guidance from God telling them *not* to go ahead! Paul's experience suggests that it takes an adventuresome spirit to recognize the doors which God opens for us. And it takes the sort of willingness to do God's will about which we have spoken at such length.

When that willingness is there, we will typically find many opportunities to employ our gifts and potential for Christ. Yet responding to these opportunities will typically require tackling certain challenges as well. With an open door comes the adversary factor—which can too easily persuade us that the door is not open at all. At some point, for instance, you might perceive a professional change which would better allow you to realize the potential which Christ has given you. Yet this might require getting further education, and that could necessitate living at a lower economic standard for a while. In real-life terms, this could be the adversary factor you have to deal with in order to walk through an open door.

The other factor of interest is the tentative nature of Paul's language in speaking to the Corinthians about his desire eventually to visit them. Consider how he expresses his future intentions in this passage (if you worked through the first study question in chapter four, you have already noticed this): "I will visit you after passing through Macedonia, for I *intend* to pass through Macedonia, and *perhaps* I will stay with you or *even* spend the winter, so that you *may* speed me on my journey, *wherever I go*. For I do not *want* to see you now just in passing; I *hope* to spend some time with you, *if the Lord permits.*"

Here we note eight words or phrases which indicate that Paul's plans for the future were tentative at best. He had a clear understanding of what God wanted him to do right now, which was to stay and minister in Ephesus. Yet his perception of God's will for the future was only provisionary. This again gives weight to the conclusion that Paul wasn't normally receiving supernatural revelations of guidance; if he had experienced such guidance here, his declaration of plans for the future would have been much more definite.

His example reinforces the point that God guides us in a step-by-step fashion and provides another fascinating biblical example of this. While Paul was comfortable speaking of the *direction* he was headed in, he didn't normally speak in absolute terms about his future. He took the Lord's guidance one step at a time. And as the passage clarifies, this gradual understanding normally came not through supernatural enlightenment but through a process of practical decision making.

Return Visits

While Paul looked for open doors in planning his missionary travels, this passage shows that he was also swayed by another strong priority as well—that of revisiting those he had ministered with before. And as the passage suggests, decisions to visit former converts were usually resolved in the same rational manner as those to break fresh evangelistic ground.

Romans 15:18-24, quoted above, speaks to this also. When Paul tells of his intention to visit the Romans, he bases it not on any extraordinary sign but on the fact that he has longed for many years to visit them and that he has run out of fresh territory to evangelize in the east. As a result he boldly declares that it will be God's will for him to visit his Roman friends (15:32) once he has fulfilled the remaining responsibility of delivering a contribution to the poor in Jerusalem (15:25-31).[1] The interplay of logical factors in his decision making is fascinating to observe.

Paul's motives in revisiting communities where he had previously ministered were several. He desired to instruct them; he was concerned to protect them from persecution and adverse influences on their faith; he was eager to receive personal refreshment and encouragement through their fellowship.

Paul, then, had several major priorities to balance in his major decisions. This brings home the fact that such decisions were not always clear-cut for Paul. He didn't solely look for an open door for ministry. The open door was always an important consideration—but it was one factor which had to be balanced among several others.

The challenge Paul sometimes faced in resolving major choices is particularly well illustrated in 2 Corinthians 2:12-13:

> When I came to Troas to preach the gospel of Christ, a door was opened for me in the Lord; but my mind could not rest because I did not find my brother Titus there. So I took leave of them and went on to Macedonia.

In this case Paul's personal concern for former converts finally overruled his intention of going ahead to fresh territory. John Allan makes some interesting observations about this incident:

> Here we have a striking minor change of plan. Paul had evidently arranged to meet Titus at Troas, and he had every inducement to adhere to that plan because the evangelistic opportunity was great "in the Lord," that is, the favourable circumstances pointed to the Will of Christ in the matter. Yet Paul went on to Macedonia, simply because his concern for the Corinthian Church tormented him so that he could not settle to work but hurried forward on the route so as to meet Titus and hear his report [on the church] the sooner. If his letter and Titus's visit had failed, the Church at Corinth would practically cease to exist as a Christian force, and he would have to excommunicate them and hand them over to Satan's realm. His passionate concern for his dear friends and his anxiety for the continuance of the Christian cause in Corinth made it impossible for him to consider any other service of Christ in the meantime. *Nothing could show more clearly that Paul was no fanatic, depending blindly on direct, particular guidance, and unshakably confident in that guidance.*[2]

What I find most eye-opening about this passage is that Paul mentions a door being opened *"in the Lord"*—almost certainly meaning that God himself opened this door—and yet in the same breath speaks of turning away from this opportunity in order to follow another priority. While we might at first glance think Paul is confessing that he reneged on what God wanted him to do, the verse which follows this passage suggests otherwise, for Paul then declares, "But thanks be to God who always leads us in triumph" (2 Cor 2:14). Paul seems to be saying, then, that in retrospect he is comfortable with the decision to leave Troas for Macedonia and believes it to have been in God's will.

We have, then, strong evidence that Paul didn't always feel compelled to respond to open doors for ministry. While he took such opportunities very seriously, he weighed them along with other factors before finally deciding whether to respond. I have often noticed in my seminars that many find this passage more liberating than any other on guidance, for it shows that we are not obliged to respond to every call for our help that comes along. It is, in short, okay to say no, and there are times when stewardship of our time and energy requires us to do so. The passage suggests that we may well be faced with more opportunities at a given time than we can legitimately fulfill.

In fact, it states things even more strongly than this. The fact that Paul turned away from a door opened "in the Lord," suggests that *God himself* may bring more opportunities into our life at a given time than he expects us to carry out. Undoubtedly he does this for a number of reasons: to encourage us to trust him to accomplish what we cannot do through our own strength, to drive us to delegate more (and thus allow others the privilege of using their gifts), and to help us grow through taking responsibility for challenging decisions.

Four Modern Proverbs

In this context, I think of four statements which Christian teachers have made that help place the weighing of open doors in healthy context.

One comes from Henrietta Mears, who was well-known for saying "the need is not a call." Mears, the notable director of Christian education for Hollywood Presbyterian Church, in her lifetime discipled some of the best known Christian leaders of today, including Bill Bright, Richard Halverson, and many others. She was speaking to the Christian who is eager to do God's will when she made this statement and not suggesting one should ever turn a hard heart to anyone's need. But she knew too well how difficult it can be for serious Christians to balance their limited reserves of time and energy. A need, she was saying, shouldn't be taken as an automatic invitation from God to meet it. Weigh the opportunity along with other priorities and feel free before the Lord to respond or not in light of your full range of commitments.

Richard Foster also put it aptly when he noted that by saying yes to an opportunity you can in effect be saying no to a commitment you've already made, for you deplete the energy you have for responding to that prior commitment.

Rev. Don MacNair in St. Louis helped me with his observation that when St. Paul talked of being fruitful in all good works, he certainly meant we should not take on more work than we can possibly be fruitful in.

Finally, there is the memorable statement which someone made, that "open doors can sometimes lead to elevator shafts!" Open doors can present marvelous opportunities; but they shouldn't be taken as guidance in themselves until all the factors are considered.

A Genuine Challenge

While Paul's example of leaving Troas for Macedonia gives us this freedom to weigh the factors, there is a challenging side to his experience as well (though it is liberating in its own way). When we look carefully at Paul's language in this passage, it becomes apparent that this was an exceedingly difficult decision for Paul. He mentions a door opened in the Lord yet also that "my mind could not rest." We're given the impression of a man who probably made up his mind and remade it a number of times before finally resolving what to do. And it's striking that in the midst of this inner struggle God didn't intervene and bail Paul out with a revelation. He allowed Paul to assume the full responsibility for a most challenging decision.

We are reminded again of our need to take responsibility for working through major choices. Yet the fact that Paul was required to do this is encouraging, for it tells us that the failure to receive supernatural guidance doesn't necessarily mean we're less spiritually mature than we should be. Paul himself, in spite of his spiritual maturity, had to work through even very difficult decisions in a normal, logical process.

Selecting Church Leaders

There is another area where we're given some helpful insight into Paul's practical approach to guidance, and that is his appointment of leaders in the early church. We find a wealth of evidence that his selection of leaders was normally based not on supernatural calls but upon rational considerations. Although Paul himself received a dramatic call to the ministry, there is no indication that he *ever* required this same experience of others. When, for instance, he gives instructions about how to choose church leaders in 1 Timothy 3:1-13 and Titus 1:5-9, there is absolutely no mention of need for a special call. Judgment is to be based purely on one's ability and the quality of one's Christian example. Likewise, where we see Paul choosing leaders himself, there is no indication he required a specific call.

Kenneth Pike observes two interesting examples of Paul's using reason in leadership selection. The first is Paul's choice of Silas and Timothy to be his missionary companions, in Acts 15:22 and Acts 16:1-3:

From Paul's point of view, why did he choose the two? By divine orders? . . . One finds no evidence of such, but rather sees consecrated judgment in confident action on the basis of the proved character of the two men. Silas had first been chosen by a council as trustworthy, and as one of the "leading men among the brethren" (Acts 15:22); Timothy was "well spoken of by the brethren" (Acts 16:2). These two missionary calls were based on sound judgment, not on feelings.[3]

Regarding Paul's disagreement with Barnabas over the selection of Mark to travel with them (Acts 16:36-41), Pike observes the following:

The first split of a "mission board" came on the basis of judgment over the fitness of a candidate. Neither Paul nor Barnabas argued that God had directly revealed to him that Mark should or should not go again to the field. The "sharp contention" was on the basis of judgment, since "Paul thought not good to take with them him who withdrew from them from Pamphylia, and went not with them to the work" (Acts 15:38). Judgment, not feeling, as to God's guidance seems to be implied by the words "thought not good."⁴

It appears, then, that Paul regarded rational judgment of a person's qualities as the prime factor constituting a call to Christian leadership. The need for a dramatic supernatural call, such as Paul himself received, was not emphasized. Likewise, our popular notion that a call may come through an inner sense of leading, without outward evidence of ability, finds no support in Paul's teaching.

It appears that in both travel planning and leadership selection Paul made use of his God-given rational faculties in solving most of his decisions. For Paul, discerning God's will was mainly a matter of making sound, logical judgments, in light of what course appeared most glorifying to God. We must conclude that this process of rational discernment should also be our normal approach to discovering God's will.

The Bottom Line
In addition to Paul's example, we could also note specific places where he exhorts believers to use logical judgment in finding God's will. Colossians 1:9 and Ephesians 5:15-17, when carefully interpreted, yield this sense.⁵ But we are in danger of belaboring the point, which is only too obvious by now. It is through our normal, rational decision processes that we discover God's leading, provided that we approach our decision making with a heart toward doing God's will. We must agree with the conclusion of James Jauncy, "Guidance is largely consecrated and sanctified thinking."⁶ While God can, if he chooses, lead us contrary to reason, we may trust that in such cases he will make his directions unmistakably clear. Apart from such dramatic guidance, our responsibility is to make as sound a decision as possible, trusting that he in his providence will give us all the information we need to decide within his will.

I sincerely hope that these biblical insights are as helpful to you as they have been to me. God has put considerable potential within you—potential for certain accomplishments, for relationships, for growth in many areas. Yet for this potential to be fully realized, you will need to take responsibility for making many important personal choices.

In the final section of this book we'll consider more specifically how we should go about making decisions which are glorifying to Christ. We'll look at how to weigh important factors such as desires, abilities, circumstances and counsel. First, however, it will be helpful to take a closer look at exceptions to the norm. When, if ever, might God be expected to bypass our normal rational process and guide us in a more direct fashion? In part three we'll look at the areas of supernatural guidance and inward guidance.

For Personal Study:

1. We referred briefly in this chapter to Acts 16:1-3, where Paul chooses Timothy to be his missionary companion, and noted Kenneth Pike's observation on the passage. Actually this passage, though very brief, reveals many practical factors which influenced Paul to choose Timothy—clearly one of the most critical personnel decisions of his ministry. Read the passage and note as many factors as you can that impressed on Paul that Timothy was God's choice (and by the same token would have persuaded Timothy to go with Paul).

☐ Note, too, what these different factors imply for our own approach to knowing God's will.

2. Read Luke 1:1-4, and note how Luke decided to write his Gospel (a helpful biblical example of a complex decision). Does he speak of supernatural guidance, or was the decision made for practical reasons? (I'm referring here to how he made the decision to compile a written record, not to how he received inspiration in the process of writing it.)

☐ What can we learn from his experience to help us in our own endeavor to realize our potential for Christ?

3. Likewise, read about Nehemiah's decision to lead the mission in rebuilding the wall of Jerusalem in Nehemiah 1:1-2:8. Is there any mention of a direct revelation from God to do this?

☐ What were the factors that led Nehemiah to make this choice?

☐ What can we learn from his example?

4. Consider the most pressing decision presently facing you. List two or three practical questions which if answered would help you understand God's will for that choice.

☐ Now note any steps you could take to help resolve those questions.

☐ Pray, asking God to guide you in dealing with these questions and in understanding his will for that decision.

Part 3
Exceptions and the Rules

11
Supernatural Guidance

Key Questions:

■ *Are there occasions where God might convey his will to me in a direct supernatural manner?*
■ *How should I determine the authenticity of a dramatic experience of guidance?*

*W*ell, it's time for another lighthouse story. . . .

A friend of mind, while in college, attended a youth revival meeting. The event was held in a picturesque oceanside setting, in view of a lighthouse some distance out in the water.

Though my friend wasn't a Christian at the time, he was becoming warm to the possibility. Yet he felt the need for proof of Christ's reality. When the speaker urged those present to give their lives to Christ, my friend bowed his head and prayed, "Lord, if you are real and what I'm hearing about you is true, please pick that lighthouse up and move it ten yards to the right." For some time he waited, believing that his request might actually be granted.

Well . . . the lighthouse never budged (sorry to disappoint you). But, thankfully, my friend eventually concluded that his request was presumptuous. He finally decided to commit himself to Christ on the basis of faith alone, without the need for supernatural proof.

Yet his example brings to mind how instinctive it is to want God to communicate with us supernaturally. Because God himself is purely supernatural, it's only natural to think he would bend the rules of nature in his effort to make contact with us. Most people, Christian or not, long to see supernatural demonstrations of the existence of God. Like my friend, they may imagine that a single convincing preternatural act would be enough to push them over the threshold of faith.

We long for the supernatural not only to persuade us of God's existence but also to convince us of what he wants us to do. For the serious Christian it's in the area of guidance that the desire for supernatural evidence is often most strongly felt. We long for God to break through the void and communicate with us in a direct, unmistakable way, removing all doubt about what his will is for us.

As I once heard a speaker aptly put it, we wish we could wake up one morning, look out the second-story window and see twenty-foot letters carved in the grass of our back yard saying, "Move to China and become a missionary."

Or, "Apply to med school and become a doctor."

Or, "Sell all you have and move to the inner city."

Or, "Marry Frank."

This desire for supernatural guidance is easy to understand. We are painfully aware that we have only one life to live and that our time is terribly limited; we dreadfully fear taking a wrong direction in any major life choice. Supernatural guidance, it seems, would give us the clarity we need for our life's direction and quench our fears over making a wrong decision.

Our desire to avoid responsibility, too, makes us susceptible to wanting supernatural guidance. While it's wonderfully freeing on the one hand to know that God wants us to take responsibility for our choices, still that means making efforts and taking risks. It would be so much easier if God would just intervene and guide us in a way that would remove the need for personal initiative and absolve us of all need to think!

Can It Happen Today?

Then there are reasons to think that perhaps we *should* receive supernatural guidance. For one thing, there are extensive examples of it in Scripture. Not a few Christians who read them conclude that they must be illustrating the normative pattern of guidance for believers today. On the surface, that conclusion is only too logical. If people of faith in Scripture were guided in a direct manner, and if we are now saints on like footing with them through the work of Christ, shouldn't we also expect direct guidance from God?

There are those Christians, too, who claim to have received supernatural guidance. They may be our friends or others we esteem as spiritual role models. In reality, many who make this claim are referring to a one-time or very occasional experience. Yet we may infer more than this from what they say. We may assume they're talking about their usual experience of guidance or implying it should be normative for us as well.

Christians do sometimes have significant and genuine experiences of supernatural guidance. Though these seem to be most common in the early stages of one's Christian walk, they can occur at other times as well.

I'm intrigued with how sometimes the most rational Christian will admit to having had a spiritual experience which defied the rational. A level-headed Baptist pastor I know speaks openly about a cherished mystical experience he once had unexpectedly while driving along in his car. Or one thinks of John Calvin's decision to return to govern Geneva a second time. Though this great proponent of rational faith wanted to decline the offer, he claimed to suddenly feel the hand of Christ on his shoulder prodding him forward. That left him with little choice about what to do.

Many of us, though, have never had such experiences, even though we may be many years into our Christian walk. We may naturally wonder whether we're less mature spiritually, or whether there's something fundamentally lacking in our approach to knowing God's will. For each of us the critical need is to have clear perspective on the area of supernatural guidance. We need to understand when—if ever—it might be reasonable to expect it, and why—if never—we are not privileged to experience it.

Let's first distinguish several possible types of supernatural guidance, as each requires some differences in perspective. There are three general ways in which individuals in Scripture sometimes experienced special guidance:

Direct supernatural guidance: This is the most common means of extraordinary guidance shown in Scripture. It includes those instances where God communicates in a *direct* and often *dramatic* way to someone, through a vision, sign, dream, audible voice, angel or the like.

Prophecy: There are also instances in Scripture where God's guidance comes *indirectly,* through another person's directive. We typically call this *prophecy* today. Though the term *prophecy* is used in other ways as well, we will employ it in this study to refer to supernatural guidance coming via someone else's revelation.

Putting out a fleece: Finally, there are examples in Scripture of individuals seeking God's will through a *predetermined* sign. This is often termed "putting out a fleece" or "fleecing" today in light of Gideon's experience in Judges 6.

Then there is the area of inward guidance—guidance through mystical impressions. This is an extremely popular approach to God's will, and one which needs to be put in careful perspective. While our feelings and impressions play an important role in guidance, we must be careful not to take them as the infallible voice of God's Spirit. They must be understood in the context of our humanity.

In the remainder of this chapter we'll look more closely at the area of direct supernatural guidance. Then we'll devote a chapter each to prophecy, putting out a fleece and inward guidance.

The Biblical Norm
Many Christians wonder if they shouldn't at least occasionally experience direct supernatural guidance. Some pastors and teachers will answer that, yes, you should expect this sort of guidance as a regular experience. The

result is that some believers end up frustrated with the lack of such experiences, if not deluded with imagined theophanies. Most pastors and teachers, however, will say that such guidance should not often be expected. The stock reason given is that unlike the saints of the Bible we now possess the full canon of Holy Scripture and we are now indwelt by the Holy Spirit.

But this answer, when considered carefully, is really beside the point. The early Christians in the book of Acts had received the Holy Spirit, yet they still experienced supernatural guidance at times. In addition, the guidance was not a revelation of moral or doctrinal truths such as comprise the canon of Scripture but directives for personal decisions which couldn't have been found in Scripture anyway. Thus, even though they were filled with the Spirit, they still needed occasional direct guidance, and this would have been necessary even if they had possessed the entire New Testament.

But while the stock answer doesn't deal adequately with the issue, there are in fact substantial reasons why we shouldn't normally expect supernatural guidance today. First, when all the instances of decision making in the New Testament are considered, we are struck by the sparsity of such guidance in the early church. It seems that in the great majority of instances where decisions were made there was no experience of supernatural guidance. This seems true even with the apostle Paul; Acts records less than ten examples of direct guidance received by him, and the evidence is overwhelming that in the bulk of his day-to-day decisions supernatural guidance played no role (see chapter ten).

Further, it's by no means evident that the typical Christian in the early church *ever* received supernatural guidance, or even, for that matter, that many of the apostles experienced it after Pentecost. It must be concluded that supernatural guidance was a decidedly exceptional experience in the New Testament church.

Even more important, there is no statement in the Old or New Testament telling us either to seek or to expect supernatural guidance. If God had wished us to rely on such guidance as a normal approach to knowing his will, he would surely have given us a command to that effect within his Word.

Furthermore, there are several common-sense reasons for not expecting supernatural guidance. For one thing, such direct, dramatic encounters with God could be terribly frightening to us. Martin Luther states, "Our nature cannot bear even a small glimmer of God's direct speaking. . . . The dreams and visions of the saints are horrifying . . . at least after they are understood."[1] The late James H. Miers, former pastor of Fourth Presbyterian Church in Washington, D.C., said that he prayed hard for a supernatural revelation from God. When it finally came, it scared him half to death! Beyond this obvious psychological hazard, we can also see that supernatural guidance could pose severe trials for our faith. We might be inclined to think of ourselves as more spiritual than others. And we wouldn't be motivated to take the sort of personal responsibility for making decisions that really develops faith.

Exceptions to the Rule
But while we must conclude that we shouldn't normally expect supernatural guidance, we should avoid going to the dispensationalist extreme of thinking such guidance *never* occurs in our present age.[2] There might be certain occasions where direct leading would be necessary, and Scripture leaves open these possibilities. The most probable would be where one is young in the faith and not ready to take full responsibility for a major personal decision. This isn't to suggest that all or even most new Christians receive supernatural guidance. But it does explain why some young believers have special experiences of guidance which are not repeated as they grow older in Christ.

Or there might be occasions when God would wish to lead us to do something which we would never consider doing on the basis of reason alone. This situation, of course, could occur at any point in our Christian experience. In most of the examples of supernatural guidance noted in Acts, it seems that believers were led to conclusions they probably wouldn't have reached through normal decision making.

In some cases the guidance was repugnant to reason. When Philip was directed by an angel to go to a desert road (Acts 8:26), it was highly doubtful he would have chosen to go there on his own. Reason would have dictated staying in Samaria where a big revival was under way and his services were needed. Likewise, when Paul was struck down on the Damascus road, the guidance given could not possibly have been further from his present intentions. And the vision to venture into Macedonia (Acts 16:9-10) probably came at a time when he was perplexed and lacking logical insight into the next step to take.

In other cases, God's purpose might be to provide an unmistakable point of reference through direct leading which would serve as reassurance in the face of future challenges or trials. Most likely this divine strategy was in God's mind at the dramatic commissioning of Paul, as Bob Mumford observes:

> Paul had the need for a strong point of reference . . . something he would never forget! God told Ananias in the vision, "For I will show him [Saul] how great things he must suffer for my name's sake." Paul was beaten, jailed, stoned, and left as dead for the sake of the gospel. But God had spoken to him in proportion to the degree of challenge he would face. . . . And he never forgot what happened to him on the road to Damascus.[3]

Finally, it is also certainly possible that God will guide supernaturally for reasons known only to him—perhaps to remind us that he is free to communicate in any way he chooses and is not bound by our preconceptions! Our purpose in outlining principles of guidance is not to box God in or to pretend that we understand everything about his nature in communicating but simply to stress what is *normative* in guidance.

But on the basis of what Scripture demonstrates as normative, we are certainly justified in concluding that supernatural guidance is not something we should normally expect or seek as Christians. Those who do receive it will probably not experience it often, and most of us will never receive it.

We shouldn't think of ourselves as less spiritual because God hasn't intervened directly in our lives in this way. Supernatural guidance, in fact, could signify spiritual immaturity as much as anything. God might use it to jar someone into realizing that he or she is headed in the wrong direction, whereas ideally the person should have reached this conclusion without dramatic aid.

Of course, experiences of supernatural guidance do not necessarily indicate spiritual immaturity, and we should refrain from judging anyone on this basis. But neither should we judge ourselves for the lack of such experiences. We should simply trust that God will provide each of us the enlightenment we need to walk within his will, and in a manner that will best contribute to our growth in faith.

Verifying Our Perception
Still an important question remains, and that is how we can determine whether an apparent experience of supernatural guidance has been genuine. Are there ways to distinguish between authentic direct guidance and an imaginary experience or hallucination?

I approach this matter cautiously, for I certainly don't want to imply that anyone claiming to experience supernatural guidance is necessarily hearing imaginary voices or seeing sixteen-foot angels. I realize, too, the stigma involved here. The very idea of hallucinating seems to imply mental instability.

In fact, though, a single episode of hallucination does not in itself suggest that one's sanity is seriously impaired. Even the most stable individual can hallucinate under certain extreme conditions, such as severe fatigue, strong medication, illness or long-term exposure to highly monotonous circumstances. The latter could include a prolonged period of straight highway driving without adequate stops for rest. Studies of sleep deprivation have shown that hallucinations are common after long intervals without sleep. Highly susceptible individuals, too, may hallucinate under the influence of someone else's suggestion.

It is also possible to experience a dream state while partially awake, a phenomenon which can produce the sense of having a vision. This wakeful dreaming can occur, for instance, in the first moments of awakening from sleep. A dream may continue as you're coming out of sleep, even though you have some awareness of your surroundings and some general sense of being awake. Though this occurrence is not uncommon, it unfortunately is not generally well understood. Not a few people who have this experience conclude they have hallucinated or seen an apparition. In fact, they have merely been dreaming, though not fully asleep.

Such lucid dreaming can occur while falling asleep, too, or at other times when fatigue takes over. Some people are simply more susceptible to this experience than others.

Given these possibilities, then, we shouldn't be afraid to confront the possibility that a visionary experience we have had was imaginary as well as that it was directly from God. Neither should we regard it as irreverent or an affront to God to raise this question. Any effort we make to determine whether our humanness has affected our understanding of God's guidance is certainly honoring to God. It is exercising good stewardship of our responsibility for wise decision making.

Thousands of years before the advent of modern psychology with its insight into the human imagination, Gideon felt the freedom to question the authenticity of a revelation he received (Judg 6). While this incident needs to be interpreted carefully, it does suggest that we are not by definition out of bounds in asking God to validate a revelation (we'll look at Gideon's experience in greater detail in chapter thirteen). Indeed, with our understanding of the human psyche being what it is today, we are if anything more justified than Gideon in questioning a visionary experience.

Considering the Source
But how should we go about doing that?

To begin with, we cannot always judge the authenticity of such an experience merely by looking at its psychological nature. Sometimes, to be sure, we do have good basis for believing an episode has been purely hallucinatory. If after spending two all-nighters cramming for finals I think I'm hearing a voice telling me to jump out my third-story dormitory window, I have good reason to conclude that a purely psychological process is taking place (and even better reason to stop and get some sleep!). Yet in other cases it may not be so easy to draw a line between hallucination and genuine vision.

Few individuals during this century have given closer attention to the study of subjective spiritual experiences than Catholic theologian Karl Rahner. In his books *The Dynamic Element in the Church* and *Visions and Prophecies* he examines the experiences of notable mystics, looking at both the psychological and spiritual aspects of their visions.[4] Rahner concludes that an authentic vision will be brought to the person as much as possible through the same psychological mechanisms that trigger dreams and hallucinations. Since God works through natural means to provide for us and guide us in other areas of life, Rahner points out, we should assume he will use the natural psychological processes he has put within us if he wishes to bring about a vision.[5]

A visionary experience, then, cannot always be discounted just because there are indications of a normal psychological process in it. On the other hand, there is nothing generic to the nature of a true vision which proves that it isn't psychologically induced. Rahner comments,

> . . . it is not to be taken as a proof of the corporeality (and divine origin) of the vision if the person seen in it "speaks," "moves"—and even lets himself "be touched" (for this happens in natural, purely imaginary processes); even if the visionary has the impression of learning something surprising and hitherto unknown to him. This division of consciousness into two personalities and the sense of surprise we all experience in dreams; we do not wonder at it there because it is familiar, but the psychological explanation of the experience is far from simple.[6]

Rahner's observations make good sense. While they don't provide a final basis for judging the validity of a vision, they do help steer us away from a futile attempt to do so purely by analyzing its psychological characteristics.

A Reasonable Test

If you do not have clear reason to think that a visionary experience has been hallucinatory, you may be on safest ground not to analyze the psychology of the experience but rather to test the content of the guidance that has come through it. Doing so will allow you the most objective standard possible for determining if in fact you've received special guidance.

Begin by considering whether the guidance aligns completely with biblical revelation. If, for instance, you're being told to do something which violates biblical norms, you may rest assured the directive is not from God. Instruction to abandon your marriage, for instance, or to do anything harmful to yourself or anyone else should be disregarded.

If the guidance is not in violation of Scripture, then you should make a further test of its authenticity. One way to do this is to ask God to provide specific help or resources which you would clearly need to carry out the guidance. Since you are trying to determine the validity of miraculous guidance, it is not unreasonable to ask God to provide what you need miraculously, or at least without your having to ask anyone else for help. The request, though, should clearly be reasonable in light of the guidance. It should not be for unnecessary luxuries and should not be for an irrelevant "fleece" (more on that in chapter thirteen).

Let's say, for instance, you believe you've been told to join a ministry of smuggling Bibles into an anti-Christian country. It could be appropriate to ask God to provide a certain level of financial support that would be needed for this mission by a particular date, but not to mention your need to anyone else. If the provision comes, you may have good reason to conclude God has directed you. If your request is not granted, you may be justified in not proceeding. The most reverent step to take at this point is to humbly express your doubts about the guidance to God and to ask him to provide compelling evidence if in fact you have reached the wrong conclusion about it.

It can also be appropriate simply to ask God to provide clear *reasons* for following the guidance you believe you have been given supernaturally. Then be open to clarification coming through ordinary means. You might discover through counsel, for instance, that you are more motivated for this sort of adventuresome mission than you realized and that you have gifts for it which you hadn't recognized. Through further investigation you find avenues open for pursuing this ministry which you hadn't known about before.

My personal belief is that the most reverent approach is to ask God to authenticate the guidance through *either* of these means. Ask him, in other words, either to grant a specific request for help *or* to provide convincing reasons for going ahead. Framing your request in this way allows God the greatest freedom to confirm things in whatever way he chooses, and best assures you are not making unreasonable demands of him.

One further point. Karl Rahner notes that even in an authentic vision human perceptions are typically mixed in. As an example, he notes how mystics throughout the centuries who have had a vision of the baby Jesus have pictured him in the clothing and settings of their own culture. Of course, the fact that Roman Catholic mystics have so often envisioned Jesus as a baby seems to give evidence to Rahner's observation, given the veneration for the infant Jesus that is unique to Catholic tradition.

There is, though, strong biblical evidence for Rahner's point in Paul's Macedonian vision in Acts 16, which we examined at length in chapter four. We noted that while Paul had a genuine vision to go to Macedonia, his perception of what God wanted him to do had to be adjusted at a number of points as he moved forward. It seems that his vision—authentic as it was—was influenced by certain human presuppositions as well.

We may conclude, then, that even if we receive a genuine vision, we are still free to question its individual elements and to continue to look to God for fresh guidance as we move forward.

In the same vein, we should remember that the impressions and images which come to our mind are often more symbolic than literal in what they reveal to us. The highly imaginative imagery of dreams, for instance, usually symbolizes our feelings and perceptions and only rarely provides a literal picture of reality. And in spite of the claims of some scholars to the contrary,[7] I find little evidence to suggest that dreams provide a literal prediction of the future except on the rarest occasions.

Charismatic Episcopal priest Morton Kelsey—an ardent Jungian and one enthusiastically open to mystical experience—has spent much of his lifetime studying the nature of dreams. In doing so he has carefully chronicled his own. Kelsey concludes that only a minute percentage of his dreams have carried valid, literal predictions of the future. The vast number have been symbolic in character. While he stresses that the symbolism of dreams is valuable in understanding our psychological makeup, he strongly cautions against taking direct guidance from dreams. Kelsey notes:

Being rather compulsive, I have kept a careful record of my dreams for the past thirty-four years; they probably number 30,000, of which no more than 20 are basically [prophetic] dreams. One never knows whether a dream is prophetic until it is confirmed by an outer event. It is nonsense to suggest that all dreams predict future events. The purpose of dreams is to reveal, correct, compensate, and direct, and *very* rarely to predict.[8]

Like dreams, a vision may also have symbolic elements or even be primarily symbolic in nature. Again, this is a further reason to test the content of an apparent vision and to feel free to adjust its guidance according to further light which God may throw on your path.

Getting Counsel

What we're seeing, then, is that it's not always easy to judge the nature and implications of a visionary experience. Not only must we determine its divine vs. human origin, but also there's the challenge of interpreting its guidance in light of both human and symbolic perceptions. Perhaps more than anything, our need is to seek out the very best counsel that is available to us and to ask for help in the process of sorting things through. In this area, especially, we are likely to be over our heads attempting to understand things merely on our own. We should take advantage of the help God provides through pastors and other gifted counselors in the body of Christ.

In chapter eighteen we'll look more closely at the importance of getting counsel and at how to evaluate the counsel we receive. At this point, though, we'll find it helpful to look at a related question, and that is how we should respond if others claim to have more than counsel to give us. What if they claim to have had a direct revelation about what God wants us to do? Is this a possible means through which God might supernaturally reveal his will to us? We'll turn our attention to this question in the next chapter.

For Personal Study:

1. Read Acts 10, which tells of Peter's rooftop vision and the events that followed. Through Peter's visionary experience God revealed a general principle of ministry to Peter and also guided him to do something specific in light of it. What was the principle that was revealed and what was the specific guidance?

☐ Are there reasons to think that Peter should not have needed a supernatural revelation to understand either the principle or the specific guidance that was given?

☐ If so, why did he in fact need such dramatic guidance?

☐ Was it complimentary to Peter, or not, that he received this vision? What lessons can we learn from Peter's experience?

2. Likewise, consider Moses' experience with the burning bush in Exodus 3. God spoke to Moses through the burning bush, telling him that he was to deliver Israel. What evidence do we have that Moses would never have remotely considered this idea at this point in his life apart from such a spectacular revelation?

☐ Note as many reasons as you can why Moses probably needed this level of guidance.

☐ Note, too, ways in which Moses' decision differs from most major decisions which we typically face.

☐ What, then, should we conclude from Moses' experience to apply to our own search for guidance?

12

The Place of Prophecy

Key Question:

■ *If someone claims to have a divine revelation of guidance for me, how am I to respond to it?*

W hat if one or more other Christians should approach you and tell you they are certain they know God's will for you? What if they are speaking not of a moral or doctrinal matter but of a *personal* choice? What if they inform you they have received a revelation from God about this? And what if the guidance is to do something you've never considered—to move to another country, to take on a responsibility you're not naturally gifted for, to marry someone you've never met?

Sound remote? Such scenarios do occur and more frequently than many Christians realize. In our popular Christian vocabulary we use the term "prophecy" to refer to a revelation of guidance which one person claims to receive for someone else. Instances of prophecy are not at all limited to charismatic circles but occur within many mainline churches as well. Marriages are entered into, engagements broken off and vocational decisions resolved, simply because one person claims a prophecy of God's will for another.

In the last chapter I suggested that while direct supernatural guidance will not be a frequent experience for most Christians, God may use it to get our attention in special circumstances. You might naturally expect a similar perspective to be presented now for prophecy. In fact, though, I'm compelled by Scripture to draw a harder line on this area. I do not find any New Testament evidence suggesting that prophecy should ever be considered a possible channel of guidance for personal decisions.

Let me hasten to say that this is not an anti-charismatic position. Many charismatic teachers will agree fully with the perspective of this chapter. The New Testament holds the gift of prophecy itself in high esteem. And, as we'll note, the imparting of prophetic pronouncements to the church—a cherished practice within many charismatic circles—can be a valid function of this gift. It's at the point of giving guidance for personal decisions that we must draw the line on what is allowed. The New Testament does not regard personal guidance as a legitimate function of prophecy.

No Biblical Basis

There is only one instance in the New Testament after Pentecost which might seem to provide a basis for prophetic guidance. In Acts 27 Paul receives a revelation that a harrowing sea voyage will end safely. He then declares to his shipmates:

> "Men, you should have listened to me, and should not have set sail from Crete and incurred this injury and loss. I now bid you take heart; for there will be no loss of life among you, but only of the ship. For this very night there stood by me an angel of the God to whom I belong and whom I worship, and he said, 'Do not be afraid, Paul; you must stand before Caesar; and lo, God has granted you all those who sail with you.' So take heart, men, for I have faith in God that it will be exactly as I have been told. But we shall have to run on some island." (vv. 21-26)

Following this announcement, the sailors seek to escape from the boat.

Paul, though, instructs the centurion: " 'Unless these men stay in the ship, you cannot be saved.' Then the soldiers cut away the ropes of the boat, and let it go" (vv. 31-32). After this, Paul gives some comforting counsel to his travel companions: "Today is the fourteenth day that you have continued in suspense and without food, having taken nothing. Therefore I urge you to take some food; it will give you strength, since not a hair is to perish from the head of any of you" (vv. 33-34).

In this passage Paul receives a valid revelation of the future. He then gives others some earnest counsel in light of it. At first sight this might seem to be a clear example of guidance through prophecy; yet when we examine it closely, we find some important differences from the popular practice today.

For one thing, Paul was not specifically told in his revelation what to advise his shipmates to do. He was told what he himself should do (stand before Caesar), and he was given a *prediction* of safety for himself and the others on the ship; but there was no *guidance* in this revelation to impart to the others, at least as far as Luke reports it.

The counsel which Paul did give them was purely logical advice—so logical, in fact, that it was akin to telling a child not to play in traffic. It was only too obvious to Paul that if the sailors escaped, the ship would lose the vital manpower needed to bring it to port. We may wonder why the centurion had to be informed of this. Yet it may be that Paul simply became aware of the problem before the centurion did, and then used emphatic language to urge the centurion—who was undoubtedly numb from days in a storm-tossed boat without food—into action.

Likewise, Paul's recommendation to his shipmates to take food was merely pragmatic counsel. Note that he did not say, "God commands you to take food," or, "It is God's will for you to eat." He simply gave them *advice:* "I urge you to take some food. . . ."

Both of these instances of counsel, too, had to do not with individual complex decisions but with emergency steps needed for the survival of a group. There is a world of difference between the counsel offered here and the prophecy which tells another person whom God wants them to marry or where he wants them to live. There is no instance of that type of prophetic guidance anywhere in the New Testament after Pentecost, nor is there any passage which hints that this sort of practice was respected as a valid approach to guidance in the early church.

Even more significantly, there is no statement in the New Testament to the effect that we should look on prophecy as a possible source of guidance.[1] Again, we must assume that if God wanted us to regard prophecy as a means for discovering his will for personal choices, there would be clear teaching to this effect in his Word.

Paul's Response to Prophecy

The New Testament also provides an intriguing report of a time when Paul received prophetic guidance—but ignored it. Acts 21:3-4 records:

When we had come in sight of Cyprus, leaving it on the left we sailed to Syria, and landed at Tyre; for there the ship was to unload its cargo. And having sought out the disciples, we stayed there for seven days. Through the Spirit they told Paul not to go on to Jerusalem.

The phrase "through the Spirit" almost certainly indicates that these people believed they had received a revelation of God's will for Paul. They were not merely predicting the future (as others did who spoke of Paul's visit to Jerusalem) but were telling him what they believed God wanted him to do. Paul, however, disregards their counsel and continues to move toward Jerusalem. There is no implication in Acts that Paul disobeyed God's will in doing this; instead the impression is given that he followed God's will by proceeding to Jerusalem. While he recognized the validity of his friends' prediction of doom (Acts 20:22-23),[2] he did not believe that the counsel stemming from their prophecy was divine.

Thus, it seems that their counsel was a human conclusion, resulting from their experience of revelation but not received as a direct part of it. F. F. Bruce's observation here is pertinent: "It was natural that his friends who by the prophetic spirit were able to foretell his tribulation and imprisonment should try to dissuade him from going on."[3]

Prophecy in Perspective

We are not denying, then, that prophecy can at times function as prediction. But we are insisting that it never has to be taken as guidance. There is just no clear New Testament mandate to this effect. We must agree with the conclusion of Michael Harper:

> Prophecies which tell other people what they are to do are to be regarded with great suspicion. "Guidance" is never indicated as one of the uses of prophecy. Paul was told what would happen to him if he went to Jerusalem, but was not told either to go or refrain from going. His friends may have advised him concerning this but the guidance did not come from the prophecy. Agabus foretold a famine, but his prophecy gave no instructions as to what should be done about it.
>
> On the whole in the New Testament guidance is given direct to the individual—not through another person as was common in the Old Testament. For instance, although Cornelius was told by an angel to send for Peter (Acts 10:5), Peter himself was told to go with them through an independent agency (Acts 10:20). There may be exceptions to this—but if so they are very rare. This gift is not intended to take the place of common sense or the wisdom which comes from God and which manifests itself through our natural faculties.[4]

It is of interest to note that Harper is a charismatic author writing with the very highest respect for the gift of prophecy. Yet he recognizes all too well how prophecy can be misused. His intent is to understand the gift in biblical context, and he finds no basis in his study for including guidance as part of the function of this gift.

The Gift of Prophecy in Scripture

What, then, is the biblical understanding of the gift of prophecy? The word *prophecy* is actually used in two ways in the New Testament. Sometimes it is simply a generic term for preaching, teaching or articulate communication. Paul uses it in this sense in 1 Corinthians 14, where he contrasts tongues-speaking with prophecy. While he respects the gift of tongues, he stresses that the use of tongues in worship situations should not supersede clear exposition of Christian truth. He uses *prophecy* here as a synonym for such lucid communication. "Make love your aim, and earnestly desire the spiritual gifts, especially that you may prophesy. For one who speaks in a tongue speaks not to men but to God . . . Now I want you all to speak in tongues, but even more to prophesy" (1 Cor 14:1-2, 5).

Elsewhere, though, Paul uses *prophecy* to refer to a distinct spiritual gift. He includes prophecy in his lists of spiritual gifts in Romans 12:6 and 1 Corinthians 12:10, and at three places he mentions "prophets" in the context of other gift lists (1 Cor 12:28; 12:29; Eph 4:11; see also Eph 2:20; 3:5).

Unfortunately, Paul never explains what precisely the gift of prophecy is, and we can only guess at what was in his mind when he spoke of prophecy as a spiritual gift.

It is easier to determine what the gift of prophecy is not than to say with full confidence what it is. In the face of such silence, the use of the term in 1 Corinthians 14 for clear communication may well hold the key. The prophet then would be one who is gifted above and beyond the ordinary person to proclaim Christian truth.

It is clear, however, that Paul saw a distinction between prophecy and teaching as spiritual gifts. In three instances he mentions both functions in the same gift lists (Rom 12:6, 1 Cor 12:29, Eph 4:11); this would not likely occur if he merely understood prophecy as a synonym for teaching. This leads us to conclude that there must be a further distinctive to this gift.

My conclusion is that prophecy is Paul's term for *preaching*.

Though there are similarities between teaching and preaching, there are differences as well. While the teacher is concerned with carefully and systematically explaining the whole of Christian truth, the preacher is more concerned with applying one aspect of it at a given time in a way that evokes a response from his hearers. Given the eminence that Paul attached to preaching, and given the fact that no other word for preaching is included in these gift lists, it's highly probable that he understood prophecy and preaching as synonymous spiritual gift terms. There is good support in the Greek usage of prophecy for this conclusion, also.[5]

This is not to say that the gift of prophecy is relegated to only those who hold the official office of preaching in a church. It is common

practice in charismatic churches for laypersons to offer a word of prophecy, or "word of wisdom," in the context of public worship services. This
custom certainly can fit within the boundaries of the New Testament
concept of prophecy.

Prophetic pronouncements in charismatic services not uncommonly
include predictions of the future. Often, though, these are not pure prophetic predictions so much as *consequential* predictions, based on moral
commandments and clear cause-and-effect teachings of Scripture. The
person who stands up in a service and proclaims, "If we give more of our
resources to helping the poor in our community, the Lord will bless us
exceedingly," for instance, is merely restating a direct command and
promise of the Bible (Ps 41:1-3).

Prophetic pronouncements do go beyond this at times to be unequivocal predictions of future events. There is nothing in the New Testament
to rule out the possibility that the one with the gift of prophecy could
be enabled to make such predictions. Our best evidence, though, is that
straightforward predictions of the future occurred only rarely in the early
church. In any case, there is no basis in Scripture for either preacher or
layperson giving a prophecy of guidance for an individual's personal decisions. That is always a case of a prophet overstepping his or her bounds.

Not Bound by Prophecy
We conclude, then, that the gift of prophecy, while an important benefit
to the body of Christ, does not impart the ability to pronounce God's will
for the unique personal decisions which individual Christians face. This
isn't to imply that the counsel of others is not important in our personal
decisions. Indeed, we'll stress in chapter eighteen that counsel is vital in
making major decisions. But we may be freed forever from the fear that
someone's counsel will have to be taken as God's will simply because they
claim a prophetic revelation.

I may assume that in all cases if the prophecy is genuine guidance, God
will make this abundantly evident to me through other means. If there
is no compelling evidence, I may feel free to disregard the counsel based
on a prophetic utterance as an unfortunate misjudgment on the part of

the one offering it.

The question naturally arises whether we at least are responsible to test a prophecy before deciding not to follow it. Since we suggested in the last chapter that certain steps should be taken to verify direct supernatural guidance, it might seem only natural now to suggest a similar approach for testing prophecies. But because the New Testament does not recognize prophecy as a potential source for personal guidance to begin with, I do not believe we are obliged to make the effort to validate a prophecy we might be given.

It should be enough merely to pray and ask God to make it abundantly clear in his own way and time whether in fact the prophecy did contain genuine guidance, and to leave it at that. We should not feel compelled beyond that to take personal responsibility for proving the prophecy.

The Need for Perspective

My pastoral experience convinces me that this hard-line perspective on personal prophecy is greatly needed not only because it is biblically accurate but also because of our psychological needs. It is hard, in fact, to exaggerate the unsettling impact which prophetic pronouncements can have upon our psyche. If we are not compelled by the sheer power of suggestion to follow a prophecy, we may still be driven to distraction with concern over its implications.

In college I once received one of those insidious chain letters. If I would mail a dollar to each of the six individuals listed, then send copies on to six new people, I would eventually be rich.

The letter carried not only a promise but a threat. If I didn't follow through, terrible things might happen. It mentioned some calamities, otherwise inexplicable, which had befallen past recipients who failed to carry out the scheme.

I didn't consider myself a superstitious person. My initial thought was, "This is ridiculous, manipulative, I'm not going to give this pyramid scam any further consideration." But thought life is not always easy to control. I couldn't get the fear out of my mind that maybe, just maybe, there is some slight possibility that catastrophe does come to those who break the chain. Perhaps the person behind all this has spiritual powers which I don't know about. I actually came close to acquiescing. Six dollars and the little effort involved to recirculate the letter seemed like good insurance.

Finally my rational sense got the better of me. To spare myself the agony of any further deliberation, I ripped the letter into shreds small enough to be digested by our antique toilet, dumped them in and pulled the lever.

But for several days the thought continued to nag me, "What if . . . ? I've burned my bridges now. Maybe terrible things will happen."

Thankfully, the next few weeks were unusually good ones for me. Perhaps God even blessed me for firmly turning my back on superstition. Yet I remember too well the ambivalence I felt at first and how I came close to caving in. It's remarkable, the persuasive power someone can have who assumes the role of prophet in your life. Even an anonymous personality in the mail. Most of us are stirred much more than we'd like to admit by anyone's unequivocal statement about our future. While our rational side says, "This is ridiculous," our intuitive side cringes. We can't get the thought out of mind, "What if?"

A firm that manufactured a popular software program greatly reduced pirating of their product by including a warning on the package. If you copy the program illegally, within thirty days the company will negotiate selling the eternal destiny of your soul to the first alien spirit that comes along.

The message adds that while this might seem ludicrous, given even the remotest possibility that it might be true, you would do best not to risk eternal disaster. A release clause is provided: if you have already violated the licensing agreement, send in $20.00 and you will be forgiven. The company reported that fifty per cent of its revenue came from guilt-singed customers mailing in $20.00 after the fact!

Prophetic messages, regardless of their nature or source, have their effect on us. It is this effect that is so well understood by the spiritualist personalities in every primitive culture and which gives them their almost unchallenged authority to direct the lives of others. But even in enlightened, scientific society, the effect can be powerful. Human psychology remains basically the same.

The Christian Context

Please understand that I'm not suggesting that those who offer personal prophecies within the body of Christ necessarily do so from a desire to manipulate or control others. Many times this is done from the most pure and benevolent intentions. The one giving the prophecy may be convinced he or she is being obedient to Christ and acting in the best interests of the other person. But regardless of the motive, those who give prophecies too often mete out emphatic advice on matters about which they have little understanding. I have seen more than a few cases where the results were tragic. Take the case of Helen, an example I also note in *Should I Get Married?*

Helen became a Christian during her freshman college year and began attending a church nearby her school. An older woman there, Margaret, whom Helen had not previously met, told her that she had received a revelation from God for her future. She was to marry Bill, a young man in the fellowship about Helen's age. Helen barely knew Bill and had no romantic leaning toward him. Yet Margaret's confidence was overwhelming. Certainly such a mature and seasoned Christian would not offer guidance like this if it were not inspired by God. Though Helen was bewildered by the prophecy, she felt she would be irreverent to question it. Finally she accepted it and opened herself to a relationship with Bill. A friendship developed, then a dating relationship. During her sophomore year Bill proposed marriage.

By now her affection for Bill had grown deep and she had no hesitation accepting. Not long afterward, however, Bill's feelings toward Helen waned. He broke the engagement and within a short time married someone else.

Helen fell apart. Not only was there the normal, brutal pain of rejection, hard enough for most people to bear. There was also mortifying confusion over why the prophecy had not worked out. Had Margaret defrauded Helen? Had Helen done something wrong which caused God to change his mind? Did God let her down? There seemed to be no reasonable answers.

When Helen shared the experience with me, she was a college senior and had only recently begun to get her bearing again, after two years of severe depression over the incident.

Helen's case is extreme. Yet it illustrates the problems which can occur. Helen was a bright woman and not a seriously repressed personality. I don't believe she was any more susceptible to manipulation than most people. Yet as a young Christian she was impressionable. And the sense of spiritual authority present in someone who had the confidence of her own infallibility to declare, "This is God's will for you" was enough to sway Helen.

Again, many experiences of prophecy are perfectly benign. John was moving to Seattle to take a position with a computer manufacturer. At his farewell party a Christian friend said, "John, I know it is God's will for you to go to Seattle. I was given confidence of this during my prayer time this morning." The prophecy in this case was not hard to swallow. It implied no change in plans for John and thus he had no need to wrestle with it. However pretentious it might have been, it served as an encouragement to John and helped him feel affirmed in his move.

But when you receive a prophecy to do something you haven't contemplated doing—especially if it is diametrically opposed to what you're inclined to do—the effect can be traumatic. I've counseled with a number of people who have received such prophecies. Most, while not as easily taken in as Helen was, have still been left terribly befuddled. Many hours have been spent mulling it over, wondering, "Should I do this? What if this is the will of God and I just don't realize it? What if I don't follow the prophecy? Will something terrible happen to me?"

What If It Happens to You?

You may go through life without ever having this experience. Yet it's possible that at some point it will happen, and when it does it can catch you off guard. Because the experience of receiving a prophecy can be so troubling, it's important to have a powerful theological perspective to deal with it. This can be of great benefit in counseling others, also, for it is likely you will at some point know someone who has been given a prophecy and is confused over how to deal with it.

How should you respond to the person who would give you a prophecy? Remember that it may be offered lovingly and from the very best motives. The one giving it may be utterly sincere in believing it to be divine revelation. Give that person the benefit of the doubt. Thank him or her, express your appreciation for his or her interest in you, and do not show disrespect toward the advice given you (1 Thess 5:20).

But feel no constraint to follow the guidance given. Look for other factors that confirm it. Trust that God will do what is necessary to persuade you to do this particular thing if in fact it really is his will. Otherwise, feel no guilt for continuing to follow whatever course wisdom suggests in the particular decision area, even if it is quite different from the prophecy given.

As unnerving as the experience can be, take comfort in knowing that it is not uncommon. Thank the Lord, too, for what you can learn from the experience and for how it will better equip you to help others who have a similar experience with prophecy.

For Personal Study:

1. Read 1 Corinthians 7:1-7. (If you wish, read the entire chapter for a fuller context; though we looked at this passage in question 1 in chapter six, it will be helpful now to examine it again in light of our discussion on prophecy.)

Paul begins the passage by indicating that he is responding to questions some in the young Corinthian church have raised to him. These questions obviously had to do with the propriety of getting married and very possibly with specific individuals marrying specific others. Paul had a golden opportunity here for offering prophecies about who should get married and about who should marry whom. We know, too, from the previous chapter that he was quite at home pronouncing God's will for individuals in moral situations. What posture does Paul in fact take to their questions about marriage? (Does he claim to know God's will for any person in this church in this matter, or does he leave it to individual discretion?)

Outside of situations where clear moral issues were involved (such as incestuous marriage), is there any evidence in the New Testament that Paul or any leader ever took a direct role in declaring God's will for any person's marriage decision?

2. Read Acts 15:36-41. In this passage Paul and Barnabas, two central leaders in the church, disagree over taking Mark on a missionary trip. Each obviously has a very strong opinion on the matter. Does either of them claim to have absolute knowledge from God (a prophecy, in other words) about what Mark should do?

☐ Does Luke (the writer of Acts) indicate that either Paul or Barnabas had such divine insight or that others in the church believed either of them to have it?

☐ Is it reasonable to think that if the practice of giving prophecy for significant personal decisions was prevalent in the early church, Paul or Barnabas would have offered a prophecy in this case?

☐ What important lessons can we learn from this passage for our decision situations today?

13
Putting Out a Fleece

Key Questions:

◼ *Is it right to ask God to confirm his will through some specific sign, even if it has no direct relation to my decision?*
◼ *What about flipping a coin, casting lots, and so on in order to find God's will?*
◼ *Is there a difference between putting out a fleece and seeking circumstantial guidance?*

I doubt there are many of us who at some time in our Christian experience have not sought to know God's will through "putting out a fleece." Putting out a fleece—or "fleecing," as it's often called—involves seeking knowledge of God's will through a predetermined sign. Because the sign is something you decide upon in advance, fleecing requires that you already have some idea about what God might want you to do. You then pray that God will bring about a particular turn of events if you're correct. The "turn of events" could be something as mundane as which way a coin lands when you toss it, or as major as whether the U.S. goes to war by 4:00 p.m. tomorrow.

A typical example: Henry has just received an unexpected bonus at work and wonders whether this is finally the time to buy a new car. It would still mean taking on some payments, though, and he isn't eager to become further encumbered financially. It is a somber, overcast winter day, and the forecast has been for a possibility of snow. Henry prays and asks that if God wants him to purchase a new vehicle, it will snow between 1:30 and 2:00 this afternoon.

The practice of fleecing is extremely popular. And many Christians—probably most—assume it has a clear basis in Scripture. But while there are examples of fleecing in the Bible, the question of what these mean for us today requires careful consideration. I will argue that when the full range of biblical evidence is understood, we find Scripture pointing us away from fleecing as a healthy approach to knowing God's will.

Once Justified, No Longer Recommended

The prime biblical text for fleecing is Judges 6. In this passage an Israelite named Gideon is asked by God to take a very small army and attack the neighboring Midianites, who have severely oppressed the Israelites for many years.

Gideon, who thinks of himself as an insignificant member of a lowly clan, finds the command so incredible that he asks God for a clear sign as evidence. He places a lamb's fleece on the barn floor and prays that the next morning it will be wet and the ground around it dry. When God grants his request, Gideon then reverses it, asking for the fleece to be dry and the ground wet. God again responds as Gideon has asked. Gideon declares it a miracle and concludes he indeed has been divinely commissioned to deliver Israel.

The incident is a fascinating one, and it has inspired many Christians to ask God to show the path they should take by some specific sign.

There is one other prominent Old Testament example where God's will is sought through a predetermined sign. When Abraham's servant comes to Nahor to look for a wife for Isaac, he prays, "Let the maiden to whom I shall say, 'Pray let down your jar that I may drink,' and who shall say, 'Drink, and I will water your camels'—let her be the one whom thou hast appointed for thy servant Isaac" (Gen 24:14). Immediately after he prays,

Rebekah comes forward and responds in the manner he requested. While he doesn't take this as the final indication she is God's choice, it definitely gets his attention. From there he confers with her and her family about her returning to Canaan with him and marrying Isaac.

Beyond these two examples, there is considerable Old Testament precedence for fleecing in the convention of casting lots. This practice was extremely common among the Israelites (see Prov 16:33). The Mosaic Law, in fact, prescribed that priests fulfill this function for persons wishing to inquire of the Lord (Deut 33:8). This practice was still common among the Jews in New Testament days; thus through casting lots Zechariah was assigned to temple duty (Lk 1:9), and the early believers chose a successor for Judas (Acts 1:15-26).

But after the day of Pentecost there is no further instance in Scripture of casting lots. Nor is there any example of an approach to God's will akin to putting out a fleece. This suggests to me that after this time the practice was no longer necessary.

This is a critical point to note. As we've observed, the overwhelming majority of decisions noted after Pentecost involved a rational process of weighing logical factors. Supernatural guidance came into play only a few times. And there is no instance of someone seeking to know God's will through a predetermined sign.

I believe this compels us to conclude that fleecing is not an appropriate practice for us as Christians today. The New Testament demonstrates that the Spirit-filled believer has all the inner resources necessary for sound decision making. Scripture wants us to understand that we put ourselves in the best position for the Lord to guide us when we take full responsibility for thinking through our choices.

It isn't hard to see how fleecing is often an abdication from this responsibility. It usually amounts to an effort to shortcut a decision, to reduce the thinking and risk involved. By its very nature, too, a fleece tries to compel God to give an answer which he may not be ready to provide or may not wish to provide at all.

In addition, fleecing often puts God in the position where he would have to give us a pledge about our personal future if he answered the fleece. The man, for instance, who puts out a fleece to find if he should marry a certain woman will probably conclude that God has promised he *will* marry her if the fleece is answered. That is more assurance about the future than God is normally willing to provide. As we've stressed, God usually guides us only one step at a time. Fleecing is typically an attempt to take too many steps at once.

This isn't to deny that God may sometimes honor a fleece which is put out in sincerity, especially by a young believer who is not in a position to know better. One respected Christian leader relates his experience as a young man seeking guidance about whom to marry. He mailed letters to two different friends, praying that if God wanted him to marry his girlfriend, he'd receive letters back from each friend on the same day. He did not tell his friends about the fleece. When responses from both arrived in the same mail delivery, he concluded that God had given him a revelation about what to do.

Though his decision to marry proved to be a good one, he now admits that he no longer believes this was a mature approach to God's will; God was simply gracious to stoop down to where he was.

Yes, God may graciously stoop to answer a fleece. Yet Scripture offers no guarantee that he will. And experience shows that he often does not. Even worse, fleecing can lead to frustrating or highly misleading results.

Fooled by Fleecing

My friend Brock, who lived in the Washington, D.C. area, had a long-distance relationship with Kelly, a Texan. For several years they corresponded, phoned and occasionally visited each other. Yet it was strictly a friendship with no romantic overtones.

Increasingly, though, Brock began to have romantic feelings for Kelly and wondered what God had in store for their future. Finally, a week before a scheduled visit from Kelly, Brock asked God for a clear indication. He prayed that if God intended the relationship to become a serious one, he would allow Brock to see a deer sometime during the next week. Brock was on a retreat at the time where the possibility of encountering a deer was good.

The weekend passed, however, and a deer never appeared. Brock returned home assuming the fleece would not be granted. Two days before Kelly was to arrive, however, he spotted a deer just off the Tyson's Corner exit as he was driving off the Beltway.

Yes, the Tyson's Corner exit of the Beltway. If you have ever driven on the Washington Beltway, you'll appreciate how startled Brock was, for deer rarely appear in the close-in suburbs of Washington. Brock was so astonished that he pulled his car off the road, stopped and stared at the animal, to be certain his eyes were not deceiving him. Sure enough, it was a deer—the first time he had ever seen one near the Beltway.

The sheer improbability of this event left Brock assuming he had been given a revelation of pleasant things ahead with Kelly. With great joy he looked forward to her visit. It would surely be a wonderful turning point in their relationship.

Unfortunately, Brock was about to go from the mountaintop to the valley. While Kelly was friendly enough during her visit, she was just as intent on spending time with other friends as with Brock. There was no indication that her feelings for him were different in any way.

Finally Brock confronted her. While discretely omitting any reference to his experience with the deer, he told her that he cared deeply for her and wondered if she was open to a serious relationship. Kelly, surprised by Brock's sudden change, responded that no, she really had no romantic leanings toward him at all.

Finally Brock asked Kelly if she felt that at least the *possibility* of a romantic relationship was there for some point in the future. Kelly answered that she was firmly convinced their relationship could never move beyond a friendship. Never after that did she change her position.

Brock was understandably crushed. Not only was there the pain of rejection, but also the baffling experience with the deer. How could a fleece so uniquely and distinctly answered not match the reality of things? How could God have allowed this mess to happen?

An Explanation

I realize I tread on speculative ground in attempting an explanation of

Brock's bizarre experience. Yet there is one which I believe makes good sense once it is understood.

It lies in a principle which every athletic coach understands well. A good coach pushes his best players the hardest, not to break them down but because he knows that they will benefit from the prodding and grow stronger from it.

Sometimes, I believe, God mercifully allows us to continue with a spiritual practice which is less than the best. He is patient with the elementary state of our faith and not willing to push us to a higher level before we are ready. Yet when he knows that we *can* handle it, psychologically and spiritually, he may allow us a hard experience with that same practice—not to break us down but to build us up.

His intent is to wake us up, to quell our enthusiasm for the practice, to prod us to look for a more mature approach to spiritual insight. I strongly suspect that this explains otherwise inexplicable experiences which some Christians have with fleeces and other improper approaches to guidance.

And it probably explains Brock's experience. Brock, a remarkably mature and sensitive Christian, agrees with me. He admits, "I realize now that I was dictating to God how he should reveal his will to me." While the experience, now eight years in his past, was extremely hard for him, it did strengthen him spiritually in the long run. And one thing is certain: he will never be inclined to put his faith in a fleece again.

Again, Scripture is consistent in teaching that God seldom gives us a purchase on our personal future. While he graciously guides our decisions, his guidance comes not in a blinding flash of insight about what's ahead but incrementally, day by day, hour by hour, step by step. Any process that would pretend to produce a more certain insight into God's plan for our future should be regarded suspiciously. And any insights that come through it shouldn't be taken as reliable.

A Vital Distinction

Fleecing should not be confused with asking God for *reasonable circumstantial guidance.* By this term I mean an indication which is logically necessary to take the next step in a decision. Fleeces often involve signs which are not in any way related to the decision at hand; Brock's request for the deer had nothing to do with insight logically needed to better understand the direction of his relationship. That is different from asking God to make a detail of the path right ahead of you black or white as an indication of whether to go ahead. This sort of request is quite appropriate to make in some instances.

Asking for circumstantial guidance is especially justified when you are at a genuine impasse in a decision. A friend of mine, for instance, was seeking God's will regarding the purchase of a particular home. After a careful analysis of the situation, he made an offer to the owner. When after some time he had not received a reply, he prayed that the owner would give him a positive response by 5:00 p.m. the next day if God wished him to purchase the home. Otherwise, he would feel free before God to begin looking elsewhere. The owner did indeed phone him, shortly before 5:00 p.m., accepting the offer, and since all other signals were positive, he took this as a remarkable confirmation of God's will.

In this case my friend made a mature and responsible request for a sign from God. He had done his homework, carefully analyzed the situation, and done what he could to get the final piece of information he needed— the owner's selling price. Now his hands were tied, and since he knew it would be irresponsible to wait indefinitely for a reply, he asked God for special guidance.

But he did not ask God for some irrelevant sign, but merely that the circumstances of his transaction would work out in a specific, positive way. Being at an impasse, he was quite justified in praying as he did.

All of us can expect occasionally to confront similar circumstances, where we face a genuine roadblock to making a decision we otherwise believe God would have us make. In such a case we are justified in asking God to remove the obstacle as a specific indication of his will. We must simply be careful not to use this sort of request to avoid responsibility for careful thinking. Only when we face a real hindrance is this approach recommended. And then it is best not to think of it as putting out a fleece but rather as asking God for some explicit circumstantial guidance.

But we should avoid the practice of asking for a sign which is not pertinent to the details of our decision. Regardless of the impasse we may be up against, that approach to guidance is inappropriate and may even set us up for greater confusion. God's concern is that we grow into people who take mature responsibility for our choices. Fleecing is almost always a diversion from that responsibility and a futile effort to oversimplify complex choices.

One final point. In the last chapter we noted that it is appropriate to ask God for miraculous confirmation in the special case where we believe we have received supernatural guidance. Even here, though, it's best not to request a sign which has no bearing on our decision. Better to ask God to provide a need directly related to what we believe he is calling us to do. In all cases we should avoid asking for a sign simply for a sign's sake. Requests for circumstantial guidance should always focus on the circumstances clearly pertinent to our decision.

For Personal Study:

1. Read Matthew 10:11-14 and Luke 14:28-32. In these passages Jesus offers advice for evaluating circumstantial indications in certain important decisions. (In the passage from Matthew he offers the advice directly; in the one from Luke he offers it indirectly by affirming some common prudent practices.)

☐ How does the process for weighing circumstances which Jesus advocates differ from our popular practice of putting out a fleece?

☐ Give real-life examples of how you might apply Jesus' principles to decisions you would face. Then show how these same decisions could be also approached improperly through fleecing.

2. Read Esther 3:6-7, where Haman casts lots in order to receive guidance on a matter of personal revenge. (If you are not familiar with the book of Esther and can take the time, read the entire book for the context of this passage.)

☐ Note as many reasons as you can find why Haman's effort to receive divine guidance through casting lots was clearly improper in this case.

☐ While Haman's example was certainly extreme, are there lessons we can learn from it to apply to our own search for guidance? Does it, for instance, help bring to light reasons why fleecing can be an unhealthy practice for us today?

14
Inward Guidance

Key Questions:
■ *What does my intuition reveal to me about God's will?*
■ *How am I to regard inner impressions, inspirations, hunches, warm feelings and so on? Are they ever the direct voice of God's Spirit?*

*O*ften, rather than look for an outward sign, Christians will seek an intuitive impression of the Holy Spirit's leading—a hunch, inspiration or "warm feeling" that something is God's will. This experience is distinguished from supernatural guidance in that there is no audible voice or visible sign, but simply a feeling about God's leading. It is different from rational thinking in that a conclusion is reached not from logical argument but from intuition.

It's popularly assumed that intuition is in some sense the direct voice of the Holy Spirit. A strong inspiration to do something is as clear a leading of the Holy Spirit as the audible voice of God itself. When someone says "God spoke to me," most often he or she does not mean hearing God's audible voice but simply feeling a sense of inspiration to move in a certain direction. Many refer to this as "the still small voice," or "inward guidance."

This inward guidance is understood to function in two significant ways. On the one hand, God's leading will be known by strong, positive feelings to go in a certain direction. Apart from the evidence of such feelings, many say, you should not proceed. On the other hand, negative feelings, or "pangs of conscience," about a certain action are considered a direct command from God not to go ahead. "When in doubt, don't," as the popular expression goes.

What is common to both aspects of inward guidance is the belief that God speaks directly through our feelings—that is, that our intuition is the direct voice of the Holy Spirit.

When we come to the question of whether there is truth to this assumption, we have to be cautious in our reply. Intuition can be important, sometimes greatly significant, in helping us understand the direction we should take in a major decision.

But many Christians place too much weight on the implications of intuition. Not a few look upon it as an infallible channel of God's speaking. Thus, to question intuition is to question God himself. This understanding reached its height in the Quaker doctrine of the "inner light," which, especially among George Fox and other early Quakers, was taken to considerable extremes. Among them the possibility of human error in knowing God's will through intuition was simply not entertained. But even among modern Christians we often find this tendency to regard intuition as a foolproof channel of guidance.

What the Bible Says

When we turn to Scripture, we find no evidence supporting this extreme notion of intuition. I can find no examples in either the Old or New Testament where it is clear that someone discerned God's will through inward guidance. This may seem surprising, but I would challenge the reader to find such an instance. You might think of places in Acts where reference is made to the Holy Spirit's guiding someone to do something— but a careful analysis of each passage shows it is more likely a reference to direct supernatural guidance or to a rational decision.[1]

There is also no clear statement in the Old or New Testament telling us that we should attempt to discern God's will merely through intuition. There are several verses which are popularly used to support inward guidance as the prime means of knowing God's will, but when examined in context they are found not to be dealing with the notion at all. Let's look at three of these.

Colossians 3:15 states: "Let the peace of Christ rule in your hearts." This is the most popular verse cited in favor of inward guidance. The Greek word for *rule* means "act as umpire," and it is claimed that Paul is saying we should let peaceful feelings umpire our decision making. Examined in context, however, it is plain that this verse is not referring to a personal, subjective feeling of peace, but rather to the corporate reality of peace which should exist among believers. The verse does not relate to personal decision making.

Another largely misunderstood verse is 1 John 4:1: "Beloved, do not believe every spirit, but test the spirits to see whether they are of God." It's widely held that the testing of spirits in this verse refers to judging personal feelings as to whether they are divinely produced or not. In context, however, the reference is to judging the doctrinal teachings of teachers who call themselves Christian.

A more complex passage is Romans 14:22-23: "The faith that you have, keep between yourself and God; happy is he who has no reason to judge himself for what he approves. But he who doubts is condemned, if he eats, because he does not act from faith; for whatever does not proceed from faith is sin." It's commonly believed that Paul is saying here that we should take no action whenever we have any reservations. It must be noted, however, that in this passage he is talking about those gray areas of morality for which the early Christians had no explicit commandment, such as drinking, eating meat that had been offered to idols or observing certain pagan holidays. In these areas, Paul says, let your conscience be your guide: if in doubt, then don't. Paul's statements in Romans 14 were not meant for application to broader, more complex personal decisions; he is simply not dealing with that subject here at all.

Not that we should ignore guilt feelings when making complex decisions. To do so would be both spiritual and psychological suicide. But at the same time we will seldom make a major decision without experiencing some guilt feelings or some sense of fear that perhaps we are choosing the wrong alternative. This is the natural response of the human psyche. If we waited for absolute peace in every major decision, we would be paralyzed. Fortunately Paul is not laying down such a difficult commandment.

But what about the rest of the Bible? Other biblical passages could be cited which, on a cursory reading, might seem to be talking about seeking God's will purely through intuition, but which on closer analysis are found not to be dealing with this at all. We must conclude that there is no biblical basis for the notion that intuition should be regarded as an infallible indication of the Holy Spirit's leading, akin to hearing the audible voice of God.

This is not to suggest that God never leads Christians through their feelings. But we must see that for most of us our feelings are so diverse and so changeable that it would be unreasonable to expect them to be the sole barometer of God's will. In any case, if we suspect God is trying to convey a special message to us through our intuition, we have the right (and really the responsibility) to check it out through other means. Oliver Barclay says that "such guidance must be checked by more objective standards, and it would seem to be our duty to pray that God will rather give us *reasons* for such actions."[2] Taking precautions with intuition should not be thought of as a lack of faith, but as our responsibility to guard against error.

Mirror of Our Minds

We have been discussing the role of intuition as a spiritual phenomenon. But it must also be seen as a *psychological* event. And it is here that its value for guidance is especially apparent. Intuition in many cases is revealing something about myself: it can be a crucial insight into my subconscious. This insight can be of immense value in understanding God's will, from two important angles.

For one thing, my intuition may be revealing what underneath I really think I ought to do. The fact is that our intuition often does a much better job processing information and reaching conclusions than our conscious mind does. Problem solving can occur on a purely conscious level, to be sure. Yet when an answer to a problem or decision is not reached quickly, a subconscious process typically takes over. The subconscious mind mulls the matter over, perhaps for weeks, months or years. Eventually a solution may make its appearance on the conscious level with all the impact of a divine revelation—the "eureka, I've found it!" sensation. This experience leads many—Christian and non-Christian alike—to conclude that God has spoken directly to them. But usually there is a psychological explanation. The subconscious mind has been working on the problem unnoticed, finally reaching a conclusion which has bubbled to the surface in the form of a conscious inspiration. I'm convinced that this explains many—probably most—of the experiences of intuition and inspiration which we typically have as Christians.

Creative thinkers from all fields have stressed the importance of this internal gestation process, and I find their testimonies of greatest interest. Consider, for instance, Amy Lowell's reflection on her process of writing poetry:

How carefully and precisely the subconscious mind functions, I have often been a witness to in my own work. An idea will come into my head for no apparent reason; "The Bronze horses," for instance. I registered the horses as a good subject for a poem; and, having so registered them, I consciously thought no more about the matter. But what I had really done was to drop my subject into the subconscious, much as one drops a letter into the mail-box. Six months later, the words of the poem began to come into my head; the poem—to use my private vocabulary—was "there."[3]

Or author Jean Cocteau's description of an inspiration in play writing:

The play that I am producing at the Theatre de l'Oeuvre, *The Knights of the Round Table,* is a visitation. I was sick and tired of writing, when one morning, after having slept poorly, I awoke with a start and witnessed, as from a seat in a theater, three acts which brought to life an epoch and characters about which I had no documentary information and which I regarded moreover as forbidding.

Long afterward, I succeeded in writing the play and I [discerned] the circumstances that must have served to incite me.[4]

Or mathematician Henri Poincaré's testimony about how he reached a critical discovery:

For fifteen days I strove to prove that there could not be any functions like those I have since called Fuchsian functions. I was then very ignorant; every day I seated myself at my work table, stayed an hour or two, tried a great number of combinations and reached no results. One evening, contrary to my custom, I drank black coffee and could not sleep. Ideas rose in crowds; I felt them collide until pairs interlocked, so to speak, making a stable combination. By the next morning I had established the existence of a class of Fuchsian functions, those which come from the hypergeometric series; I had only to write out the results, which took but a few hours.[5]

Well, so much for black coffee. Yet such descriptions of the internal creative process from both artistic and scientific thinkers are common. What is significant for our study is that this same subconscious process is often in operation in our personal decision making. Understanding this, more than any other single factor, helps to put the matter of inward guidance into meaningful perspective. Our bursts of intuition about what we should do often reflect an internal gestation process which has been going on for some time.

This does not in any way leave God out of the guidance picture. The God who providentially directs and sustains our lives guides the subconscious process as fully as he guides our conscious thinking. We can give him the full honor and glory for any wise insights that come through this process and acknowledge with confidence that he has directed us to a good conclusion. Yet saying that God guides our subconscious process is quite different from saying that our intuition is the *direct voice* of God—and thus not open to critique or further revision.

As vital as our intuitive insights are, they are always only as good as the information to which we have been exposed. Our intuition is merely light onto our path—a helpful insight into what our best conclusion may be at the time, but not necessarily the best conclusion we are capable of reaching. We are always free to get further information, and new information may lead to a new sense of intuition on the decision at hand.

A Glimpse of Our Desires

Intuition is valuable not only in helping us determine what underneath we think we *should* do but also in helping us understand what we really *want* to do. Our subconscious is the seat of our feelings, and intuitive hunches not infrequently reveal our deepest and most significant emotions.

Here again intuition plays an important role in guidance. My deepest desires are often significant in finding God's will. They tell me something about how God has made me and thus about the kind of responsibilities he might want me to assume.

On the other hand, no desire is ever an infallible sign in itself of God's will. It's merely one factor to be considered along with others. Even my deepest-seated feelings can change; and even where they are consistent, they may or may not be significant indicators of God's will. And while intuition is an important signal of my feelings, it's not an infallible gauge of them. Most important, it does not reveal how I might feel if I had further information.

In the next chapter we'll look more closely at the matter of understanding our desires in light of God's guidance. For now, let us merely say that feelings are important in knowing God's will but not the infallible voice of God. When I feel a strong sense of intuition, rather than say, "God has spoken to me," I would better say, "My subconscious has spoken—and this *may* indicate what God is saying."

For Personal Study:

1. Read 1 Kings 19:9-18. This is the one passage in Scripture which uses the term *still small voice* (v. 12). In the context of the passage, what is the still small voice which Elijah hears—his own inner impression or an actual audible voice of God?

☐ How, then, does our contemporary use of the term *still small voice* to refer to inner impressions go beyond the boundaries of this passage?

2. There are eleven references in Acts to people being inspired or led by the Holy Spirit: Acts 8:26, 39; 10:19-20; 11:28; 13:2; 15:28; 16:6-7; 19:21; 20:22-23; 21:4, 11-14. These instances are sometimes cited as examples of guidance through inward impressions. Read each example carefully in context.

☐ Does any passage clearly indicate that an inner impression was involved?

☐ Consider what other means of guidance may be indicated in each of these examples.

3. Tracing the words *feel* and *felt* through Scripture with a concordance reveals a number of instances where individuals experienced impressions, some accurate, many not so. While these instances are never directly tied to divine inspiration, they do give us a picture of the psychological process involved in intuition and how this can work for us or against us.

☐ Using the NIV, read the following three examples where individuals experienced inaccurate impressions either of what God wanted them to do or of their life situation (the term *I felt* signifies the impression in each of these passages): 1 Samuel 12:12-13; Psalm 30:6-7; 2 Corinthians 1:9.

☐ What warnings can we take from these examples?

☐ What encouragement can we take as well?

☐ On the other hand, Jude 1:3 gives a positive example. Jude states that he was convicted (again, "I felt") that he must write words of warning even though he would have preferred to write a more encouraging treatise on salvation. In this case Jude reached a redemptive conclusion through an impression. What factors may have led Jude to make a good decision in this case, and what can we learn from his example?

Part **4**
Beginning to Decide

15
Considering Personal Desires

■ *What do my desires tell me about God's will?*
■ *Is God's will likely to be what I most want to do? what I least want to do?*
■ *How do I discover what my desires really are?*

*T*o this point in our study we've emphasized the importance of clear, practical thinking when it comes to knowing God's will. While we've noted exceptions to this pattern, we've stressed that in most decisions God guides us through our logical thought process; discerning his will boils down to making a rational decision.

Still, we have not yet addressed the question of exactly *how* we should think through a decision in a way that is most honoring to Christ. How should we weigh the various factors that are almost always involved in major personal decisions?

Tremendous confusion exists over this question of *how*. In the remaining chapters we will look at the process of decision making more closely.

I admit that I approach this section with certain reservations, for I don't want to imply that there is an easy answer to our complicated decisions.

Our decision making as believers, at least in major areas, must always be a somewhat difficult process, and we have to be leery of oversimplified approaches and pat formulas.

At the same time, we do often make it more complicated than necessary. There are certain principles which can simplify our understanding of God's will and help us focus our thinking more clearly. Understanding these will also increase our confidence that we are seeing our alternatives with the mind of Christ.

Covering the Bases

To begin with, it is helpful to think of all of the factors we have to weigh in a major decision as falling under four basic areas. I term these "the four providential factors in decision making":

Desires: my personal feelings about a particular alternative.

Abilities: my skill for handling the responsibilities of a particular alternative, or my potential for developing the ability needed.

Circumstances: opportunities available to me (open doors, closed doors).

Counsel: the opinions of other people about my decision, and the advice which they offer me.

These four areas include every factor we normally have to consider in a complex decision beyond the direct guidance which is already given us in Scripture. Apart from problems in our attitude, our confusion in understanding God's will almost always results from difficulty in understanding the role that one or more of these four factors should play. We will take a close look at each of them, noting how they interrelate and how they should influence our understanding of God's will.

Big and Small Decisions

From this point on, too, it will be helpful to distinguish more carefully between major and minor decisions. In drawing this distinction, we'll employ a word whose original sense has practically vanished from our popular vocabulary, the term *vocation.* We use this word today to refer to a person's profession. But during the Protestant Reformation the term was used by the Reformers in a much broader sense to refer to *any major commitment or station in a person's life*. Not only was a person's profession a vocation, but also his or her family relationship, citizenship, church affiliation, community involvement, hobbies and so on.

We will make use of this term to distinguish between major and minor decisions. A major decision will mean a decision *for* a vocation, that is, to enter a major area of commitment. A minor decision will be one made *within* a vocation, that is, to fulfill the responsibilities entailed by taking on the vocation. A decision to marry, to have children, to choose a certain profession or job or to attend a certain college would be a major decision. A minor decision, on the other hand, would be one to carry out the commitment already made to the vocation—for example, the decision to take a vacation with the family, to make a certain business deal, to take a certain course at school.

While this distinction may seem simplistic, we will find it helpful in understanding how various factors should relate in our decision making. It will be particularly helpful as we turn now to look at the role of personal desires.

How Desires Fit In

No one area creates more confusion in knowing God's will than the role of personal wishes. Does doing God's will mean that my desires should be affirmed, or denied? This is an area where Christians are especially prone to go to extremes.

On the one hand, many assume that personal desire is the all-important sign of God's will. "Love God and do what you please," as the popular expression goes. But this assumes that if we love God our wishes will automatically conform to his will. In fact, because we are sinners, this will not always be the case. The Bible confirms that Christians will have to choose alternatives at times which do not immediately seem attractive.

Jesus said that the person who walks with him must pick up his or her cross *daily* (Lk 9:23). So there will be a daily element of self-denial in the mature Christian life.

On the other hand, I find that some Christians go to the opposite extreme and believe that a Spirit-led decision must always be the one that involves suffering. They think that God's will and their wishes will never coincide.

I'm reminded of Malcolm, a man who spoke with me when I was a pastor in St. Louis. Malcolm hated his job as a house painter. Though some would find the occupation enjoyable, to him it was drudgery and monotony. He sat slumped in the chair across from my desk, lamenting his lot. Finally I stopped him and asked, "If God rolled out the red carpet and said that you could have any job you wanted, what would it be?"

"I'd like to be an English teacher," he shot back.

At age twenty-five Malcolm had two years of college under his belt. From what I knew of him he could go back and finish and find a teaching job. So I said, "Why don't you pursue a teaching vocation with all the passion and energy you can muster?"

His reply was unforgettable. "I know that God doesn't want me teaching. I'd enjoy the experience too much, and the affirmation of students would be more than I could handle." Then he added the clincher. He was sure God wanted him painting houses, for he thoroughly disliked his work!

Malcolm's example is extreme. Yet it reflects a pattern of thinking which I've often observed in Christians—the belief that being in God's will means *a priori* choosing a path that is repugnant to you. Just recently I received a card from a ministry which endorses this perspective. Inside it declares, *"God's way: Exactly the opposite of my natural inclinations."*

But such thinking is every bit as distorted as the notion of loving God and doing what you wish, for it ignores the biblical evidence that God sometimes creates desires within us in order to guide us. In both cases an important biblical truth is carried to an unhealthy extreme. What is really needed is an understanding of the truth on *both* sides of this coin. There is a strong sense in which self-denial must operate in our decisions as Christians, but there is also a sense in which our desires must be affirmed in order to recognize God's will. A mature Christian perspective demands that we see the relationship between self-denial and self-affirmation and how these two areas interrelate.

Affirming Our Desires

On the positive side, the biblical doctrine of providence suggests that God works within the redeemed believer to form desires which accord with his will. Consider Paul's familiar statement in Philippians 2:12-13: "Work out your own salvation with fear and trembling; for God is at work in you, both to will and to work for his good pleasure."

Here Paul implies that God is working within us to create certain feelings. This is clear from Paul's use of the word *work*, which in the Greek is *energeō*, from which we get our word *energy*. When Paul says, "God is at work in you," he means literally that God is *energizing* you in the direction of his will. God is *motivating* you, in other words. He is giving you the creative inspiration you need to make decisions which agree with his will. He is providentially forming in you certain desires which will move you in the direction he wants you to go.

We have already pointed out that Paul's missionary itineraries were strongly influenced by the desire to spend time with former converts (see chapter ten). When the urge to be with his friends got too strong, Paul assumed that God was leading him to spend time with them.

Likewise, in his teachings Paul implies that desire is a key sign of God's will in two important vocations—marriage and spiritual leadership. Regarding marriage, Paul indicates that one recognizes God's will for whether or not to marry, in part, through a desire for sexual fulfillment (1 Cor 7:1-9). We must conclude that desire is a vital factor in the choice of whether to marry and whom to marry. Marrying someone out of sympathy or out of a sense of duty is not recommended by Scripture. Not that desire is the only factor to consider—there must be compatibility on several levels. But if the *desire* for a marital relationship is not there, no amount of compatibility in other areas will make up for it.

Regarding spiritual leadership, Paul notes the qualifications needed in 1 Timothy 3, beginning the section by saying, "If any one aspires to the office of bishop, he desires a noble task" (v. 1; *bishop* is a general term for overseer or spiritual leader). Notice the words *aspires* and *desires* in this verse. Paul simply assumes that the person who takes on the role of spiritual leader should have a significant desire to be in that position—

a sense of aspiration toward it.

Paul, then, indicates that our desires are important. The point is that God exercises his providence in creating our personalities. I may trust that he has not allowed my particular personality to develop by accident but has fashioned my inclinations and preferences as a means of motivating me in certain directions. By looking to the desires that are most basic to my personality, I can gain vital insights into where God is leading me.

Where Self-Denial Fits In

But if this is true, where does the responsibility for self-denial come in? We must begin by stressing that willingness to deny our desires must always be present if we hope to know and do God's will.

While God will not necessarily call me to self-denial in a given decision, I must always be willing to respond if he does. There will be times when circumstances force me to accept an alternative I little desire. Or God could reveal supernaturally that I should go in a direction I would never choose on the basis of personal preference. I must determine in advance that I will follow if God should so lead.

But apart from such direct leading, and whenever circumstances allow freedom of choice, I believe there is a critical rule of thumb to follow. *Generally speaking, a major decision should be based on personal desire as much as possible.* A decision for a particular vocation, in other words, should be based on my desires. But decisions made *within* the vocation (in order to fulfill its responsibilities) may often involve sacrifice and considerable self-denial.

Let me explain. Under most conditions we tend to do our best work when it's a reflection of what we most want to do. The person who really enjoys being a security guard, for instance, will do a better job than the one who dislikes the role. The man who loves being with his wife and family will be a better husband and father than the one who spends time with them out of a sense of duty.

I conclude, then, that I'll do my best work for Christ when I'm doing what I most enjoy. I'll be able to invest my total personality, and I'll be most helpful to other people, since others tend to relate to me best when they sense that I enjoy what I do.

Since a decision for a vocation means a long-range commitment of time and energy, it makes sense that it should be based on desire as much as possible. Without a basic desire to be in the vocation, I'll lack the creative energy to carry it out fruitfully.

On the other hand, once I have entered a vocation, my desires will often have to be sacrificed in order to fulfill its short-range responsibilities. By committing myself to a vocation I've pledged myself to a long-range desire—that of successfully meeting the goals of the vocation. In order to satisfy that long-range ambition, I'll often have to forsake short-range desires which conflict with it.

For example, the men and women who choose the medical profession should be very sure they will enjoy medical work. If they do not experience a basic fulfillment through this vocation, they will lack the momentum to carry out the intensive responsibilities of the work. They will constantly have to sacrifice otherwise worthwhile desires to fulfill the daily demands of the job. While a physician may strongly desire to spend Saturday evening with a church group, the call to do an emergency operation will leave little question as to where the will of God lies, in spite of the intrusion this will be on a well-deserved time of fellowship.

It is clear, then, that the more enduring or time-consuming a vocation, the greater should be our certainty that we really want to be in it. With respect to the most permanent vocation of all, that of marriage, the highest degree of certainty should be demanded. A couple seeking God's will for marriage should look closely at their desire to spend their lives together. This desire must be very strong before they begin to seriously consider marrying.

By the same token, the shorter the commitment, the greater the freedom we may feel to experiment. We should look on our desires as reflective of how God has made us and as key indicators of the type of responsibilities he would have us assume.

We should see it as bad stewardship not to make a careful assessment of our desires. Only someone with a martyr complex would go into a particular vocation just because he or she thinks it would be a miserable kind of work. We may trust that as we choose a vocation that best matches our deepest desires, God will provide abundant opportunity to practice self-denial through the demands of the vocation.

Weighing Our Desires

At this point we are still left with a major question: How do we really know what our deepest desires are? All of us experience myriad desires, from fleeting urges to monumental passions. How are we to sort out from all of these which ones are most significant in knowing God's will?

To begin with, no desire which contradicts Scripture should be heeded. This should go without saying. But beyond this, there are some practical steps which I believe will improve our understanding of where our most significant desires lie. I recommend the following six points of consideration when making a major decision:

1. Pray. Discuss your desires with Christ, and ask him to clarify which are most significant. This is not to spiritualize the matter of considering desires but to remember that everything in the Christian life comes back to the never-ending necessity of prayer. Remember that Christ is even more concerned that you understand and respond to the desires he has put within you than you are. Pray and assess your desires from that confidence.

2. Look for a broad level of desire. Not only should desire for personal fulfillment be present, but there should also be a genuine urge to see other people helped through your vocation. We are happiest when we are helping others. But we are of limited value to others unless we also feel creatively fulfilled through what we are doing. So, look for a vocation which will allow you creative fulfillment *and* enable you to help others.

In addition, there should be a desire for personal growth through the challenges of the vocation. In other words, I should desire the personal qualities which the vocation will produce in me. If I'm considering a vocation in music, for instance, I should desire not only to perform, but also to become as proficient in my area as possible.

3. Experiment! Basically all thinking about a vocation is speculation until you actually become involved in it. So whenever possible, get involved with a vocation before making a long-range commitment to it. In some cases you may discover that what you thought would be abhorrent work is actually very fulfilling. This has been the case with many missionaries, for instance. Or you might discover just the opposite. I would especially encourage young Christians who are free to do so to experiment with areas of service which might not seem naturally attractive but where the human need is great. There are many short-term missionary projects in this country and abroad, for instance.

4. Look to intuition. As we stressed in the chapter on inward guidance, your intuition may often be a signal of what you are most deeply feeling.

5. Put desires to a time test. If at all possible, avoid choosing a vocation until you have experienced a significant desire toward it for a reasonable period of time. The greater the commitment involved in the vocation, the longer should be the time allowed for your desires to "season." Needless to say, this speaks of the importance of a reasonable engagement period before marriage.

6. Ask yourself, "How would I advise someone else faced with the same facts?" Your answer to this question may well give insight into your deepest feelings.

These six steps will provide a helpful basis for evaluating personal feelings. Remember, though, that regardless of how well you understand your personal desires, you should never read them as an infallible source of guidance. While they are a vital factor to consider, they will not tell you God's will beyond question.

Even an obviously God-honoring desire should not be taken uncritically as his leading. Remember that King David of Israel greatly desired to build a temple for God, but God replied that while this was a noble intention, it was simply not in his present timetable for it to be built (1 Kings 8:17-19; 2 Chron 6:8-9). Ultimately, you should take your desires seriously only when they have been carefully considered along with the other factors of ability, circumstances and counsel. We move on now to look at these other areas.

For Personal Study:
1. Going to the cross was agony for Jesus, as all the gospel narratives

indicate. Yet Hebrews 12:2 shows a different side to Jesus' perception of the experience. Read this revealing verse, and then note how Jesus' decision to go to the cross reinforces a major point we have made in this chapter.

☐ In light of this verse, what parallel can we draw between his decision to endure the cross and the vocational choices we face?

2. Read Colossians 1:28-29 and Galatians 2:8. The Greek verb for *work*, used several times in these verses, is *energeō*. What points made in this chapter do we find illustrated or reinforced in these verses?

☐ In what way do these verses give us freedom? In what way do they call us to responsibility?

3. This question is for the serious student and requires some knowledge of David's life, as described in 1 and 2 Samuel and elsewhere in the Old Testament. Note different ways in which David demonstrated both the positive and negative role of desires in various situations.

☐ On the negative side, note at least two major instances where David by following his desires made a bad decision (in addition to his decision to build the temple, which we've already mentioned).

☐ Why did his desires mislead him in these cases, and what can we learn from his mistakes?

☐ On the positive side, note how desire played a healthy role and helped him in different vocational areas he was involved in. What can we learn from his example in this respect?

4. If you could have your ultimate choice, what would you most desire to be doing five or ten years from now?

16

Evaluating Abilities and Gifts

Key Questions:

■ *Do I need evidence of ability before concluding that God is leading me to take on a certain responsibility?*
■ *What is the difference between abilities and spiritual gifts?*
■ *If I have a significant ability or spiritual gift in some area, does that mean that God wants me to put it into use?*

*I*n addition to indication of desire, we should also have evidence of personal potential before choosing a vocation. This would only seem logical. But a surprising number of Christians actually challenge this assumption. Many feel that God's calling to a vocation comes irrespective of personal qualifications. They feel that walking in faith means moving ahead in spite of a lack of ability, trusting God to provide the necessary skills when they are needed and not before.

As a result, many Christians enter vocations without carefully assessing their skills and potential for future development. This is typical in the area of marriage. So many Christians enter marriage simply "in faith," without seriously considering whether they are capable of living with one another or whether they have the maturity for marriage.

Likewise, it's common for Christians to enter professions, especially in the area of Christian ministry, without really considering their competence for the work they will face. They trust that God will give them the skills they need once they are in the work, even though they might have shown no previous potential in the area.

But this kind of thinking has little basis in Scripture. More often than not it is based on a faulty understanding of spiritual gifts. The Bible records that God sometimes manifests his power by enabling people to perform in ways in which they previously showed no aptitude. From this it is concluded that God can be expected to lead us into major areas of commitment before we have reasonable assurance of our potential in the area. This is an unfortunate misunderstanding of biblical teaching. In order to correct it, we will now take a look at the nature and purpose of spiritual gifts in biblical teaching, and then consider the relevance of gifts and abilities to guidance.

Spiritual Gifts

It is considerably beyond my purposes to present an exhaustive study of spiritual gifts. Doing so with any thoroughness would require a full volume, and some excellent books on the subject already exist.[1] Here we will simply note some basic facts about spiritual gifts that are pertinent to understanding their role in guidance.

Although teaching on spiritual gifts permeates the entire New Testament, the most extensive passages dealing with them are Romans 12:3-8, 1 Corinthians 12—14 and Ephesians 4:7-14, all Pauline writings. If the reader is not familiar with these passages, I recommend reading them as a background to the discussion which follows.

In light of Paul teaching in these passages, we should note five facts about spiritual gifts:

1. Spiritual gifts are given to every believer. Paul is about as explicit concerning this as you can get, in 1 Corinthians 12. "To each is given the manifestation of the Spirit for the common good," he says in verse

7, and throughout the passage it is clear that "the manifestation of the Spirit" refers to spiritual gifts. There is no room in Paul's thinking for the notion that these gifts are the special possession of the ordained clergy; spiritual gifts are given to each member of Christ's body and have no direct relation to a person's official status within the ecclesiastical structure. Each of us must begin with the assumption that we are a recipient of this remarkable endowment.

2. *Spiritual gifts are a present-day reality and not merely a phenomenon of the first-century church.* Although some within the dispensational camp of theology would claim that the gifts (or some of the gifts) ceased with the formulation of the full canon of Scripture, there is no direct statement to this effect in the Bible, and certainly the evidence in the contemporary church would point to the contrary. Here we must agree with Charles Hummel:

> The New Testament nowhere teaches that these spiritual gifts would be withdrawn. Paul devotes three chapters of his first letter to the Corinthians to the nature, purpose and use of spiritual gifts. Here, if anywhere, one would expect him to identify any temporary gifts and prepare the believers for their phasing out. On the contrary, he not only emphasizes the importance of each charism, but also takes pains to instruct this new Christian community in the proper use of prophecy and tongues in public worship.[2]

3. *Spiritual gifts are not human abilities but special manifestations of the Holy Spirit.* A great deal of confusion exists among Christians regarding the exact nature of a spiritual gift. And this confusion is understandable in light of the diversity of gifts which Paul lists in the various passages. Some, such as the gift of administration or the gift of teaching, would appear simply to be the Spirit's use of one's natural ability, leading many to conclude that a spiritual gift is merely an intensification by the Spirit of an innate ability. But on the other hand, there are those gifts which are clearly miraculous in nature (such as faith, tongues, healing), leading many to conclude that a spiritual gift has no real relation to a person's natural talents.

If Paul's complete teaching on gifts is considered, we must conclude that the truth lies in neither of these extremes. Paul "makes no distinction between what we call supernatural and natural, spectacular and ordinary, logical and emotional."[3] Paul is concerned not with what personal channel the Holy Spirit used, but rather that the Holy Spirit worked in a special way.

In 1 Corinthians 12:7 Paul describes the spiritual gift as a "manifestation of the Spirit," and this is really his conception of a gift—nothing more, nothing less. The spiritual gift is a special working of God's Spirit through the believer which makes use of innate ability and personality but is not limited by any of these personal characteristics and often transcends them. Hummel describes one view of *charism:*

> A charism is neither a natural ability nor a new impartation which a person *possesses,* but a new functioning of what God has already given, activated and exercised by the power of the Spirit. Arnold Bittlinger defines a charism as "a gracious manifestation of the Holy Spirit, working in and through but going beyond, the believer's natural ability for the common good of the people of God." The charism is a gift because that ability has a new function and power. In its exercise the unity of the divine and the human should be recognized.[4]

4. Spiritual gifts are given specifically for building up the body of Christ. Personal edification, while inevitably a result, is not the primary reason God bestows spiritual gifts. If we look at the specific gifts listed by Paul in various passages, we see in every case, either from the obvious nature of the gift or from the context in which it is presented, that its purpose is to contribute to the edification of Christ's body in a special way. This occurs either through directly contributing to the well-being of other Christians (most of the gifts clearly do this) or through bringing nonbelievers into the fold (the gift of evangelism, especially). In every case the spiritual gift strengthens the body of Christ.

Thus we can see the criterion by which we are to judge whether we have a spiritual gift: if some service I'm performing is helping other Christians in a significant way or bringing others to Christ, then it's quite likely I'm making use of a spiritual gift.

It should not be supposed, however, that the spiritual gift by definition must be exercised within the context of the Christian community. While the person teaching a Bible class at church may be making obvious use of a spiritual gift, it's also possible that the one teaching math at a public school is using a spiritual gift as well, if through that teaching people are being drawn to Christ. Ultimately, the test of a spiritual gift is not the activity itself nor the location where it is exercised, but its *effect*— is it making a significant contribution to the body of Christ?

5. A believer may have more than one spiritual gift. There is an unfortunate assumption among many Christians that each believer has only one gift. Thus it happens that I decide what "my gift" is and then close myself off to the possibility of ministry in other areas. "Well, my gift is teaching, so I really can't consider helping with the hunger mission." But such a perspective is a narrow understanding of Paul's teaching. In two places (1 Cor 12:31; 14:1) Paul tells his readers to desire the *gifts* (plural).

Paul himself demonstrated more than one of the gifts he talks about. He laid claim to both the gift of apostleship (1 Cor 1:1) and the gift of tongues (1 Cor 14:18); and he certainly demonstrated contributions to the church of his day in numerous areas which align with spiritual gifts, such as administration, giving, exhortation and teaching. Paul was open to ministering to people on a wide variety of fronts, and this openness is probably best described by his statement, "I have become all things to all men, that I might by all means save some" (1 Cor 9:22).

Paul saw his work not as narrowly dictated by one particular gift but as a need-centered ministry, where he was willing to involve himself in many different sorts of activity in order to advance the gospel and build others up in Christ. Certainly this indicates that Paul left himself open to the possibility that new gifts would be given to him when needs arose.

Spiritual gifts are given, as we've said, to meet needs in the body of Christ. With this purpose in view, it's only logical that one may experience a variety of gifts throughout a lifetime. Each of us must stay open to the possibility of experiencing new gifts for new needs.

Then, when is it right to expect Christ to give a gift for a particular ministry and when is it presumptuous? This brings us back to the question of guidance.

Gifts, Abilities and Guidance

Must I have clear evidence of a spiritual gift before I assume God would want me to take on service in a certain area where that ability is needed? Or should I in faith take on certain responsibilities even though to this point I have had no clear evidence of God's desire to gift me in that area?

Here we have to see the answer as depending on the dimension of the commitment involved. In the case of more limited, short-range commitments where we are not locking ourselves into anything permanent, we should be willing to experiment with areas of service where we are not certain of our qualifications.

Ultimately, the only way I can discover whether or not God wishes to gift me in a certain area is to experiment. As I try out an area of service, I discover through the results and through the confirmation of others in the body whether I truly do have a gift in the area. If I'm interested in finding out about my gifts, it's essential that I have regular involvement in a Christian community, where I can receive feedback from others as I endeavor to meet the needs in the fellowship.

In this context the most important question becomes not, "What is my gift?" but rather, "How can I be of service?" My thinking should not begin with myself but with the needs of others in the body.[5]

I may find that there are significant needs which demand gifts I do not have. In such cases it may be well to experiment in a new area to see if the Lord might give me a fruitful ministry in it. The results will often be surprising. Countless Christians have discovered a gift for teaching through responding reluctantly to a need within the fellowship, even though underneath they thought teaching would be the last way the Spirit would manifest himself through them.

Experimenting is necessary in areas of Christian service where the commitment is limited, and we have the freedom without embarrassment to withdraw if we sense we're not being fruitful. But the greater a commitment of time and service becomes, the lesser should be the sense of freedom to experiment, and the greater should be our advance assurance that we already possess the potential for the work.

Here we should note the advice of Paul in Romans 12:3, where he introduces his discussion of spiritual gifts: "For by the grace given to me I bid every one among you not to think of himself more highly than he ought to think, but to think with sober judgment, each according to the measure of faith which God has assigned him." In the context of the passage, "the measure of faith" refers to the manifestation of the spiritual gifts which one has experienced, that is, the evidence of spiritual gifts. Paul then proceeds in the next several verses to exhort his readers to use their particular gifts.

It is interesting that in verse 3 Paul precedes the exhortation not by telling the readers to take bold ventures of faith into areas where they are not certain of their capacities, but to think soberly about how they will serve one another in light of the gifts they already have. Paul is not ruling out the need for experimentation with interests in order to find out what one's gifts are, but his statement indicates that there is a point at which sober thinking must take over and one must avoid venturing into areas where aptitude has not already been evidenced.

Paul doesn't get technical about just where this point is reached. But we must conclude that the point is unquestionably reached in major vocational decisions. We can see this, for instance, in the advice Paul gives Timothy about choosing church leaders in 1 Timothy 3:2-7:

> Now a bishop must be above reproach, the husband of one wife, temperate, sensible, dignified, hospitable, an apt teacher, no drunkard, not violent but gentle, not quarrelsome, and no lover of money. He must manage his own household well, keeping his children submissive and respectful in every way; for if a man does not know how to manage his own household, how can he care for God's church? He must not be a recent convert, or he may be puffed up with conceit and fall into the condemnation of the devil; moreover he must be well thought of by outsiders, or he may fall into reproach and the snare of the devil.[6]

Here we see Paul giving a very specific list of qualifications which must be met *in advance* before a particular person would be called into service. There was a similar list of qualifications for deacons (vv. 8-13). Paul does not suggest that a person should be put in a leadership position simply as an experiment to see if he or she might acquire the gifts. He says the qualifications must be in evidence *before* the appointment is made.

Paul notably does not make a fine distinction between spiritual gifts and natural endowments in this passage. He simply mentions *qualifications* which must be met. Paul seems more concerned with character traits than with talent (although talent is definitely important: one must be an "apt teacher" and able to administer). What the list really shows is that in assessing God's call to a vocation of church leadership I am to take everything I know about my personality and potential into account. Not to do this is to act presumptuously. And it's not too great an inference, I believe, to say that this is true with respect to any vocation we would consider as believers.

In Scripture where God calls a person into a major area of service, while there are cases of further gifts being given after the call, we see few clear examples where the person did not possess at least some basic qualifications for the call before receiving it. One might cite Moses as an exception, since at first he resisted God's call to deliver Israel due to his lack of speaking ability. But it should not be overlooked that Moses grew up in Pharaoh's court and was son-in-law of the priest of Midian, two circumstances which uniquely prepared him for the unusual mission into which God called him. And when we look through the Old Testament we find numerous examples where personal abilities clearly preceded God's call to a particular responsibility.[7]

In the New Testament the prime example is Paul. While Paul received special gifts after conversion, the fact remains that he had numerous qualifications before conversion that uniquely suited him for apostleship. Paul was by nature a person of unusual energy and vision, and his background included considerable administrative experience, a faculty for public speaking, and theological training under one of the most respected Jewish scholars of the day. Thus, while his call to apostleship required a profound reorientation of his mind and heart, it did not by any means plunge him into an area of work incompatible with his personality.

The Scriptures do not give basis to the popular notion that God's call to a vocation is unrelated to our personal qualifications. Evaluate your gifts, abilities and personality to see whether you have the qualifications needed for a particular vocation. Don't look at this evaluation as a lack of faith, but rather as part of the process God would have you go through in making a mature, responsible decision.

This isn't to suggest that you must be completely assured of your competence in advance and that you must be able to handle every minor duty of a vocation before entering it; in most cases, there will still be plenty of room for trusting God for further development. But you must at least be certain you have the capacity to develop the basic skills needed in the vocation, if you do not already possess those skills.

We can trust that God will make any exception to this general rule abundantly clear through supernatural guidance. Otherwise, we should assume he will guide us into areas where we can use the gifts and abilities we already have.

When Is a Gift Not a Guide?
Knowing that God will normally lead me only into vocational areas in which I already show some aptitude may not answer all of my questions. How do I know when a particular gift or ability indicates God's call to a vocation?

Within the context of Christian fellowship, I am to invest my energies in order to meet the needs of my brothers and sisters in Christ. But what about the broader question of a long-range vocational commitment? When should I assume that a particular gift or ability is an indication from God to pursue the vocation? If I find, for instance, that I have a definite gift for public speaking, would this indicate the pulpit ministry, or public relations? Or if I enjoy tinkering with electricity, does this mean I am to become an electrical contractor?

Here we have to say that a gift or ability never should be taken in and of itself as a vocational calling. For one thing, most of us have more areas of potential than we could ever pursue. We will always be forced to make choices between various abilities, investing in one at the expense of another. Our gifts and abilities are simply one factor to be considered along with others in guidance.

Another vital consideration is whether I desire to use a particular talent. To this should be added my assessment of the opportunities before me and how other people counsel me. These factors will be discussed in chapters seventeen and eighteen.

But another key question remains: Is it best, as a general principle, for me as a Christian to choose a profession or job which makes obvious use of a spiritual gift?

Here I will say two things. On the one hand, it is very clear from Scripture that each of us has a responsibility to make use of spiritual gifts. 1 Peter 4:10 states, "As each has received a gift, employ it for one another, as good stewards of God's varied grace." Most of us as Christians do not begin to take this responsibility as seriously as we should.

But on the other hand, there is nothing in Scripture which commands us to choose a profession or job merely because it provides the opportunity to make direct use of a spiritual gift. We should, in fact, see that such a requirement would actually hurt Christ's ministry rather than advance it. If we chose our professions on the basis of the opportunities they provide to use spiritual gifts, we would all be inclined to choose "Christian" jobs such as the pastorate, missionary work or teaching in a Christian school.

In general, the best rule of thumb is simply to pursue the occupation I most desire to be in. If this happens to allow me to use a spiritual gift, then fine. But if I would rather work in a department store than be a pastor, it would be a mistake to enter the pastorate simply because this is the most "spiritual" job that challenges my gift for administration. I would do better to enter business and trust that God will give me a ministry there. That ministry will occur in part through my being a channel of Christ to meet the temporal needs of people, a vital aspect of Christ's purpose on earth. And I may well discover that within the context of the secular business world I'll be given a special gift for bringing others to Christ.

Once we find the vocational field we most desire, we should continually look to Christ to give us a fruitful ministry in our daily work, and we must be open to whatever gifts for ministry he may want to give us in that context. Likewise, we must continue to seek every opportunity within a local church or fellowship to use our spiritual gifts in direct service to those in the body of Christ.

For Personal Study:

1. Read Exodus 35:30—36:3, which tells of people called to perform certain tasks in the construction of the sanctuary in the desert. It is of interest that this is the first situation in Scripture where individuals are spoken of as filled with God's Spirit.

☐ What is the indwelling of the Holy Spirit directly connected with in this passage?

☐ What does this say to us personally about how we should look upon the abilities, gifts and potential that we have?

☐ What role did personal abilities play in this passage in helping individuals understand God's leading?

☐ What role did their desires play?

☐ What other factors played a role?

☐ What practical help or inspiration can we take from this passage?

2. Again read 1 Corinthians 7:1-9. We noted earlier that this passage teaches that desire is an important consideration in a decision to marry. In what way does Paul indicate that *ability* is also a factor to consider in deciding whether to marry or stay single?

3. Read Luke 10:38-41, which describes a time when Martha and Mary hosted Jesus for dinner.

☐ What gift or ability does Martha demonstrate in this passage?

☐ What weakness does she exhibit?

☐ Martha later comes to a profound point of faith in Christ, through experiencing his raising her brother Lazarus from the dead (described in detail in Jn 11). Following this, she and Mary host Jesus again for a meal; read John 12:1-7 for a description of it. What personal trait does Martha continue to demonstrate at this second meal?

☐ What seems to have changed about Martha?

☐ What principle that we've emphasized in this chapter does Martha demonstrate?

4. List three areas where you feel you are the most gifted (or the most potentially gifted). Do any of these areas align with what you most want to do?

17
Assessing Open and Closed Doors

Key Questions:

■ *When are open and closed doors indicative of God's guidance, and when are they not?*
■ *Is there a difference between the role of open or closed doors in major and minor decisions?*

*U*p to this point we have discussed desires and abilities, which refer to everything *about myself* I must consider in making a decision. Now it will help to look at those things *outside myself* which I must consider, in other words, my circumstances.

Actually, we face two types of circumstances. *Constraining circumstances* prevent us from taking certain actions; they do this either through physical force or through making our line of duty extremely plain.

A house on fire leaves me little choice but to get out of it; a flat tire on a trip forces me to stop and repair it. Many of our circumstances are of this nature, and they simplify our decision making.

In some instances closed doors are God's way of showing us that we must sacrifice otherwise worthwhile desires. If I'm unemployed and waiting for a particular type of job, but my family runs out of money in the process, I should trust that God would have me at least temporarily settle for a less appealing job in order to keep my family from going hungry.

We also experience *nonconstraining circumstances,* which offer us opportunities to which we can freely respond or not. If I am considering a certain profession, for instance, and the job market is wide open, I may wonder whether this is a sign from God for me to move ahead or merely a diversion from Satan to sidetrack me. Or, if the job market is unfavorable, I may wonder whether this is God's way of telling me not to enter the profession or whether he wants me to grow in faith by moving ahead in the face of apparently closed doors.

Actually we face these sorts of dilemmas in practically every major decision we make; interpreting circumstances is almost always a problem if we are thinking as deeply as we should. Unfortunately, there is no ultimate way of removing all confusion in this area, and we must recognize that circumstances can have radically different significance in different decisions, depending upon God's purpose for us at the time.

If, for instance, God wishes to deepen my trust in him, he may want me to make a decision in the face of less than favorable circumstances. But if, on the other hand, he wants to move me in a direction I would probably not consider taking, he might do it by closing off all the other possible alternatives and providing a wide-open door.

More than any other factor in guidance, the question of circumstances shows our need to be yielded to Christ and in communion with him through Bible study and prayer. If we are yielded, we may trust that God will guide our decisions, as Romans 12:1-2 promises. In major decisions there is simply no way of knowing the implication of circumstances with unbending certainty, and only as we yield ourselves to God's will can we expect to evaluate these circumstances correctly.

But there are two basic principles which can reduce our confusion and make it easier to recognize God's leading. As these principles refer to the role of circumstances in major and minor decisions, it will be helpful to look at each of the two separately.

Circumstances and Major Decisions

In a major decision (a decision for a vocation), circumstances should play only a limited role in discerning God's will. At best, we should let them play either a suggestive or confirming role.

By *suggestive role* I mean letting circumstances suggest a possibility which should then be judged on the basis of desire, ability and the counsel of others. If, for instance, I am considering going to college, and a university offers me a generous scholarship, there is good reason to consider this circumstance as God's leading to attend the school. But it would be wrong to take this encouraging opportunity as guidance *in and of itself.* Only if after carefully considering the matter I conclude that I really want to attend the college and would profit from its training should I decide to enroll there.

By *confirming role* I mean letting circumstances confirm a choice we already have good reason to think might be God's will. If, for instance, I desire to marry a certain woman, and I believe we complement each other, then I have reason to think God may be leading toward marriage. But I'd better not finally conclude this until I ask her to marry me and she accepts! This would be the confirming circumstance. (In a real sense, of course, circumstances must always play a confirming role in our knowledge of God's will; whatever we might suspect God's will to be, we can know with certainty only when he confirms the possibility through circumstances.)

By saying we should limit the role of circumstances to suggestion or confirmation, we are really saying something quite important, for as Christians we too often attach undue significance to circumstances, regarding them uncritically as an infallible indicator of God's will.

There is a tendency to do this when circumstances are quite favorable, and especially when circumstances are highly coincidental. I find again and again that Christians want to regard such circumstances as God's clear leading without considering any other factors.

As an extreme example, I know of a Christian couple who decided God was leading them to marry because they first met in Europe and then later happened to encounter each other in a church in America. Since they had not made any plans to get together again after their first meeting, this unexpected encounter in America was taken as God's direct guidance to get married. Unfortunately they didn't take the time necessary to find out if they were really suited to be married to one another, and not surprisingly they were divorced less than a year after the wedding.

In this instance the mistake came in taking circumstances alone as divine guidance. While the coincidental meeting certainly gave them good reason to consider further possibilities for their relationship, it was wrong to make as dramatic a move as marriage without a more thorough consideration of their capacities for living together.

But to what extent, then, must circumstances appear favorable in advance of the decision we are considering? To what extent must they confirm our desires and abilities before we move ahead? Obviously they must always eventually confirm our choices, but to what extent must they do so *in advance?*

Here, unfortunately, there is no pat answer. While in a major decision desire and ability must normally be present to indicate guidance, the degree to which circumstances must appear favorable in advance cannot be stated as a general principle, and it will vary greatly from decision to decision. On the one hand, we can say that if circumstances are in strong agreement with desire and ability, that is a good indication of guidance. But on the other hand, even when they do not seem in agreement, it might still be God's will to move ahead, especially if desire and ability are strong. There is no easy formula for resolving this dilemma.

I wish it were possible to provide a more helpful insight for evaluating circumstances in major decisions, but this is where we really reach our limit in what can reasonably be said about divine guidance. We can say how circumstances should not function in these decisions, and this is helpful in narrowing our focus. But the light we can shed from a positive angle is limited.

Open Doors and Minor Decisions

In the area of minor decisions (that is, decisions within a vocation), we should see circumstances as playing a much more defined role. In fact, whereas circumstances should play only a limited role in major decisions, in minor decisions they are God's primary means of conveying his will.

In a major decision we decide for a particular vocation. This decision may be quite complex and the role of circumstances in the decision somewhat ambiguous. But once the decision is resolved and a commitment made to the vocation, the role of circumstances becomes much clearer.

It is through the circumstances of the vocation to which you commit yourself that God shows his will for your everyday decisions.

This is vital, for we have a tendency as Christians to spiritualize minor decisions—to look for some dramatic sign or intuitive impulse to resolve the most insignificant matters. But we need to see that once we have resolved a major area of commitment, God will seldom give us guidance which takes us out of the clear course of that commitment. We must trust that the normal responsibilities entailed by the commitment are by definition a part of his will.

This principle was a central theme of the Reformation doctrine of vocation, and one which we too quickly lose sight of today. Martin Luther referred to the details of a Christian's vocation as a "daily sermon."[1] We should think of God as virtually preaching his will to us through the responsibilities of our vocations. We need not look further for guidance.

By the same token, we should assume that any opportunity which is not clearly related to a vocation we have chosen and which might distract us from our present commitment is probably not God's leading. We should trust that if God wants to divert us from responsibilities to which we are already committed, he will make this strikingly clear.

For me the decision to become a pastor in St. Louis was a difficult one. But once it was resolved, much of God's will was clearly defined by it. There were the weekly sermons to write, people needing counsel, hospital visits to make, various programs to plan and other responsibilities clearly implied by the commitment.

It would have been foolish for me to expect God to make his will more plain to me than this. I didn't have to pray about whether to visit the church members who were ill or whether to play golf on a certain Sunday morning.

And it would have been foolish for me to look beyond these responsibilities to find God's will. If a friend offered me an intriguing business opportunity, I would have known that it simply was not God's will, since it would divert me from my pastoral commitment.

This principle does not make all minor decisions simple. It does not tell us what to do when faced with conflicting responsibilities within a vocation or between vocations. Deciding between conflicting responsibilities will often be difficult. God may allow many conflicting opportunities to come our way so that we will learn to make intelligent decisions and to trust him to do what we cannot do.

This principle narrows our focus in discerning God's will. But it doesn't mean we are rigidly locked into a vocation once we have chosen it. If we find circumstances extremely unfavorable, then we may have reason to explore changing our situation.

But until we have made a responsible decision to leave a vocation, we should assume that its details are a daily sermon—clear guidance and a precious trust from God.

For Personal Study:

1. Read Acts 16:6-10 (this is part of a longer passage which we looked at in detail in chapter four). In this passage Paul is confronted twice with closed doors. In what important way, though, did Paul *not* recognize the door of opportunity as closed?

☐ What vital lesson do we learn from Paul's example in this respect? (For a similar lesson, read Genesis 26:16-22.)

2. One of the major challenges we face in evaluating circumstances is seeing them realistically. In 1 Kings 19:1-8, Elijah, in spite of his deep spirituality, reaches some unfortunate conclusions about circumstances in his own life. Read this passage. (The previous chapter, 1 Kings 18, provides the context for this incident; read that too if you are not already familiar with it.)

☐ What inaccurate perceptions does Elijah reach?

☐ Why does he come to these unreasonable conclusions?

☐ What steps does he take that bring him back to a point of seeing his circumstances more realistically?

☐ What lessons can we learn from Elijah's experience? (Note as many as you can—both positive and negative.)

3. Read Mark 1:35-39 (we also looked at this passage in question 1 of chapter eight). In this passage Jesus is presented with an open door for ministry yet declines it. Why was he in a good position to make this judgment?

☐ What important lesson with respect to weighing our circumstances are we reminded of through Jesus' example here?

18
Weighing the Counsel of Others

Key Questions:

■ *How important is the counsel of others in understanding God's will?*
■ *How should I evaluate the counsel I receive?*
■ *How should I go about getting counsel?*
■ *Can I develop an unhealthy dependence upon others' counsel?*

*W*e have discussed the roles of desires, abilities and circumstances in knowing the will of God. But there is a vital remaining factor in decision making—the counsel of other people. Counsel should play a key role in practically all of our major decisions and sometimes in our minor decisions as well.

It's sometimes assumed in Christian circles that we are each in various authority relationships where one person's counsel is to be taken as God's will by definition. This is sometimes referred to as a "chain-of-command" relationship. Regardless of what other factors might seem to suggest, this person's counsel is considered the final word in knowing God's will.

Because this is an important issue with many Christians, and because the Bible has some pertinent teachings in this area, we will devote appendix one to this subject. In this chapter, we will look at the more general aspects of counsel. Those interested in the specific subject of chain-of-command relationships will want to work through the study in the appendix.

Members of a Body

The great tragedy of evangelical Christianity has been a tendency toward individualism. We have tended to stress our individual relationship with Christ to the exclusion of our relationships with other Christians.

We have emphasized commitment to Christ as the only essential in the Christian life and fellowship as a nicety but not a necessity. We think of fellowship as potluck dinners and other social events rather than as the building of significant personal relationships. The result has been a pietistic sort of Christianity where even though we spend time together as Christians we are isolated from one another in the deeper matters of life, reluctant to share struggles and important decisions with each other.

When we turn to the New Testament, we find a strikingly different picture of Christian community.

In the early church, commitment to Jesus Christ was not thought of apart from commitment to one another—the two notions were inseparable. The church was understood as the body of Christ, and to be committed to Jesus Christ, the head, meant also to be committed to his body, the company of those who believe in him.

Thus we find John saying, "he who does not love his brother [in Christ] whom he has seen, cannot love God whom he has not seen" (1 Jn 4:20). And we often find Paul talking about love for Christ and love for fellow believers in the same breath (for example, see 2 Thess 1:3; Col 1:4; 2 Cor 8:3-5; Philem 1:4-5).

When we observe the examples of Christian community described in Acts 2:41-47 and elsewhere, we see an infectious sort of fellowship between believers who have the closeness of being brothers and sisters in God's family.

If we take this New Testament emphasis on fellowship seriously, it should have profound implications for the way we live as Christians. We realize that we are called to live our lives not only for Jesus Christ but also for one another. This entails an intimate sort of caring for and sharing with one another in all aspects of our lives.

Specifically, it means that any serious endeavor to know God's will should not be an isolated effort but one shared with other Christians. If my commitment to Christ is inseparable from my commitment to other believers, then I must not expect to understand his will fully apart from being in relationship with other Christians, and I should expect that he will often convey his will to me through others. I should regard any attempt to resolve an important decision without the counsel of other Christians as a short circuit of my relationship with Christ.

It is important that we have regular involvement in Christian fellowship. This is vital to our spiritual health in all areas, and especially to gaining the desire to do God's will. We will find that through regular fellowship with other Christians our thinking in many areas becomes clarified.

We stressed in chapter sixteen how this happens, for instance, in the area of spiritual gifts. Sometimes we will find that simply through casual dialog with others we discover strengths and weaknesses in ourselves which were hidden to us but which have a bearing on a decision with which we are wrestling. The spiritual stimulation in fellowship is such that it inevitably has a positive influence on our thought processes.

When we're faced with a major decision it's especially important to go to other Christians and share this decision openly, seeking their thoughts and reflections on it. As believers we do not take this responsibility seriously enough. Not only does the New Testament emphasis on fellowship give us a strong mandate to seek counsel in our decision making, but it also makes good sense for purely practical reasons. Dialog on a subject stimulates us to think more deeply about it. There is a certain chemistry in the process of communication that invariably broadens our thinking, even if talking things over adds nothing new to our understanding of the problem. From this angle we can see that verbalization in and of itself— whether with a Christian or not—is generally a healthy process.

Thus, in the practical admonitions of Proverbs the importance of seeking counsel is a recurring theme:

"Where there is no guidance, a people falls; but in an abundance of counselors there is safety" (11:14).

"The way of a fool is right in his own eyes, but a wise man listens to advice" (12:15).

"Without counsel plans go wrong, but with many advisers they succeed" (15:22).

"Listen to advice and accept instruction, that you may gain wisdom for the future" (19:20).

"The purpose in a man's mind is like deep water, but a man of understanding will draw it out" (20:5).

"Plans are established by counsel; by wise guidance wage war" (20:18).

"By wise guidance you can wage your war, and in abundance of counselors there is victory" (24:6).

"Iron sharpens iron, and one man sharpens another" (27:17).[1]

All in all, then, we must conclude from both theological and practical standpoints that the counsel of other people is indispensable to responsible Christian decision making. We must see counsel as one of God's prime channels of guidance.

Assimilating Advice

But we need to understand how to evaluate the recommendations we receive in light of God's will. Should we suppose that if counsel from many people points unanimously in a certain direction, that's where God is leading? Or what if the advice we receive is contradictory?

With the exception of certain chain-of-command situations (discussed in the appendix), I do not believe we are ever under obligation to regard any counsel as God's will by definition, regardless of how many people might agree with the advice and regardless of the spiritual maturity of the one giving it. The value of counsel, in my opinion, lies not in providing direct insight into God's will, but in the fact that through counsel a healthy mental process occurs in which we are inspired to think more creatively, to see new alternatives and to see old alternatives in a new light. The end result is a deeper understanding of the issues at stake in our decisions. Ultimately, we must make our own decision in light of our desires, abilities and circumstances, even if it flies in the face of the counsel we've received.

None of the proverbs listed above say we must accept counsel as unerring divine leading. When they stress that there is strength in a multitude of counselors, for instance, there's no suggestion that the strength comes from the content of the counsel. There's little indication that from the counsel of many people a certain course of action will be consistently advised which will be the direction we must take.

The proverbs simply are not that specific. They stress that there is an advantage to many advisers and imply that through counseling we're helped to think more deeply, and we're strengthened to make wiser decisions.

I believe, to be sure, that if a large number of people concur in their advice, we should seriously consider whether it is indeed God's will. The burden of proof should be on us to show why it would not be God's leading. But we need to remember that there are many times in Scripture where one person was right against the multitude. We are not ultimately obliged to look on any counsel as the will of God, but merely as a help from God in responsibly thinking through our decisions.

By the same token, as mature Christians we should not lean on other people to make our decisions for us. While God gives us counsel as a help in understanding his will, he never wants it to become a crutch. We must remember that he expects us to grow through taking responsibility for our own decisions.

Obtaining Counsel

In addition to talking about how to evaluate counsel, we need to say something about how we should go about seeking counsel when making an important decision. From what sort of persons should we seek counsel, and how many should we consult?

It is difficult to lay down hard and fast rules at this point. The type of counsel we should seek will vary greatly from decision to decision and from person to person. But there are some general guidelines we can follow.

1. Seek counsel only when making a major decision or one which requires significant deliberation. Most minor decisions will not require seeking counsel.

2. Consult more people on more momentous decisions. The more critical the choice, the greater should be the number of persons from whom counsel is sought. In deciding on a major in college or a particular course of vocational training, for instance, you might ask the advice of a dozen people who would be likely to take your decision seriously. On deciding whether or not to teach a Sunday-school class or sit on a church committee, you might need only the advice of one or two close friends.

3. Seek counsel from a variety of persons, including those you do not expect will agree with you. The purpose of advice is not to simply confirm a decision you've already made.

4. Give greater emphasis to getting counsel from Christians than from non-Christians, because the former are part of the body of Christ through whom God gives special insight into his will. Also, Christians are more likely to identify with the spiritual aspects of your decision. But remember that God can guide through the wisdom of nonbelievers as well.

5. Get counsel from those who know you particularly well, such as parents, other family members, close friends and so on. If you are married, top priority should of course be given to the counsel of your spouse, and there should normally be strong agreement between you and your spouse on any major decision.

6. Consult spiritual leaders with whom you are in contact. Find a pastor, chaplain, Inter-Varsity staff member or other Christian leader whom you feel can add perspective to your decision.

7. Seek counsel from a psychologist, psychiatrist or other person specially trained in counseling if your decision is causing you particular emotional difficulties. Big decisions can be expected to induce a certain amount of anxiety. But if your emotions prevent you from making a rational decision or carrying that decision through, it might be best to talk with a professional counselor. A pastor, teacher or friend may be able

to recommend a good one.

In laying down guidelines for seeking counsel, one word of caution is perhaps in order. We cannot go on endlessly getting counsel for any particular decision. We reach a point where seeking counsel amounts to an escape from dealing head on with our problems. The fear of taking responsibility for our decisions can lead us to seek counsel in an effort to delay the decision or perhaps in the hope of being persuaded to depart from what we see to be our clear line of duty.

While there is no easy way of judging just when this point has been reached, the important thing is to be alert to the danger and to be praying for wisdom and balance in the whole process.

For most of us, however, I believe the danger lies not in seeking too much counsel, but in not taking the need for counsel seriously enough. We must forever fight the tendency to think that we have a private pipeline to God and can discover his will for our lives without the help of others. God has made us as social creatures, who find identity and purpose only in relationships with other people. And we cannot expect to understand God's direction in our lives apart from the experience of sharing our lives and decisions with those who bear his image on this earth.

For Personal Study:

1. Read 1 Kings 12:1-19. What fatal mistake did Rehoboam make in seeking counsel, and what can we learn from his experience?

2. Exodus 18 describes a time when Moses decided to make a critical change in his approach to life as a result of the counsel of Jethro, his father-in-law (who was also the priest of Midian). Read this chapter. What was the conclusion Moses reached through Jethro's counsel?

☐ It is interesting that in spite of his considerable wisdom and experiences of supernatural guidance, Moses had not reached this conclusion on his own. Do you think he would have done so without Jethro's help? Why or why not?

☐ What important principle for seeking counsel is underscored by this passage?

3. On the other hand, 1 Samuel 17:31-37 shows another side to the matter. Read this passage. Here David consults with Saul (at the time a highly respected leader) about fighting Goliath. What is Saul's initial counsel to David?

☐ Why did Saul misjudge David, and what can we learn from this?

☐ Why did David see his own potential differently than Saul did, and why was David right in not letting Saul dissuade him from confronting Goliath?

☐ What important lessons do we learn from David about interacting with those who counsel us?

19
Finally Deciding

Key Question:

■ *How do the principles we've discussed fit together in real-life decisions?*

I n concluding our study of guidance, it may help if we consider a couple of examples which tie together many of the points we've discussed.

First, let's look at the case of Jamie. When Jamie entered the university, her intention was to become a missionary doctor. Her decision had been based not on personal motivation as much as on a sense of obligation. Her father was a surgeon, and ever since she could remember her family had encouraged her to pursue a medical career. Also, she had long been a member of a church which put an unhealthy emphasis on denying natural aspirations. You should enter a profession mainly for the opportunity it presents to serve others, she had been taught, even if this means doing the very thing you don't want to do.

While she was in high school, a missionary nurse spoke to Jamie's youth group. The woman's presentation was inspiring, and Jamie found herself becoming excited about the prospect of missionary medical service. "Surely God must want me to do this," she thought. From then on, she simply assumed that God had called her to enter the field, even though she increasingly doubted that this was what she really desired to do.

Jamie's first year in college was a sobering experience. She found her zoology and chemistry courses uninteresting and the required memorization tedious. Her grades were poor, and more and more she dreaded going to class. During her second semester, however, she decided to try an elective course in accounting. She discovered a genuine interest in the subject, and while other students struggled with the material, she grasped it well.

During the summer she took a job with an accounting firm. She enjoyed the work immensely and found the business environment stimulating. The following semester she took a standard interest test at the vocational counseling center of her university. It revealed a distinct interest in the areas of business analysis and management . . . and minimal motivation for medical work.

At this point Jamie sought counsel from a campus minister. She shared with him that she felt a growing interest in pursuing an accounting career but feared that God had already given his final word on her profession. She also admitted that she felt extremely guilty about entering a profession she enjoyed so much.

The campus minister explained to her that God had not made her the way she was by accident. He showed her various passages of Scripture which suggested that her interests and potential were a strong sign of God's vocational direction. He also explained that she was under no obligation to regard the sense of inspiration she had felt during the missionary's talk as a final call from God. "God may have used your thoughts about a medical career to bring you to this college where you would find out that you should be an accountant," he suggested.

Jamie left the session much relieved and with a new sense of freedom in Christ to follow a profession that suited her personality. Upon graduation she found employment as an accountant with a hospital. Her background had uniquely suited her to employ her business skills within a medical environment. Her managerial skills were also noticed by her supervisors, and eventually she was promoted to a management position.

And her interest in medical missionary work continued; she found several ways to support it, though she didn't end up actually going to the field.

In another situation God might use the same factors in Jamie's background to lead someone else into a career of medical missions. But then the person's temperament would probably be clearly inclined in that direction. In any case, a person in a similar situation would have the right and responsibility to consider his or her personality make-up a vital indication of God's leading.

Making the First Move

John's experience of guidance was different. Through studying the biblical teaching on the role of church leaders and carefully considering his interests and abilities, he concluded that he could productively serve Christ as a pastor. He took this to be God's will and negotiated the first steps toward this goal by attending seminary. Then John faced the complex question of where and in what way God wanted him to serve.

This is a problem for any high-school or college graduate entering the job market for the first time. It's one thing to follow a particular course of study because you believe that is where God wants you. But facing the realities of the job market can be a great strain on your faith. We must not underestimate this problem for seminary graduates either. In many denominations, for instance, there is no organized system of placement, so one must simply depend upon being chosen by a particular congregation.

John was a member of such a denomination and was without a job offer. Graduation was coming up in three months. John wrestled with the very real question of what was God's responsibility and what was his own. He knew he must pray earnestly for God's direction. But beyond this, would faith demand that he do nothing but wait patiently and trust that

God would drop the ideal opportunity into his lap? Or would this be presumptuous? Should he instead take the initiative himself by following the practical steps taken by most other people who are looking for jobs?

Although less than fully convinced, he finally decided on the latter course, partly out of restlessness, and partly because he felt it would be lazy not to make some effort toward finding employment. He filled out his denomination's complicated dossier, contacted the seminary placement office and then sent his résumé to churches with open positions.

While John was open to a wide range of possibilities in the area of pastoral work, he had concluded through long and prayerful consideration that because of his interest in preaching the most ideal job would include a regular opportunity to preach. Likewise, because he had been successful in working with college students, he felt it would be especially good if he could serve a church located near a university. Yet, recognizing that the job market was quite crowded and that he must be open to new areas into which the Lord might lead him, John sent his résumé to a large variety of churches.

John continued his daily devotional time and prayed for God's wisdom and grace in the matter of finding pastoral work. But by graduation time he had contacted more than fifty churches with no positive response.

Then, two weeks after graduation, an extraordinary coincidence occurred. He received an encouraging letter from a friend in Detroit whom he hadn't heard from in over a year. On the next day a church in Detroit to which he had sent his dossier called him and asked him to visit as a candidate. His immediate response was that surely this coincidence was a sign from God that he should go to Detroit.

But a pastor friend encouraged him to take a close look at the situation first. As he did, John discovered that the church wanted him to serve primarily as a youth assistant with limited opportunities for preaching. Also, there would be little chance to minister to college students. He knew in his heart that he was open to going there if Christ wanted him to go. But from the evidence he had, he concluded that this situation wouldn't be a wise investment of his potential or a challenging atmosphere for growth. He cautiously decided not to go, but asked Christ to make it clear if he was wrong.

A week later another invitation came, this time from a church in Richmond, Virginia, which had heard about John through the seminary placement office.

From the phone call John found out that the church was located several blocks from a university and provided an outstanding location for college ministry. In addition, as an assistant, John would be expected to preach regularly in the Sunday evening service.

John then made a further, careful investigation of the situation by phoning a friend in Richmond who had attended this church for some time. John also sought counsel from several friends and pastors. Finally, he flew to Richmond to candidate officially at the church and spent several days there. He enjoyed the people of the church and felt they were open to his ideas and gifts. At the end of his visit they gave him an official "call." After several more days of thinking, praying and reading Scripture, John accepted the offer.

From Jamie's and John's experiences we can learn several things.

The first inquiry John received, from the church in Detroit, was a classic example of a coincidental circumstance, since he had received an unrelated letter from a friend there on the preceding day. And John's immediate reaction was a typical one—to assume God was giving special guidance through the coincidence.

But, on the advice of others, John backed up and took a second look. When he did, he logically concluded that the opportunity did not reasonably fit his interests and abilities, and he turned it down. It was only his first "nibble"; there would be others. To have looked on the coincidental circumstance as extraordinary guidance would have been an unfortunate assumption.

In a similar manner, Jamie was encouraged not to assume that her feelings during the missionary's presentation were an indication of God's will. Instead, she took a more careful look at her interests and abilities and made a decision based on them.

John may be commended for making a mature and responsible effort to investigate the Richmond church before finally responding to the invitation. But what comes through loud and clear is that God took an amazing amount of responsibility for guidance. He brought John to a position which he had not even sought. John had not sent his résumé to the church in Virginia, and it turned out to be ideal. This did much to deepen John's trust in Christ.

Still a hard question remains: Were John and Jamie wrong to try hard to find the right job and the right major? Would they have shown greater faith if they had just sat still and waited for God to bring things about?

We must say no. In John's case, the preparation of the résumé itself was clearly worthwhile, as this was the information which the Richmond church received from the placement office. Beyond that, even though no positive response came from sending the résumés out, this effort allowed him to accept the Richmond call with the assurance that he had reasonably covered the bases elsewhere and was not being impulsive in accepting the position.

I would like to suggest that there is truth in the adage: *God can't steer a parked car.* In many cases, God waits until he sees us taking responsibility before he brings the right opportunity along, even though that opportunity might not be directly related to our personal efforts. God did not force Jamie into an accounting major. She first tried out a course in the subject, then took a summer job in business. She made the moves and God used them to reveal his will.

All of this is not to imply, of course, that God does not sometimes make the process of finding his will considerably easier or harder than it was for Jamie and John. Unlike Jamie, some college students are sure of exactly what they want to do when they begin college. And they stick to that goal through their four years. Others change majors in college or courses of study in high school several times before settling on one interest. Some seminary graduates receive offers before they ever start to look; others who are very qualified look for six months or a year before receiving a call. There is no normal pattern.

God's ways of leading different persons are drastically different. Jamie's and John's experiences are simply examples of the correct approach to seeking God's will. When we're faced with a decision where God's will isn't clear, whether in employment or any other area, we must normally expect that he wants us to take some initiative to figure it out. This is part of our process of maturing in Christ.

The Abundant Life Is Not an Easy One

Finally, I would like to return to a point we emphasized earlier in our study. Some Christians believe that as we grow in Christ we should find it easier and easier to recognize his will. In one sense this is obviously true. The more we learn about how Christ guides, the less time we will spend looking for his guidance in the wrong ways.

But from another angle we may well find the reverse to be true. Growing in Christ means growing in responsibility, and as he sees that we are able to handle it, he allows us greater and greater responsibility. This means that we will have a greater part in decision making and that the decisions God allows us to tackle may in many cases be more difficult rather than less so.

This has been a common experience among people who have lived their lives for Christ on the growing edge. D. E. Hoste, for instance, refers to a conversation with Hudson Taylor, one of the greatest missionaries in recent history: "We were talking about guidance. He said how in his younger days, things used to come so clearly, so quickly to him. 'But,' he said, 'now as I have gone on, and God has used me more and more, I seem often to be like a man going along in a fog. I do not know what to do.' "[1]

This is not to imply that God ever wants his will to be hopelessly enigmatic to us. It's merely to emphasize that as we grow in Christ, he often makes us more accountable for our own decisions than we were when we were younger in the faith. We should welcome this opportunity, for it means a maturing in Christ which can come in no other way.

And we can have complete confidence that whether we feel God's guiding presence or not, he remains every bit as near, giving us all the direction we need to walk in the path of his will.

God's will is not simply meant to be discerned, it is meant to be affirmed. As we seek through prayer a heart that longs for his will and devote the best of our rational efforts toward finding his will, we may make the decisions of life with great conviction that he is guiding them. While there is never room for the presumptuous spirit which thinks it has a final grasp on God's will, neither is there room for the faint-hearted spirit which is afraid to make decisions and to trust that Christ is in control of them.

My prayer is that you would receive from this book not only a deeper understanding of the principles of knowing God's will, but also a spirit of courage to make decisions when they must be made, trusting Christ that even when the answer does not seem obvious, he is working out his will through the mind that seeks it and the heart that is truly open to him.

For Personal Study:

1. Note five ways in which you have grown in your understanding of biblical principles of guidance through this study.

2. Go back and review your goals from question 1 of chapter one; note whether and how any of these have been realized.

3. Have you reached any significant conclusion about a personal decision—either about what to do or about how to go about working it through? If so, write it down; then pray for courage to move forward in light of what you have decided.

Appendix 1

Authority Relationships and the Will of God

In this section we want to look at the biblical teaching on authority. In chapter eighteen, on counsel, we showed that counsel should play an important role in finding God's will. We stressed that it should function as advice and as stimulation for our thinking, but not as a final authority in our decisions.

But we are left with the question of *whether there are certain relationships where final authority exists*—that is, so-called chain-of-command relationships where one person's counsel is to be taken without question as God's will. Some Christians, for instance, believe that an unmarried person should follow the counsel of his or her parents, and married women should be led by the counsel of their husbands in all matters.

Obviously we must always be in certain limited authority relationships, such as with employers, teachers and civil authorities. But authority here does not generally extend beyond a restricted area, and certainly not to our important personal decisions. Furthermore, these relationships ordinarily can be broken at will.

A chain-of-command relationship, however, is a binding one, where there is final authority even over major life decisions. In popular thinking there are three relationships where this sort of authority is often believed to exist: the relationships between parents and children, between husbands and wives, and between spiritual leaders and those under them.

Although Christians by no means agree in any of these areas, in each case there are many who believe the Scriptures teach a hierarchy of authority. We need, then, to give close attention to the biblical teachings on each of these relationships to determine what role, if any, strict authority should play in them.

Parents and Children

The issue of obedience to parents has left many Christians confused in recent years. Bill Gothard, in his popular seminar, "Institute in Basic Youth Conflicts," has laid considerable stress on the obedience due from the Christian child even to non-Christian parents.[1] Other Christian teachers have countered that the Christian child is free in Christ to make his or her own decisions—while the counsel of parents should be respected, it is not binding.

To come to grips with the biblical teaching on this matter, we will look at the two most explicit statements in the Bible about the obedience due to parents, as they are the passages most often quoted in support of parental authority:

Children, obey your parents in the Lord, for this is right. "Honor your father and mother" (this is the first commandment with a promise), "that it may be well with you and that you may live long on the earth." Fathers, do not provoke your children to anger, but bring them up in the discipline and instruction of the Lord. (Eph 6:1-4)

Children, obey your parents in everything, for this pleases the Lord. Fathers, do not provoke your children, lest they become discouraged. (Col 3:20-21)

Both of these passages obviously give strong support to parental authority.

To begin with, the type of obedience Paul is talking about in these verses is absolute: children are to obey parents "in everything" (Col 9:20). While Paul would surely make an exception if the parent commanded the child to sin,[2] it does not appear that any other exception would be entertained.

In all other cases the child should simply assume that his or her parents' wishes indicate the will of God. The phrase *in the Lord* in Ephesians 6:1 does not, I believe, indicate that parents are to be obeyed only when their counsel appears to be the Lord's leading. I would agree with T. K. Abbott that this phrase is not to be taken "as defining the limits of obedience . . . but rather showing the spirit in which the obedience is to be yielded."[3]

Paul is saying that obedience is to be rendered in a reverent spirit.

In addition, Paul does not seem to be making any distinction between Christian and non-Christian parents in these passages. He does not say that one must obey only Christian parents. And while we might think he assumed only children of Christian parents would read the Epistles,[4] this is unlikely, for it appears that many children of unbelieving parents had become Christians in the early years of the church.

Also, in Romans 1:30 and 2 Timothy 3:2 Paul expresses disgust with the disobedience to parents present in pagan society, showing that he views obedience to parents as a human virtue irrespective of a family's religious status. Thus it appears that the command to obey parents is to be followed by all children, regardless of their parents' Christian commitment. Children should assume that their parents' counsel indicates God's will, even though their parents might not have the slightest concern about what God would will.

But while the passages support parental authority at these points, at another point they force us to qualify strongly the chain-of-command notion.

The passages do not say that *any* unmarried person is to render this obedience to parents, but that it is due from *children*. "*Children,* obey your parents," they tell us. There is a chronological distinction here which is overlooked by many Christians and vital to the meaning of the passage. The Greek word for children *(ta tekna)* used in these passages indicates not any son or daughter, but a person who is still dependent upon his or her parents.[5]

This is a crucial distinction, for it shows that the unmarried adult is no longer under the obligation of these verses, for that person by definition is no longer a child. Also it suggests that for young people in the later teens the chain-of-command requirement is less clearly defined.

Most young people today go through a transitional stage between being a dependent child and a self-supporting adult. During this stage their parental dependence gradually lessens. The person, for instance, who leaves home for college right after high school may still have strong financial dependence upon his or her parents but may be forced into a new independence in many other areas. It would certainly be wrong to think of such a person as a child. This person is in an ambiguous state where childish dependence is decreasing and adult self-reliance increasing.

Thus, while a college student should continue to value greatly the counsel of his or her parents, the student should not feel obligated to regard their advice as God's will by definition. Also, from a practical standpoint, the person in such a transitional state will never develop the maturity to make independent decisions if he or she continues to rely solely on parental counsel. A weaning period must occur, simply for the sake of personal growth.

Exactly where this transitional stage begins cannot be laid down with any rigidity. Most young people probably reach it somewhere in high school, and Christian parents should generally by eleventh or twelfth grade begin to encourage their children to take greater and greater responsibility for their own decisions. I would think that normally children in the early high-school years should continue to think of themselves as children with respect to the biblical commands, and trust that their parents' wishes convey God's will.

In summary, then, the chain-of-command relationship exists between parents and children, but ceases during the adolescent years when the child begins making adult decisions. This does not belittle the importance of parental counsel for those beyond the chain-of-command stage. As Christians—regardless of age or marital status—*the command to honor our parents always applies,* and this certainly suggests that we should give serious consideration to their counsel. Our parents are often much better equipped to understand and counsel us than we give them credit for. Generally, I believe the burden of proof rests on us to show why we should not follow our parents' advice in a particular major decision. But no adult or late adolescent needs to feel that his or her parents' advice must be taken as God's will if other factors clearly point in a different direction. To follow parental direction in such an instance could be to put parents above Christ, a tendency we are warned against in Luke 14:26 and elsewhere. Ultimately, we must accept the fact that Christ has called us to a life of responsible thinking, and we must beware lest we rely too heavily on our parents to make our decisions for us.

Husbands and Wives

There are two prevailing views among Christians today about New Testament teachings on order in marriage. These often result in different ideas about authority in the marriage relationship.

In various passages a pattern of authority is set forth: the husband is declared head of the wife as Christ is head of the church (for instance, Eph 5:21-33; Col 3:18-19) and as Abraham was master of Sarah (1 Pet 3:1-7). Thus, the wife is to submit to her husband. Many Christians feel that these statements are to be interpreted as God's command for hierarchy in marriage today and that no cultural considerations will affect their meaning and application. This has been the traditional interpretation.

On the other hand, an increasing number of Christians with a high view of biblical authority have concluded that these commands were not meant to be binding for Christians of all times. They were rather intended to correct some unfortunate circumstances in the early churches or as an acquiescence to the culture of that time. Wives were told to submit to their husbands so that Christians would not challenge a social custom in a way that would hinder the spread of the gospel. In the same way Christian women were instructed to wear veils and not to talk during worship.

These commands, it is argued, should be seen in the same class as those about slaves obeying their masters. They had their place in the culture of the first century. But just as we would not look upon slavery as God's perfect will, neither should we insist on male headship in marriage as God's ideal.

In this view, God's highest design for marriage is reflected in Galatians 3:28, where Paul says, "There is neither Jew nor Greek, there is neither slave nor free, there is neither male nor female; for you are all one in Christ Jesus." The unity portrayed in that passage should be understood as touching all aspects of life, not simply the spiritual. Within marriage the ideal pattern is one of partnership, where the husband and wife delegate authority as they choose.

The issues involved in this question are complex, and it is well beyond my purposes to go deeply into them or to argue for one side against the other. Much helpful material has been written on both sides, and I would encourage you to study the subject carefully, examine the biblical passages closely and work through your own position.[6] My only caution would be not to be judgmental of someone who reaches a different conclusion from yours, as the best minds are divided on this matter. It is vital that we maintain respect for each other's viewpoints in this area.

I do want to argue, however, that regardless of which position you hold, there is no basis for a rigid chain-of-command situation. I believe these passages should be seen as presenting a balanced picture of authority. They have sometimes been used to justify situations of extreme male dominance, where the husband is the final authority in all decisions and the wife is always expected to accept his opinion passively. That is not the spirit I see conveyed in these passages.

Paul, for instance, begins his teaching on marriage in Ephesians 5 with the statement, "Be subject to one another out of reverence for Christ" (v. 21). He does not separate the wife's submission to her husband from the thought that the husband must also demonstrate submission to his wife. He goes on to tell husbands to love their wives as Christ loved the church. While Christ was the perfect example of a leader, he was also the perfect servant, and the implications for the husband's role are profound.

Cultural considerations aside, then, Paul is saying that there must be *mutual* submission within marriage. This is stated perhaps even more plainly in 1 Corinthians 7:4: "For the wife does not rule over her own body, but the husband does; likewise the husband does not rule over his own body, but the wife does." While this verse has obvious reference to the sexual act, it certainly implies the broader principle that husbands and wives have authority to influence their spouse's decisions in all areas.

In addition, we might note that Peter closes his statement on marital order in 1 Peter 3:1-7 by referring to husbands and wives as "joint heirs of the grace of life" (v. 7) and follows with an appeal for unity of spirit (v. 8).

In short, the straightforward teaching of these passages affirms male headship only within the context of mutual submission. Couples who wish to be consistent with this teaching should strive for agreement in their decision making. Regardless of which position is held on the application and interpretation of these passages, one must conclude that discerning God's will in marriage is a mutual matter. While a couple should feel the freedom to delegate in small decisions, certainly in broad vocational decisions they should be in agreement before they decide that a certain option is God's leading.

For the couple that accepts male headship, I would think that it would apply only if after much discussion they find themselves at a genuine impasse, where a decision must be made even though agreement cannot be reached. Then it would be right for the husband's opinion to prevail. But hopefully this would be the rare exception in the normal marriage.

Ordinarily couples should recognize their obligation before Christ to make a concerted effort to reach accord in major decisions. This admittedly can be a painful and prolonged process. It takes much more time and effort than simply letting the husband decide and the wife passively follow. But I do not see any other process as true to the spirit of the Scriptures. The dividends in the long run will be closer companionship between husband and wife and greater sensitivity to the Lord's leading.

Spiritual Leaders

We come finally to the question of the authority of spiritual leaders. Most Christians find themselves in a relationship with one or more spiritual leaders, whether within a church or a fellowship group outside of the church. Inevitably, the question arises, is this person's counsel to be taken as only advice, or does his or her opinion carry special weight by virtue of position?

Interestingly, when we turn to the New Testament we find no evidence that a spiritual leader's counsel should ever be taken as more than advice in major complex decisions.

To begin with, there is no clear indication that leaders in the early church were regarded as special interpreters of God's will in such decisions. If we look, for instance, at the various passages regarding the appointment of leaders, we find no evidence that positions of leadership included authority in the area of complex decisions (see Acts 6:1-6; 14:23; 1 Tim 3:1-13; 5:17-22; Tit 1:5-10; compare Rom 12:3-8; 1 Cor 12; Eph 4:11-14).

The leader was to be respected in decisions regarding the life of the church, to be sure. But there is no indication that the leader's word had to be followed in personal matters such as career, marriage and so on. (And even in matters directly pertinent to the church's life it is not evident that the leader's directions were to be taken as God's will beyond question.)

It becomes evident in Acts 15:36-41 that not even the apostles were regarded as infallible interpreters of God's will. When Paul and Barnabas disagreed over the question of taking John Mark with them on further missionary travels, Luke's record gives no indication that Barnabas was disobedient to God's will because he disagreed with Paul.

It is sometimes claimed that Paul's commands to his disciples to be imitators *(mimētēs)* of him implies that they were expected to obey him in their personal, complex decisions (1 Cor 4:16; 11:1; Phil 3:17; 2 Thess 3:7, 9; compare 1 Thess 1:6). Willis P. DeBoer, however, in an exhaustive study of these passages, concludes, "The primary thought in Paul's speaking of his readers as *mimētai* [imitators] is not that they are obliged to be obedient to him and to act in accordance with his instructions."[7] Paul rather seems to be referring to an imitation of his virtuous lifestyle.

The lack of emphasis upon obedience to spiritual leaders in major personal decisions in the New Testament is strikingly underlined by the fact that while Paul and Peter both set forth very specific statements regarding certain authority relationships, there is no specific command given in these passages regarding obedience due to a spiritual leader (Eph 5:21—6:9; Col 3:18—4:1; 1 Pet 2:13—3:7).

There are in the New Testament only two passages where a direct command regarding obedience to spiritual leaders is given, Matthew 23:2-3 and Hebrews 13:17. In the former passage Jesus tells his disciples, "The scribes and the Pharisees sit on Moses' seat; so practice and observe whatever they tell you, but not what they do; for they preach, but do not practice." Here Jesus sets forth a command which can rightly be understood as an injunction to respect the authority of religious leaders, whether their behavior is commendable or not. It is doubtful, however, that this command pertains to the area of complex decisions.

Jesus refers to the scribes and Pharisees as sitting on Moses' seat, that is, they were interpreters of the law of Moses. Thus he seems merely to be telling his disciples to follow the laws of the Pentateuch as interpreted to them by the scribes and Pharisees. And even more, he is pointing out how hypocritical the scribes and Pharisees are because they do not practice what they preach. Jesus wants his disciples' lifestyles to conform to the spirit of the law.

The injunction of Hebrews 13:17 is: "Obey your leaders and submit to them; for they are keeping watch over your souls, as men who will have to give account." Here Christians are explicitly commanded to obey their spiritual leaders. And yet the writer of Hebrews does not explain precisely what this obedience involves. It is frankly impossible to know with certainty what this command meant. There is, however, no basis for concluding that it necessarily meant an unbending sort of obedience.

Today we often use the expression *obey your leader* in situations where obvious boundaries are implicit. Thus, a student is told simply, "Obey your teacher," even though certain limits to that obedience are understood. If the teacher gave an unreasonable homework assignment—"do some shoplifting tonight and bring in your loot tomorrow to show the class"—the student would not be expected to comply. Likewise, no matter how strongly the teacher might urge the student to participate in some extracurricular activity, the student would still be free to do as he or she wished.

I believe that the author of Hebrews similarly was telling readers to obey their leaders in a limited sense. This is most apparent from the Greek term rendered "obey" in verse 17; it is actually better interpreted "be persuaded." W. E. Vine comments, "The obedience suggested is not by submission to authority, but resulting from persuasion."[8] If the author had meant to imply a rigid authority in any sense, a stronger term surely would have been used.[9]

I believe that most likely the passage was merely urging readers to a general obedience in matters touching the corporate life of the church and the command had nothing to do with personal complex decisions. Probably the statement was understood by readers in this sense, in the same way that we understand what is meant if someone says, "Obey your teacher."

Even in this area of the church's corporate life, there is no reason to assume it was implying an absolute authority for the leaders. The writer was probably just encouraging readers toward a reasonable measure of respect and submission, which must exist in order for leaders to function.

Whatever the case, we have to say that if God wanted to convey the fact that Christian leaders should have chain-of-command authority over decisions in any area, it would have been stated more explicitly here or elsewhere.

As it is, we have no clear New Testament evidence to this effect. We must conclude that a Christian is not required to regard the counsel of a spiritual leader as the will of God by definition. While we should seek counsel from qualified spiritual leaders in making major personal decisions, we must not feel under any compulsion to regard this counsel uncritically as divine guidance. We may feel free to weigh it along with other factors which appear to be pointing toward God's will.

Chains-of-Command

We have looked at relationships between parents and children, husbands and wives, and spiritual leaders and their followers. We have discovered that the same spirit of reasonable decision making that permeated our discussion of knowing God's will also applies here.

Parents are to direct their children's decisions until the children show that they are ready to begin making choices on their own. Husbands and wives, likewise, are to labor together to choose alternatives which seem reasonable to both of them. And we are all to listen with respect to the advice of our spiritual leaders and then to weigh this advice along with other factors to come up with a rational choice. God wants to give us as much responsibility for finding his will as we can handle. He wants us not to be robots for him, but living, thinking, reasoning beings willing to follow his leading.

Appendix 2

Does God Have a Will for Our Personal Decisions?

(With Reflections on Garry Friesen's *Decision Making and the Will of God*)

Is it really accurate to claim that God has a will for our personal decisions? Does Scripture actually provide evidence that he is concerned about which person we marry or which job we choose? Is it not perhaps better to say that within certain moral boundaries he gives us freedom of choice in these areas? Is not all this concern for personal guidance an elaborate straw man, akin to sending believers on an impossible search for the emperor's new clothes?

Christians are more inclined to raise this question today than they were when I wrote the first edition of this book, due especially to the influence of Garry Friesen's *Decision Making and the Will of God,* published about a year after my own book.[1] In this landmark work Friesen argues that guidance as we traditionally think of it is a non-issue.

God in fact does not have an individual will for our decisions, Friesen insists. He does have an ultimate sovereign will which governs every aspect of life but which cannot be known except as the events of life unfold. He has, too, a detailed moral will which is fully revealed in Scripture and which must be respected in all of our decisions. Yet he does not typically have a preference for the unique, individual choices which we face. As long as we are operating within the bounds of God's moral will, there are usually a variety of options in any personal decision area which are potentially pleasing to God.

Friesen's purpose in advocating this position is clearly as much pastoral as it is theological. He is moved by the plight of many (including himself) who have been frustrated or led down the primrose path by the traditional view of guidance.

As Friesen sees it, the traditional view fosters confusion over God's will and in general promotes an immature approach to decision making. Those who bank on finding God's one ideal choice in a decision either spin their wheels in a fruitless search for the perfect center of God's will (the "missing dot") or become deluded into thinking God has given them special guidance. In the meantime, they don't do what they actually *can* do, which is to use their God-given rational capabilities and make a sensible, practical decision. In short, they fail to act responsibly and to use the capacity for good judgment which God has given them.

The Real Issue

Actually, I agree wholeheartedly with Friesen's pastoral concerns. They were the very factors which motivated me to write my own book. I saw from my own experience, and from that of many others, that traditional views of guidance often did not work well and led to misleading ideas about what God is directing you to do.

Yet it didn't seem to me that the problem resulted from the idea of God's having an individual will itself but rather from the approaches Christians took to discerning it. Like Friesen, I also saw an emphasis upon personal responsibility and practical thinking in Scripture which wasn't being brought out well in popular teaching on guidance.

This was a liberating discovery to me, as it was to Friesen, for it said that it was okay for me to take initiative for important life choices even when no special guidance was present.

Yet this never suggested to me that God has no will for our personal decisions. Rather, I understood the biblical emphasis on personal responsibility as showing the approach Christians should take in finding God's will.

While Friesen gives many examples of Christians who were liberated by finding that God wasn't holding them to an individual will, I frankly suspect that what helped these people most was discovering the freedom to take personal initiative in their decisions. I have personally taught and counseled with many who have come to a similar point of freedom *without* letting go of the belief that God has a personal will for them.

We are freed not so much by the idea God has no will for us as we are by the confidence that it's okay to take responsibility for our lives. Many Christians are able to hold onto both the idea of God's personal will and the conviction that he wants them to take responsibility for their choices. These notions don't have to be mutually exclusive.

The Benefits of the Concept of God's Personal Will

Frankly, I don't find Friesen's study giving adequate attention either to the problems which discarding the belief in God's individual will can cause or to the positive value which this notion actually has for many.

For many Christians the thought of God's having a personal will is foundational to an intimate, personal relationship with Christ. It drives them to pray, to study God's Word and to take all the steps necessary to know Christ better. One man confessed to me that he lost the incentive to pray after letting go of the idea of God's personal will. While this does not have to be the result of such a change in perspective (Friesen himself stresses the importance of prayer), it does bring out the connection some make between their devotional life and their belief in God's personal will.

Belief in God's individual will also bolsters personal confidence for many Christians. The belief that God is leading them to take a particular step of faith helps them gain the courage to take it. A friend of mine who has struggled throughout his life with low self-esteem admitted to me that he is constantly buoyed by the conviction that Christ is leading him to do what he does. His accomplishments have been impressive and have included the building of a major conference center. Knowing him as I do, it's clear that his perspective on God's will has had enormous benefit for his personal confidence. Without the conviction of God's personal will, many like him would less likely find the courage to take important steps of faith.

There is another contribution which the concept of God's personal will makes to our psyche, and I'm sure that for many this is the most important one. Each of us has a fundamental need to know we are distinctive. Part of this urge for distinctiveness is the desire to know that we can make a contribution to human life which no one else is as well equipped to make—that there is significant work to be accomplished which simply won't get done unless we do it. We find it demeaning to think that we are merely carrying out roles which others could fill just as well. We long to know that there is *purpose* to what we do, that there is justification to our existence.

If you remove the concept of God's personal will, you remove an important basis for believing your work does have ultimate significance. If in considering a job choice, for instance, there are a number of alternatives which are equally pleasing to God, how can I be assured that any of them amount to roles which others couldn't carry out just as effectively? If, however, I believe that God does have a "best" choice for me, this aids my conviction that there is a mission which won't be accomplished (or accomplished as well) unless I take it on.

One of my concerns with Friesen's book is that he gives scant attention to the area of personal distinctiveness.[2] In general his counsel for making vocational choices focuses mainly on carrying out biblical moral commands and doing what is expedient; there is minimal discussion along the lines of "finding your niche," for instance. While on one level this is a forgivable omission (a writer can only concentrate on so much), I can't help but wonder whether, if the matter of personal distinctiveness had been more in the forefront of Friesen's thinking, it would have led him to any different conclusions.

An Exemplary Book

Let me hasten to say that in general I have the greatest respect and appreciation for Friesen's book. I have often recommended his book to others and will continue to do so. It is far and away the most scholarly and stimulating book on the will of God which I have seen. Friesen displays considerable humility and much good humor in his book, too, and avoids the divisive polemical tone so common in theological writings of this sort. And in fact, I agree with a large portion of Friesen's perspective. His book provides a wealth of inspiring biblical insight, including observations which were a particular help to me personally.

I do disagree, though, with his basic thesis that God has no personal will for us. My purpose in critiquing this point is not to discredit his book but rather to carry forward the dialog on this subject which Friesen himself encourages.[3]

Friesen's Argument

Friesen bases his conclusion about God's having no individual will on a number of critical observations. To begin with, he can find no clear statement in Scripture declaring that God does have such a will for our decisions. Further, he notes extensive evidence that individuals in the New Testament did not normally wait for extraordinary guidance but followed a rational process in their important life choices. In the occasional situations in Scripture when God did give direct personal guidance, it was always through a supernatural revelation.

We need, then, to be careful about deducing a theology of guidance from these exceptional examples; Friesen can find no instance in Scripture of guidance through mystical impressions. In addition, he notes that the traditional view of guidance carried to its logical extreme lays the impossible requirement on us of seeking God's will for every minute choice of life. Since it appears God has given us freedom of choice in small areas (choosing Cheerios vs. Pop-Tarts for breakfast, for instance), it would seem he has done so in broader areas as well.

It is well beyond my scope to go into a point-by-point critique of Friesen's study, which would require another book as long as his 450-page tome. I do want, though, to address several of his major concerns.

Friesen's most significant argument is that Scripture never directly states that God has a personal will for his people. While he admits that the Bible never denies this either, he does place more weight on the (seeming) biblical silence about this matter than any other point.

My own study of Scripture, though, leads me to a different conclusion about the biblical testimony here. Part of Friesen's study, for instance, focuses on the specific use of the biblical term *will of God* (actually *thelēma* of God in his examples; he does not examine the term *boulē* in his main text). He argues that this term is used in an obvious sense only to signify either God's sovereign will or his moral will; he finds no clear case where the term is used with reference to God's individual will.

God's Personal Will in the New Testament

In looking carefully at the instances of *thelēma* as God's will in the New Testament, however, I am persuaded that the notion of an individual will is sometimes implied. It appears to be used in this sense in the synoptic Gospels, for instance. The term *thelēma* is used with reference to God's will for human behavior three times:

> *Matthew 7:21:* "Not every one who says to me, 'Lord, Lord,' shall enter the kingdom of heaven, but he who does the will of my Father who is in heaven."
> *Matthew 12:50:* "For whoever does the will of my Father in heaven is my

brother, and sister, and mother."

Mark 3:35: "Whoever does the will of God is my brother, and sister, and mother."

In none of these passages is the notion of God's will *(thelēma)* defined, and the context could allow for either a moral will, a personal will or both. But while God's moral will is probably intended in each of these verses (the first, for instance, occurs during the Sermon on the Mount, which is largely a series of moralistic exhortations), a personal will is probably intended as well.

This is most evident from the fact that *thelēma* is the word used for God's will in the Gethsemane passages in Matthew and Luke (Mt 26:42; Lk 22:42: "not my will but thine be done"). Here God's will clearly refers to a unique matter of personal guidance for Jesus.

Further, *thelēma* is used of the will of a human master who symbolizes God in the parable of the repentant son in Matthew 21:28-32 (v. 31), and the parable of the master who delays in coming in Luke 12:35-48 (v. 47). In each of these parables the moral is that obedience to God is required, and in each the analogy is not to a universal moral commandment but to a matter of unique, individual responsibility: tilling a vineyard in the first and guarding a house in the second.

I believe that we have good reason to agree with C. Leslie Mitton, who in a study of *thelēma* in the Synoptics concludes:

> Jesus not only enlarged and clarified our understanding of the will of God for His people in terms of their general conduct towards one another, but He was insistent that this Will was something which must be obeyed. It was the supreme authority in His own life, and the characteristic mark of a disciple of Christ was that a man accepted the same authority for himself. No doubt in this sense the Will of God included . . . general principles of conduct . . . but also included the particular course of action God might require of one particular man at any one special moment.[4]

In the Johannine writings it is also probable that *thelēma* has reference to God's personal will. *Thelēma* is used of God's will for people in three instances:

John 7:17: . . . if any man's will is to do his will, he shall know whether the teaching is from God or whether I am speaking on my own authority.

John 9:31: (the parents of the healed blind man are speaking) "We know that God does not listen to sinners, but if any one is a worshiper of God and does his will, God listens to him."

1 John 2:17: And the world passes away, and the lust of it; but he who does the will of God abides for ever.

The strongest clue to John's intended meaning for *thelēma* in these passages comes from the fact that on three occasions in John's Gospel Jesus refers to himself doing the *thelēma* of God (4:34; 5:30; 6:38-39). It is clear that God's *thelēma* for Jesus did not refer merely to moral commandments but to his unique mission (thus, in Jn 4:34, Jesus appears to identify doing the will of God with accomplishing the work of God, and in Jn 6:38-39 he directly identifies the will of God as a specific responsibility of his calling). In light of this, it is likely that John's references to believers doing the *thelēma* of God imply a will for matters of personal guidance and not simply for areas of moral conduct.

In Paul's writings, *thelēma* is used in several places where I believe the notion of God's personal will is implied.

> *Ephesians 5:15-17:* Be very careful, then, how you live—not as unwise but as wise, making the most of every opportunity, because the days are evil. Therefore do not be foolish, but understand what the Lord's will is.

Here the term *the Lord's will* most likely has reference to the counsel immediately preceding it to be "wise, making the most of every opportunity . . . do not be foolish." These injunctions command believers to manage their time carefully and to make the best possible use of all circumstances to God's glory. These clearly go beyond moral commands and provide a principle for confronting all situations of life—the nonmoral as well as the moral.[5]

> *Romans 12:1-2:* I appeal to you therefore, brethren, by the mercies of God, to present your bodies as a living sacrifice, holy and acceptable to God, which is your spiritual worship. Do not be conformed to this world but be transformed by the renewal of your mind, that you may prove what is the will of God, what is good and acceptable and perfect.

In this passage Paul exhorts believers to "prove what is the will of God." In the verses which immediately follow this exhortation, he commands them to have a clear view of their own distinctiveness,[6] then proceeds to encourage them to make use of the unique spiritual gifts which they possess (vv. 3-8).

Paul is indicating that the will of God which we are to prove is discovered in part through the individuality which God has put within us. It suggests that God has created us each differently, that we are to serve Christ in light of this individuality, and that we are to recognize our individuality as an important key to understanding God's will for us. All of this points, then, to God's having not merely a universal moral will for all believers but also a distinctive will for the service of each Christian.[7]

There are two other places in Romans where I believe Paul uses *thelēma* to refer to God's personal will. In Romans 1:10 he speaks of his desire to visit the Romans "by God's will" and then he makes a similar statement in Romans 15:32. At first sight it appears that he merely has God's sovereign will in mind in these statements, especially since he ties the first reference to the fact that he has previously been hindered in his efforts to visit the Romans.

In Romans 15, however, it becomes clear what exactly this hindrance involved. It's not that God has physically prevented Paul from coming to Rome, but rather that Paul has had other responsibilities to fulfill (v. 22). It is because he has now finished these tasks that he can consider it to be God's will for him to visit Rome (vv. 23-24). Thus he seems to be connecting God's will with his own personal decision here.

I could note other places in Paul's writings where I believe he implies God's personal will in his use of *thelēma*. Hopefully, though, the ones we have noted will be sufficient to illustrate that Paul did at times use the term in this sense. When these are coupled with the examples from the synoptic Gospels and John's writings, we have good evidence that the New Testament teaches the concept of an individual will of God.

Different Niches
Actually, though, the most succinct statement in the New Testament about God's having a personal will occurs in a passage where the term *thelēma* is not used. In 1 Corinthians 12:4-7 Paul declares,

There are different kinds of gifts, but the same Spirit. There are different kinds of service, but the same Lord. There are different kinds of working, but the same God works all of them in all men.

Now to each one the manifestation of the Spirit is given for the common good. (NIV)

Here in the introduction to a lengthy excursion on spiritual gifts Paul refers to three characteristics of the believer's life: "gifts," "service" and "working." Paul notes, too, that God *intentionally* endows the Christian at these points: "the same God *works* all of them in all men." When this passage is read in the context of 1 Corinthians 12, it could not be clearer that Paul is declaring these to be *distinctive* endowments of the Christian. His overriding intent in this chapter is to encourage positive acceptance of those areas of giftedness where we are different:

Now the body is not made up of one part but of many. . . . The eye cannot say to the hand, "I don't need you!" And the head cannot say to the feet, "I don't need you!" On the contrary, those parts of the body that seem to be weaker are indispensable, and the parts that we think are less honorable we treat with special honor. (vv. 14, 21-22 NIV)

The three terms *gifts, service* and *working* refer to specific ways God endows believers for serving Christ. *Gifts* denotes abilities and personal potential. *Service* refers to the specific responsibilities we assume—the situations and vocations of life where our gifts are exercised. The literal Greek verb for *working* is *energizing.* As we noted in chapter fifteen, it conveys the thought of God inspiring and motivating the believer. It indicates, then, that God provides the believer with distinctive desires to serve Christ in specific ways.

It is abundantly clear that Paul's intent in teaching on spiritual gifts is not to reflect on hidden mysteries of God's sovereign will into which we have no business delving, but to present a significant aspect of God's will which we are to make every effort to understand. His motive is that believers would come to the clearest possible understanding of their unique gifts, that they can use them to the glory of Christ and have a healthy self-image as well.

It is clear, too, that he wants us to regard these gifts not as happenstance but as a clear indication of the hand of God upon our lives, nothing less than a "manifestation of the Spirit." Paul obviously has the same intent in his reference to "service" and "working." Each of us, then, should view our gifts, situations and motivational patterns as critical indications of God's guidance for our lives. It will not do to simply say (as I believe Friesen would) that these are signposts to be considered in making a wise decision. They are that, to be sure; but they are also indications of a unique personal will which God has for each child of Christ.

Working the Works

Finally, there is another important way in which the New Testament points to God's having an individual will for believers, and that is through Jesus' use of the twin concepts of *work* and *works* in the Gospel of John. Jesus speaks both of his work and his works growing out of the most intimate relationship possible with God (Jn 5:19-20; 17:4). There was nothing random in what he did; his work reflected a distinct, personal will of God at every level. He also specifically declared that his disciples would do "the works of God" (Jn 9:1-5) and "greater works" than he himself performed (Jn 14:10-12). It is highly probable that this has reference to Christians carrying out activities which are distinctively willed for them by God.[8]

The New Testament, then, in a number of important ways points to God's having a personal will for Christians. Other biblical data could be provided in support of the notion of a personal will of God. My purpose, though, is not to provide an exhaustive treatment of this topic, which would severely overburden this book with analytical material, but simply to provide enough evidence to show that the concept of God's personal will exists in Scripture and is an important article of biblical doctrine. While I respect Garry Friesen's lines of argument against this point, I don't believe they hold up when the fuller range of biblical evidence is examined.

Wisdom Guidance

I want to note one other difficulty which I have with Friesen's thesis. His concept of "wisdom guidance," when fully understood, does not reconcile well with his general tenet that God has no individual will for our decisions. In fact, it does more to convince me that God does have such a will than to dissuade me!

To explain more carefully what I mean: While Friesen gives much of his attention to refuting the concept of a personal will of God, he devotes over half of his book to providing what he sees to be a healthy basis for making decisions as disciples of Christ.

While we as Christians are free from the tyranny of having to find God's one ideal choice in a decision, Friesen stresses, we are by no means free from responsibility. Quite to the contrary, we must make every effort to make our decisions sensibly. Many times he speaks of our need to find the "best" alternative before us in a given decision. To do this successfully, our ongoing need is for wisdom to see the best option available. To this end he describes the mature Christian decision process as "the way of wisdom."

He speaks also of our need for "wisdom guidance." God is not aloof from our decision process, Friesen emphasizes; he does guide us, and we cannot function effectively apart from his guidance. In fact, God alone can give wisdom, and we have a weighty responsibility to seek this wisdom from God through prayer. Because God is omniscient, he is much more capable than we are of knowing what the best alternative is for a choice we are facing.

It is here that I have my greatest problem with Friesen's logic. If there is a *best* alternative in a decision, and if God alone ultimately knows what it is, this seems to be tantamount to saying that God has an ideal choice in our decisions.

Friesen does note that we sometimes face decisions where there are two or more *equal* alternatives. Yet he seems to be saying that this is the way we perceive the situation from a human standpoint; he never goes so far as to say that *God* ever sees two alternatives as equally matched. I don't think this would stand up well to his understanding of God as infinitely sovereign and knowing. It is hard to imagine that a God who sees the minutest intricacies of all human events in precise detail would ever perceive two alternatives as having absolutely equal value for his purposes. He would surely see that one of them would help tilt the balance of history at least slightly better toward the accomplishment of his mission. I believe Friesen would agree with this assessment of God's perception of things.

If that is true, then we do end up saying that God ultimately does have a best choice for us in any decision area. This is virtually synonymous with saying that he has a personal will. Friesen, though, studiously avoids drawing his argument out to such a point, which would of course contradict the central thesis of the first part of his book. To my mind, he leaves his main points hanging here. While he says that we are to follow the course of wisdom in a decision and that God alone gives wisdom, he never fully reconciles this with his insistence that God has no personal will for our choices. Ironically, his line of argument seems ultimately to speak more *for* God's having an individual will than *against* it.

Not Either-Or

I would contend that Scripture gives us the basis for embracing the full level of human freedom in decision making which Friesen campaigns for—*without* letting go of the cherished concept of a personal will of God.

I find Scripture giving emphasis to *both* of these realities; they are *not* fundamentally contradictory. It is not basically contradictory, for instance, to say that God has an ideal choice among several alternatives I'm facing but that from my vantage point the choices are equally weighed—even that I am free before God to choose any one of them and that *any* of them will be equally glorifying to God.

The reconciliation of these thoughts comes here: As I seek God's will through prayer, and as I come to the point where I am willing to accept his will, I can rest assured that he will preveniently (ahead of time) guide my thinking so that the choice I make is the one he wants me to make. This will happen even though from the psychological standpoint I seem to be choosing among equal options. I believe this is a more accurate way of explaining the paradox of human freedom vs. God's personal will than to dispense with the latter altogether. In reality we need *both* of these concepts—that we are free to choose *and* that God ultimately has a personal will for our choice. We need them both for healthy emotional life and for healthy spirituality. Fortunately Scripture gives us a solid basis to embrace both of them.

My concern in this book has been to give appropriate emphasis to both sides of this equation. To this end, I agree fully with the human concerns which underlie Friesen's book. I agree, too, with much of his biblical analysis—especially his observation that Christians in New Testament times generally made their decisions through a rational process. His documentation of this point is superb and I strongly recommend it for your study.

But I do not find the fact that early Christians took a rational approach to their decisions supporting his overriding thesis that they didn't recognize God having a personal will for these decisions. I believe, rather, that this rational process gives testimony to the way they went about discovering God's will.

When we look for it, there is plenty of New Testament evidence that early believers did assume God had a will for their individual choices. The evidence, too, points to the fact that we should continue to embrace that assumption today. It does not have to rob us of the psychological freedom we need to approach our decisions rationally and responsibly; indeed, when rightly understood it bolsters that freedom. And it adds immensely to our sense of personal significance as well.

Notes

Chapter 1: A Critical Concern
[1]Joseph Bayly et al., *Essays on Guidance* (Downers Grove, Ill.: InterVarsity Press, 1968), preface.
[2]Study leaders, though, should think through the questions in advance of a meeting; in some cases you will probably find that a single question will provide an adequate basis for group discussion in a particular meeting.

Chapter 2: Types of Decisions We Face
[1]Look at books on the subject of guidance in Christian bookstores, and you will find in almost every case that the subject is complex decisions, not simple moral issues. One exception is that some books on guidance also deal with gray area decisions.
[2]The gray area decision, as we have said, is a decision about moral behavior where the Bible clearly leaves us liberty of choice. Paul discusses this area specifically in Romans 14, 1 Corinthians 8 and 1 Corinthians 10:23-33. In these passages there are set forth two basic guidelines for gray area decisions which can often make such decisions simple:

First, *if I have strong reservations of conscience* about a certain gray area activity, then I should not participate (Rom 14:14, 23; 1 Cor 8:7). Likewise, *if my participation would create problems of conscience for another Christian,* then I must respect that person's scruples (Rom 14:13-23; 1 Cor 8:7-13; 10:23-33). If my friend is offended by my drinking a glass of wine with dinner, for instance, I must at least refrain in his presence.

Our broader complex decisions, however, are seldom that simple. The fact that my friend is offended by my desire to enter business, for example, does not necessarily tell me a thing. And the significance of my feelings of conscience about such a decision is often more difficult to assess than in a gray area decision.

In this book we will be concerned with complex decisions, which normally cannot be resolved simply through the two biblical guidelines for gray areas. In addition, it may be said that gray area decisions which are not affected by the restrictions these guidelines set forth can be regarded as complex decisions. If, in other words, a gray area activity causes conscience problems for neither myself nor my Christian friends, then I may approach it as I would a complex decision.

³As eminent a Christian as John Wesley followed this approach!

⁴Paul Little, *Affirming the Will of God* (Downers Grove, Ill.: InterVarsity Press, 1971), pp. 28-29.

Chapter 3: Seeing God's Will Dynamically
¹The incident is related by Dr. Richard C. Halverson, chaplain of the United States Senate.

Chapter 4: Step-by-Step Guidance in Scripture
¹New Testament instances of *thelēma* as God's will: Matthew 6:10; 7:21; 12:50; 18:14; 26:42; Mark 3:35; Luke 11:2; 22:42; John 1:13; 4:34; 5:30; 6:38-40; 7:17; 9:31; Acts 13:22; 21:14; 22:14; Romans 1:10; 2:18; 12:2; 15:32; 1 Corinthians 1:1; 16:12 (probably); 2 Corinthians 1:1; 8:5; Galatians 1:4; Ephesians 1:1, 5, 9, 11; 5:17; 6:6; Colossians 1:1, 9; 4:12; 1 Thessalonians 4:3; 5:18; 2 Timothy 1:1; Hebrews 10:7, 9-10, 36; 13:21; 1 Peter 2:15; 3:17; 4:2, 19; 1 John 2:17; 5:14; Revelation 4:11.

²New Testament instances of *boulē* as God's *will* (sometimes rendered *counsel* or *purpose)*: Acts 2:23; 5:38-39; 13:36; 20:27; Romans 9:19 (actually *boulēma,* a derivative noun); Ephesians 1:11 (rendered *counsel; will* in this verse is *thelēma)*; Hebrews 6:17. Also Luke 7:30, which is an exception to the general usage of *boulē.*

³For a helpful discussion of New Testament words translated as *God's will,* see Marion Nelson, *How to Know God's Will* (Chicago: Moody Press, 1969), pp. 10-14.

⁴See Romans 12:6; 1 Corinthians 12:10, 28-29; 14:1-6; Ephesians 4:11.

⁵Gerhard Friedrich, *"prophētēs"* in *The Theological Dictionary of the New Testament (TDNT),* vol. VI (trans. G. W. Bromiley [Grand Rapids: Eerdmans, 1968], 829), states regarding the Greek word for prophecy: "In Paul the word has a predominantly ethical and hortatory character. It denotes teaching, admonishing and comforting, 1 Cor 14:3, 31. The one who prophesies utters the divine call of judgment and repentance which is burdensome and tormenting to many (Rev 11:3, 10) but which convicts others of sin and leads them to the worship of God (1 Cor 14:24-33)."

⁶See Exodus 22:18; Leviticus 19:26, 31; 20:6; 22:27; Deuteronomy 18:10-11; Isaiah 2:6; 8:19-20; 44:25; 47:12-13; Micah 5:12; Zechariah 10:2; Malachi 3:5.

Chapter 5: The Promise of Guidance
¹See Genesis 49:24; Psalms 23; 79:13; 80:1; 95:7; 100:3; Isaiah 40:11; Jeremiah 31:10; Ezekiel 34; 37:24.

²William Barclay, *The Gospel of John, Daily Study Bible,* vol. 2 (Philadelphia: Westminster Press, 1956), 68.

³I would refer the reader to two excellent and readable discussions of the shepherd's role in New Testament times and its implications: Barclay, *The Gospel of John,* pp. 60-62, and Leon Morris, *The Gospel According to John,* New International Commentary on the New

Testament, (Grand Rapids: Eerdmans, 1971), pp. 498ff.
[4]This is precisely Morris's term in describing an important aspect of the biblical picture of God as a shepherd, ibid., p. 498.
[5]See Barclay, *The Gospel of John*, p. 64.
[6]See, for example, Matthew 9:36; 10:6; 15:24; 18:12.

Chapter 6: The Call to Responsibility
[1]Paul Tournier, *The Adventure of Living* (New York: Harper & Row, 1965).

Chapter 7: Are You Willing?
[1]Jonah is the most notable exception, but the overwhelming majority of people called by God were willing to obey.
[2]*dokimazō.*
[3]The verb is *paristēmi,* in the 1 aorist infinitive.
[4]The verbs are *syschēmatizō* (be conformed) and *metamorphoō* (be transformed), both in the present passive imperative.
[5]Johannes Behm, "Nous," vol. IV, *TDNT*, p. 958.
[6]George Eldon Ladd, *A Theology of the New Testament* (Grand Rapids: Eerdmans, 1974), pp. 524-25.
[7]F. B. Meyer, *The Secret of Guidance* (Chicago: Moody Press, n.d.) p. 12.
[8]Oliver R. Barclay, *Guidance,* 5th ed. (Downers Grove, Ill.: InterVarsity Press, 1978), p. 49.

Chapter 8: The Unique Role of Prayer
[1]C. S. Lewis, "The Efficacy of Prayer" in *The World's Last Night and Other Essays* (New York: Harcourt, Brace & World, 1959), p. 9; and "Work and Prayer" in *God in the Dock* (Grand Rapids: Eerdmans, 1970), pp. 104-7.
[2]John Calvin, *Institutes of the Christian Religion,* 3. 20. 2.
[3]Andrew Murray, *With Christ in the School of Prayer* (Old Tappan, N.J.: Revell, 1974), p. 103.
[4]Albert Barnes, *Barnes Notes on the New Testament* (Grand Rapids: Kregel, 1962), p. 1356.
[5]Paul Little, *Affirming the Will of God* (Downers Grove, Ill.: InterVarsity Press, 1971), pp. 17-18.
[6]Ibid., p. 7.
[7]Paul asked Christ to reveal his will when he appeared to Paul on the Damascus road. Paul asked, "What shall I do, Lord?" (Acts 22:10).

Chapter 9: Searching the Scriptures
[1]Stolen with appreciation from a sermon preached by Dr. Robert Norris, pastor of Fourth Presbyterian Church, Bethesda, Maryland, January 6, 1991.
[2]John White, *The Fight* (Downers Grove, Ill.: InterVarsity Press, 1976), pp. 157-58.

Chapter 10: Thinking Things Through
[1]". . . that I may be delivered from the unbelievers in Judea, and that my service for

Jerusalem may be acceptable to the saints, so that by God's will I may come to you with joy and be refreshed in your company" (Rom 15:31-32). The verb *come* in verse 32 is *elthōn*, an aorist participle, which gives the sense of *having come;* the literal sense, then, is *having come to you through the will of God.* This phrase is introduced by *hina* ("in order that"), which most likely makes verse 32 an effect of which verse 31 is the cause. Paul seems to be saying, then, that if the conditions of verse 31 are fulfilled (his being delivered from unbelievers and delivering the contribution to Jerusalem), he will then come to Rome in the will of God. See F. J. Leenhardt, *The Epistle to the Romans* (London: Lutterworth Press, 1961), pp. 376-77.

[2]John A. Allan, "The Will of God in Paul," in *Expository Times,* vol. LXXII, no. 5 (1961), p. 145, emphasis added.

[3]Kenneth Pike, "God's Guidance and Your Life Work," in Bayly et al., *Essays on Guidance,* p. 69.

[4]Ibid., pp. 69-70.

[5]Colossians 1:9 states: "We have not ceased to pray for you, asking that you may be filled with the knowledge of his will in all spiritual wisdom and understanding." Ralph Martin *(Colossians and Philemon,* New Century Bible [London: Oliphants, 1974], p. 50) notes that the prayer Paul mentions is really best understood as an exhortation to the Colossians. Paul is in effect telling them to "be filled with the knowledge of God's will in all spiritual wisdom and understanding." The readers, then, are being exhorted to make full use of all rational faculties to discern God's will.

Ephesians 5:15-17 states: "Look carefully then how you walk, not as unwise men but as wise, making the most of the time, because the days are evil. Therefore do not be foolish, but understand what the will of the Lord is." Paul here is giving his readers a command to be practical. "Making the most of the time" implies taking the best and most logical advantage of circumstances for the Lord's glory. "Understand" in verse 17 is the Greek term *suniete,* implying a rational process of discernment.

[6]James H. Jauncy, *Guidance by God* (Grand Rapids: Zondervan, 1969), p. 71.

Chapter 11: Supernatural Guidance

[1]Martin Luther, *Letters, Luther's Works,* vol. 1 (Philadelphia: Fortress, 1963), pp. 366-67.

[2]Dispensationalism, which is a particular form of conservative theology, divides history into several ages. Particular biblical passages are believed to apply only to particular periods. Thus, the experiences of supernatural guidance found in the New Testament are said to apply only to the apostolic age. Any claims to direct guidance by modern Christians would be considered false. In this book, I have taken a more moderate approach.

[3]Bob Mumford, *Take Another Look at Guidance* (Plainfield, N. J.: Logos, 1971), p. 127.

[4]Karl Rahner, *The Dynamic Element in the Church,* translated by W. J. O'Hara (New York: Herder and Herder, 1964); Karl Rahner, *Visions and Prophecies,* translated by Charles Henkey and Richard Strachan (New York: Herder and Herder, 1963).

[5]Rahner, *Visions and Prophecies,* pp. 31ff.

[6]Ibid., pp 36-37.

[7]See, for example, David Ryback, Ph.D., with Letitia Sweitzer, *Dreams That Come True:*

Their Psychic and Transforming Powers (New York: Ivy Books, 1988).

[8]Morton Kelsey, *Christo-Psychology* (New York: Crossroads, 1982), p. 123.

Chapter 12: The Place of Prophecy

[1]When Paul talks about the gift of prophecy, he makes no statement to the effect that it should be thought of as a channel of guidance. There are plenty of examples of prediction in the New Testament, such as Agabus's prediction of the famine (Acts 11:28) and predictions by various New Testament writers about God's future acts in history. But with the exception of Acts 21:4, noted immediately below, there is no clear instance where someone attempted to connect prophecy with advice for another's complex decision.

And in Acts 21:4, the one exception where this did happen, Paul did not take the advice as God's will. This is not to argue from silence that prophecy never did function as guidance in the New Testament church. But certainly if God had wanted it to be a normal channel of guidance for us today it would have been made more apparent in the New Testament. Some references to the gift of prophecy in Paul's writings are Romans 12:6; 1 Corinthians 12:10; 13:2, 9; 14:3-6, 22, 24-25, 31, 39-40. Compare Ephesians 4:11-12.

[2]I am assuming that Paul's statement in Acts 20:23—"the Holy Spirit testifies to me in every city that imprisonment and afflictions await me"—implies that this warning came through the prophecy of friends. This assumption has the support of the following commentaries: F. F. Bruce, *Commentary on the Book of Acts* (Grand Rapids: Eerdmans, 1974), p. 414; Richard B. Rackham, *The Acts of the Apostles* (London: Methuen, 1904), p. 390; Ernst Haenchen, *The Acts of the Apostles: A Commentary* (Oxford: Basil Blackwell, 1971), p. 591.

[3]Bruce, *Commentary on the Book of Acts*, p. 421.

[4]Michael Harper, *Prophecy: A Gift for the Body of Christ* (Plainfield, N.J.: Logos, 1970), pp. 26-27.

[5]See note 5, chapter four.

Chapter 14: Inward Guidance

[1]Acts references to the inspiration of the Holy Spirit are 8:26, 39; 10:19-20; 11:28; 13:2; 15:28; 16:6-7; 19:21; 20:22-23; 21:4, 11-14.

[2]Barclay, *Guidance*, p. 40.

[3]Amy Lowell, "The Process of Making Poetry," in *The Creative Process*, edited by Brewster Ghiselin (New York: Mentor Books, 1952) pp. 109-110.

[4]Jean Cocteau, "The Process of Inspiration," in ibid., p. 82.

[5]Henri Poincaré, "Mathematical Creation," in ibid., p. 36.

Chapter 16: Evaluating Abilities and Gifts

[1]The best treatment of spiritual gifts currently available, in my estimation, is C. Peter Wagner's *Your Spiritual Gifts Can Help Your Church Grow* (Ventura, Calif.: Regal Books), 1979. Charles E. Hummel's *Fire in the Fireplace: Contemporary Charismatic Renewal* (Downers Grove, Ill.: InterVarsity Press, 1978) also has many helpful insights.

[2]Ibid., pp. 168-69.

[3]Ibid., p. 190.

[4]Ibid., p. 228.

[5]Again, a helpful comment from Hummel: "Therefore, the believer does not struggle to discover his or her individual gift and then wonder where to use it. Instead the Christian participates in the body and, sensitive to the needs of others, trusts the sovereign Spirit to manifest whatever gifts will meet the needs of the community. The community benefits from and controls the exercise of gifts" (ibid., p. 171).

[6]The term *bishop* in this passage should be understood as meaning "overseer"; it does not have the ecclesiastical connotations of the contemporary term. *Bishop (episkopos)* and *elder (presbyteros)* were in New Testament times alternative names for the same officer (see Tit 1:5, 7; Acts 20:17, 28), the first term indicating function or duty and the second indicating dignity or status. Each local congregation had several persons functioning as overseers. (A. M. Stibbs, "The Pastoral Epistles," in Donald Guthrie and J. A. Motyer, eds., *The New Bible Commentary: Revised* [Grand Rapids: Eerdmans, 1970], p. 1171.) See Titus 1:5-9 for another Pauline example of qualifications for church leadership, and Acts 6:2-5 for an example from Luke of qualifications required for a deacon.

[7]Joseph is exalted to high positions in Egypt because of his gifts (Gen 39—50). Aaron is chosen to be Moses' mouthpiece because he can speak well (Ex 4:14-16). Moses' choice of men to be rulers under him is based purely on consideration of their ability (Ex 18:21), as is his choice of persons to make Aaron's garments (Ex 28:3) and of people to construct the temple (Ex 31:1-11; 35:10; 35:30—36:2). Joshua is chosen as Moses' successor because of the spirit in him (Num 27:18). Gideon chooses the men for his small army on the basis of their courage (Judg 7:2-3). Saul brings David into his court because of his musical ability (1 Sam 16:14-23) and hires Hiram (1 Kings 7:13-14) and Jeroboam (1 Kings 11:28) for special service because of their talents. David in choosing his officers from the Gadites puts "the lesser over a hundred and the greater over a thousand" (1 Chron 12:14) and makes Chenaniah director of music "for he understood it" (1 Chron. 15:22).

Chapter 17: Assessing Open and Closed Doors
[1]Martin Luther, *The Sermon on the Mount,* Luther's Works, vol. 21 (St. Louis: Concordia, 1956), 239.

Chapter 18: Weighing the Counsel of Others
[1]See also Proverbs 13:10, 18, 20; 15:31-32; 17:10; 19:25.

Chapter 19: Finally Deciding
[1]Quoted by J. Oswald Sanders, *Spiritual Leadership* (Chicago: Moody Press, 1967), p. 113.

Appendix 1: Authority Relationships and the Will of God
[1]Bill Gothard, subsection "Chain-of-Command" in "Family" section in *Institute in Basic Youth Conflicts* manual (LaGrange, Ill.: Institute in Basic Youth Conflicts, 1969 and Campus Teams Inc., 1968).

[2]See F. F. Bruce and E. K. Simpson, *Commentary on the Epistles to the Ephesians and the Colossians,* New International Commentary on the New Testament (Grand Rapids: Eerd-

mans, 1957), p. 291.

[3]Thomas K. Abbott, *The Epistles to the Ephesians and to the Colossians*, International Critical Commentary (New York: Scribner's, 1903), p. 176.

[4]John Eadie, *A Commentary on the Greek Text of the Epistle of Paul to the Colossians* (Edinburgh: T. & T. Clark, 1884), p. 255.

[5]See Eduard Lohse, *A Commentary on the Epistles to the Colossians and to Philemon*, Hermeneia Commentary (Philadelphia: Fortress, 1971), p. 159. This conclusion is highly probable on the basis of Ephesians 6:4, where Paul certainly employs *ta tekna* with the same intended meaning as in 6:1, and he states, "Fathers, do not provoke your children to anger, but *bring them up* in the discipline and instruction of the Lord," indicating that he has in mind an adolescent dependency relationship in this use of *tekna*.

[6]A scholarly treatment of the subject is given by Paul K. Jewett, *Man as Male and Female* (Grand Rapids: Eerdmans, 1975). He advocates the position that the commands concerning marital authority are not binding on modern Christians. A good argument for the traditional interpretation is given in George W. Knight III, *The New Testament Teaching on the Role Relationship of Men and Women* (Grand Rapids: Baker Book House, 1977).

[7]Willis Peter DeBoer, *The Imitation of Paul: An Exegetical Study* (Amsterdam: Vrije University, 1962), p. vi.

[8]W. E. Vine, *An Expository Dictionary of New Testament Words*, Vol. III (Old Tappan, N. J.: Revell, 1966), p. 124.

[9]The verb *obey* is coupled with the verb *submit*, which in the Greek is *hypeikō*. Unlike the verb for *obey (peithō)* this word is not used elsewhere in the New Testament, so it is more difficult to determine its precise meaning. It is perhaps intended to give depth to *obey*, suggesting that one should not only strive to agree with a leader's (reasonable) directives but should also put these into practice when one is persuaded they are valid. Again, there is no evidence that this word implies compliance with a leader's counsel in the area of complex decisions.

Appendix 2: Does God Have a Will for Our Personal Decisions?

[1]Garry Friesen, with J. Robin Maxson, *Decision Making and the Will of God: A Biblical Alternative to the Traditional View* (Portland: Multnomah Press, 1980).

[2]There is no treatment of spiritual gifts as a topic until page 338, for instance; the term *gifts* is mentioned only a handful of times prior to that and usually in passing, and the treatment he does give to this critical topic is very brief compared to other topics in his book. The term *personal distinctiveness* occurs only once in his study (p. 378).

[3]See the conclusion to his book, pp. 427-430.

[4]Leslie Mitton, "The Will of God in the Synoptic Tradition of the Words of Jesus" *(The Expository Times*, 72:5, 1961) p. 69.

[5]Friesen examines this passage (pp. 110-11) and concludes that because it occurs in a chapter where moral exhortations are given, the Lord's will in verse 17 has reference not to an individual will but to God's moral will. I believe, though, that this is forcing the point, and that it more obviously refers to the counsel immediately preceding it to make the most of every opportunity.

Friesen agrees that the verse does enjoin wise decision making and cites verses 15-16 in his discussion of wisdom in several later places in his book as a biblical mandate to make wise choices in nonmoral areas. Yet he is careful not to connect the idea of wisdom so clearly enjoined in the first part of this passage with the term *the Lord's will* in verse 17. I believe that this connection is required and that it gives an important biblical basis for the notion of God's personal will.

[6]"For by the grace given me I say to every one of you: Do not think of yourself more highly than you ought, but rather think of yourself with sober judgment, in accordance with the measure of faith God has given you. Just as each of us has one body with many members, and these members do not all have the same function, so in Christ we who are many form one body, and each member belongs to all the others."

[7]Friesen examines Romans 12:1-2 but concludes that because this passage occurs in the context of Romans 12, a chapter with many moral exhortations, *thelēma* in verse 2 must refer to the moral and not the individual will of God. He notes:

> In Romans 12:1, Paul is saying on the basis of God's mercies, which have just been explained in detail, surrender your body to God for obedient living. Then, beginning with verse three, and extending on into the next four chapters, he spells out the commands that ought to be obeyed. In other words, as soon as he completes his exhortation to "prove what the will of God is," he begins giving specific examples of that will. Significantly, they are moral commands addressed to all believers. The immediate context says nothing about such things as finding one's vocation, choosing one's mate, or anything else that is so specific as to be part of God's individual will. (p. 106)

Friesen, though, for reasons I don't understand, does not examine verses 3-5 immediately following Paul's command to prove God's will, where Paul enjoins us to have a clear understanding of our individuality. Friesen's only reference to verses 6-8 occurs as he lists the different types of moral commands given in this chapter, noting that "there are commands concerning the use of one's gift." Here he seems to be lumping the commands to use your gift into the same category with moral commands which follow the passage on gifts. Yet his argument simply doesn't hold up here. The teaching on gifts speaks to the ways in which God has created and sustained us *individually*. While one can argue that this is merely part of God's moral will (just as one could say semantically that God's individual will is part of his moral will), the point really does not follow well. It makes much more sense to say that Paul's teaching on individuality speaks to God's individual ways of guiding people, i.e., to a personal will.

[8]Friesen makes only passing references in his book to passages in John where Jesus uses the terms *work* and *works* and provides no detailed analysis of the concepts underlying them. Most significantly, he makes no attempt to relate Jesus' own conception of himself doing the work of God with statements Jesus makes about his disciples doing God's work (or works). He does have a lengthy footnote where he considers the hypothesis that Jesus' life is meant to demonstrate that God has a personal will for Christians (pp. 94-95). He notes that traditional works on guidance often make this parallel but argues that it is not justified, given the fact that there are so many differences between Jesus and ordinary

Christian mortals. Yet while he makes some good points, he fails to give Jesus' use of *work* and *works* the consideration it deserves.

Friesen examines in detail only one New Testament passage which speaks of works, Ephesians 2:10 (pp. 108-9). Here Paul states, "For we are God's workmanship, created in Christ Jesus to do good works, which God prepared in advance for us to do."

Interestingly, Friesen concedes that this verse "offers stronger possibilities" for supporting the traditional view of guidance "than many of the verses that are used" (p. 108). He considers three possible interpretations of Paul's statement, concluding that he prefers to think Paul is pointing purely to God's sovereign will. Just as Paul has declared in the previous two verses (Eph 2:8-9) that salvation itself is a gift of God and not a result of our own effort, Friesen notes, he may now be insisting that even our good works are sovereignly ordained by God (and thus not a basis for personal boasting). Yet Friesen confesses that it is *possible* that Paul could also have the notion of an individual will of God in mind in this statement.

Given this admission by Friesen, I believe he should have given closer attention to Jesus' teaching on works.

About the Author

Blaine Smith, a Presbyterian pastor, is director of Nehemiah Ministries, a resource ministry based in the Washington, D.C., area. He gives lectures, leads seminars and conferences, and does counseling and writing. He is author of *Should I Get Married?* and *One of a Kind* (both InterVarsity Press books) and numerous articles. He is also the lecturer for "Guidance By The Book," a home study course with audio cassettes produced by the Christian Broadcasting Network as part of its Living By The Book series. (For information about this course, write Blaine at the address below.)

Blaine is a graduate of Georgetown University. He holds a master of divinity degree from Wesley Theological Seminary and a doctor of ministry degree from Fuller Theological Seminary. He lives in Damascus, Maryland, with his wife, Evie, and their two sons, Benjamin and Nathan.

You Can Receive Blaine's Newsletter
Blaine authors a monthly newsletter, "Nehemiah Notes." It lists his ministry activities and always includes an article on a topic related to realizing your potential in Christ and keeping a grace-centered perspective in the Christian life. It is sent free to anyone requesting it.

To request the newsletter or correspond with Blaine, write:
Nehemiah Ministries
P.O. Box 448
Damascus, MD 20872